THE
EVERYTHING
HEALTHY TEA BOOK

Dear Reader,

As a southern girl, I was a tea lover from way back, growing up on sweet tea, enjoying afternoon teatimes with my grandmother, and soaking up the wisdom of her herbal remedies. Attending the University of Texas, I became an official *Texas Tea Sipper* (an intended insult that UT students are bookish lightweights). It wasn't until thirty years later that I discovered the vast world of tea beyond those roots and claimed my true Tea Sipper-ness.

In 1989, a San Francisco merchant prepared a whole-leaf green tea for me, shared the legend, and described how Chinese women had hand-picked more than seven thousand individual sprigs to make a pound of the dry tea. It was the first time I experienced the connection with the farms in faraway countries, the people who picked the tiny leaves, and the ancient legacies they preserved. That experience was a portal to a beautiful and elegant world that seemed to connect almost every culture with traditions of hospitality and generosity.

On a very personal level, the thread that weaves together tea's five thousand year history also includes teatimes with my grandmother and our traditions; the hospitality and generous spirit that sharing tea inspires. As exciting and reassuring as it is to follow the latest scientific research on the health benefits of *Camellia sinensis*, I'm glad that my passion for tea began at home and grew to include the worldwide family of tea people.

I'm equally grateful for the opportunity to share it.

Welcome to Tea Land.

Babette

Welcome to the EVERYTHING® Series!

These handy, accessible books give you all you need to tackle a difficult project, gain a new hobby, comprehend a fascinating topic, prepare for an exam, or even brush up on something you learned back in school but have since forgotten.

You can choose to read an Everything® book from cover to cover or just pick out the information you want from our four useful boxes: e-questions, e-facts, e-alerts, and e-ssentials.

We give you everything you need to know on the subject, but throw in a lot of fun stuff along the way, too.

We now have more than 400 Everything® books in print, spanning such wide-ranging categories as weddings, pregnancy, cooking, music instruction, foreign language, crafts, pets, New Age, and so much more. When you're done reading them all, you can finally say you know Everything®!

QUESTION

Answers to
common questions

FACT

Important snippets
of information

ALERT

Urgent
warnings

ESSENTIAL

Quick
handy tips

PUBLISHER Karen Cooper

MANAGING EDITOR, EVERYTHING® SERIES Lisa Laing

COPY CHIEF Casey Ebert

ASSISTANT PRODUCTION EDITOR Alex Guarco

ACQUISITIONS EDITOR Pamela Wissman

DEVELOPMENT EDITOR Brett Palana-Shanahan

EVERYTHING® SERIES COVER DESIGNER Erin Alexander

Visit the entire Everything® series at *www.everything.com*

THE EVERYTHING® HEALTHY TEA BOOK

Discover the healing benefits of tea

Babette Donaldson

Avon, Massachusetts

*Dedicated to my tea mentors: Donna Fellman,
Roy Fong, Richard Guzauskas, Ip Wingchi,
Radjiv Lochan, Nigel Milican, Philip Parda, James
Norwood Pratt, and Dan Robertson.*

An Everything® Series Book.
Everything® and everything.com® are registered trademarks of F+W Media, Inc.

Published by
Adams Media, a division of F+W Media, Inc.
57 Littlefield Street, Avon, MA 02322. U.S.A.
www.adamsmedia.com

ISBN 10: 1-4405-7459-6
ISBN 13: 978-1-4405-7459-7
eISBN 10: 1-4405-7460-X
eISBN 13: 978-1-4405-7460-3

Printed in the United States of America.

10 9 8 7 6 5 4 3 2 1

Library of Congress Cataloging-in-Publication Data
Donaldson, Babette, author.
 The everything healthy tea book / Babette Donaldson.
     pages cm. -- (An everything series book)
 Includes bibliographical references and index.
 ISBN-13: 978-1-4405-7459-7 (pb)
 ISBN-10: 1-4405-7459-6 (pb)
 ISBN-13: 978-1-4405-7460-3 (ebook)
 ISBN-10: 1-4405-7460-X (ebook)
1. Tea--Health aspects. 2. Tea--Therapeutic use. 3. Tea. I. Title. II. Title: Tea book.
 RM251.D66 2014
 615.3'21--dc23
                    2013051351

Cover images © Alex Bramwell/subbotina/Olga Miltsova/cokemomo/Paul Grecaud/kostrez/123RF.

*This book is available at quantity discounts for bulk purchases.
For information, please call 1-800-289-0963.*

Contents

Acknowledgments

A special thank-you goes to Frederic Rector, a dedicated reader who remained cool under the pressure of short deadlines; to Colleen Shipler who generously contributed her tea expertise; to Pamela Wissman, an enthusiastic editor, and to George and Kim Jage whose support for me with this book is in the same spirit as the opportunities they create for tea education through World Tea Media.

Top 10 Tea Myths

1. Tea doesn't go bad. (In reality, the compounds that produce flavor and health benefits degrade with time and exposure to light, moisture, and air.)

2. Green, black, oolong, pu'erh, and white teas all come from different plants. (All true teas come from varietals of the *Camellia sinensis* plant. Processing creates the differences between the categories.)

3. Green tea is healthier than black tea. (More research has been done on green tea than black tea, making it seem healthier.)

4. All tea has equal health benefits, so buy the least expensive. (The healthiest tea is the freshest and least degraded by poor packaging or inadequate storage.)

5. Drinking tea can help you lose weight. (Drinking tea can increase metabolism and energy to encourage more activity, and can also replace high calorie beverages.)

6. Black tea has the most caffeine and white tea the least. (It is nearly impossible to predict the amount of caffeine in brewed tea. White tea with a high percentage of whole buds may contain more caffeine than black tea.)

7. Decaffeinated tea is completely free of caffeine. (It is impossible to remove all caffeine from tea. There will always be a trace amount, usually less than 5 percent.)

8. Tea bags are filled with "dust" swept from the factory floor. (Tea "dust" is a byproduct of tea production, where the leaves that have broken or been ground into a dust-like powder are used to fill tea bags for quick infusion.)

9. Green tea is bitter. (Green tea has more astringency than other teas and can be bitter if it is brewed improperly. If brewed correctly, it can be very sweet.)

10. Tea causes dehydration. (An astringent green tea can sometimes leave a feeling of dryness in the mouth, but this has been shown to cause only slightly more fluid loss than water.)

Introduction

THERE ARE MANY HERBS, in addition to *Camellia sinensis*, the true tea, which brew healthy and flavorful hot beverages. There are also many fruits and vegetables with high antioxidants values that contribute to a healthy diet. But no other food product casts as wide an umbrella over your potential for good health as does tea. Distinguishing it even more are the cultural and spiritual values it contributes to people's lives. The potential for wellness is not limited to our physical bodies. Tea also nurtures the spirit with beauty through tradition and ceremony.

> *"Our thirst for tea is never far from our craving for beauty."*
> —James Norwood Pratt, author of The Ultimate Tea Lover's Treasury (2011).

Five thousand years ago, the legendary Chinese Emperor, Shen Nong, is said to have accidentally brewed the first cup of tea when a leaf fell into his boiling water. The story goes on to say that he recognized some of the beneficial properties of *Camellia sinensis*, and included it in his compendium of healthy plants. Many different practices using tea as a "tonic" became part of traditional folk medicine. Modern science is gradually accumulating a body of evidence through which they can finally confirm what ancient healers discovered by observation and experience.

Two thousand years after Shen Nong's discovery, the Greek physician Hippocrates, the father of western medicine, said, "Let food be your medicine and medicine be your food." Our modern diets are a long way from following Hippocrates' advice. Food is often our entertainment, and cooking is sometimes a hobby with less concern for the number of calories or the nutritional value. The desire for convenience can inspire unhealthy habits and aggressive marketing plays into that vulnerability to the point that some eating habits can become dangerous. But, for all of its 5,000-year history,

Camellia sinensis has continued to be valued as both healer and beverage; a cultural icon and a spiritual companion. All of this contributes to making it the second most consumed beverage in the world—second only to water.

This book blends tea's folklore and science to demonstrate how it can fit into every lifestyle. It focuses more on loose-leaf tea rather than bagged tea for three reasons. First, loose-leaf tea can seem complex and intimidating to someone completely new to tea. Secondly, there are circumstances in which it may offer greater health benefits. Lastly, many of the nonscientific health benefits are the ways tea inspires a healthier lifestyle, and the artisan teas may have more to contribute in this respect. Hopefully, understanding how tea plants are grown and processed will help make selection and brewing feel like an exciting adventure; more enjoyable and more meaningful.

"Tea began as a medicine and grew into a beverage."
—*Kakuzo Okakura, author of The Book of Tea (1906).*

Ironically, the greatest percentage of tea drinkers do not base their daily teatime on the health benefits. It is far more likely, even if they are first attracted by the media's coverage of new research on weight loss or cardio-vascular health, that they quickly become drawn into the experience.

But, art and culture aside, *Camellia sinensis*, the true tea plant, continues to be one of the most researched botanicals in the health sciences, and the results are promising. There are those who believe that, with more research, the antioxidant EGCG in green tea will one day provide a cure for some cancers. And, in the months between final editing and printing this book, many new studies will be published, hopefully bringing us even closer to that dream.

So, as Kenneth Graeme, author of *The Wind in the Willows*, said, "Come along inside . . . We'll see if tea and buns can make the world a better place."

CHAPTER 1

What Is Tea?

Thousands of years before the beginning of what is now referred to as C.E. (the Common Era), humans gathered plants for food and medicine. In China and possibly India, the tea plant, *Camellia sinensis,* was one of those green, leafy medicinal options. Anyone chewing on a leaf would probably have grimaced at the bitter taste but might have then noticed a sudden rush of energy and a feeling of invigoration. One can imagine that, once this ancient human shared his discovery with family and friends, they would have tested it on various ailments.

A 5,000-Year-Old Medicine

The true tea, *Camellia sinensis*, is one of the few plants with a long history as a medicinal. There are also several colorful legends about the first ancient brewed tea. The oldest and most often told is the legend of China's "Divine Healer," Emperor Shen Nong, who lived 5,000 years ago and is credited with discovering hundreds of healing herbs, then sharing his "prescriptions" with his subjects. (For Shen Nong's story, see Chapter 2.)

ESSENTIAL

"Tea began as a medicine and grew into a beverage" are the first words of *The Book of Tea* by Kakuzo Okakura, published in 1906 and considered one of the classic books on the subject of the little green leaf. For centuries, tea has been valued for its healthful qualities and enjoyed as a versatile beverage.

It is a combination of the history, the cultural traditions that cover the globe, and the growing statistics about the amount of tea consumed that remind tea lovers that they have chosen a popular and interesting lifestyle. Only in the last few decades has scientific medical research begun to examine the effects of tea on the human body. Results are beginning to confirm these health benefits, and the popular media is regularly filled with affirmations that this ancient history is, for the most part, true.

Tea Is the Second Most Popular Beverage in the World

Because this statement is so surprising and attention-grabbing, it is frequently the opening remark by speakers on the subject. What raises a few more eyebrows is the clarification that "tea" refers only to the leaf of the *Camellia sinensis* plant, the only true tea. In these modern times, many popular teas are blended with other ingredients, and it would be tempting to assume that when people say "tea" they are including all beverages infused in hot water except coffee. But even after we filter out the true tea (*Camellia sinensis*) from the bits of fruit and flowers, and then eliminate other infused herbs like rooibos and yerba mate, the little green leaf continues to sprint ahead of coffee, juice, and sodas in worldwide preferences and consumption.

FACT

In 2011, approximately 4,000,000 tons of tea were produced worldwide. This does not include small farmers growing only for local use. The Tea Council of the USA reports that, in the same year, Americans consumed more than 5 billion gallons of tea, and 85 percent of that was iced.

Camellia Sinensis—The True Tea

The true tea plant is a flowering evergreen that, when left to grow wild, can reach a height of fifty feet or fifteen meters—taller than a four-story building. In the wild, it can live more than a thousand years, but it is more commonly grown on small family farms or large commercial plantations where it is pruned as a shrub, limiting height to make it easy to harvest. Small farms may grow tea alongside other crops in small patchwork fields cultivated by hand, while more commercial plantations may cover steep hillsides or spread out over fields that look like an ocean of green.

ESSENTIAL

What was considered by many to be the oldest known tea tree, at more than 1,700 years old, was located in the remote jungle, south of Xishaungbanna in Yunnan Province on the southern border with Myanmar, and died in 2011. Devoted tea lovers from all over the world used to endure the two-hour hike on the overgrown jungle path to visit the "Old King Tree."

The scientific name for the tea plant was originally *Thea sinensis*, first named so in the mid-1700s. The botanical name was changed to the current *Camellia sinensis* in 1818. Tea's taxonomy shares the genus *Camellia* with a large number of flowering shrubs in the botanical family Theaceae—however, only two main varietals are considered safe for tea production.

Within each of these two varietals are thousands of specialized types, localized for their geographic position and also as a preference for the type of tea that will be produced.

Camellia Sinensis var. *Sinensis*

The Latin word *sinensis* means "of China." This varietal is a small leafed plant, native to provinces in Southern China, that has proven to adapt by hybridization to cooler climates. The mature leaves generally grow to approximately five centimeters or two inches long.

Camellia Sinensis var. *Assamica*

The Latin word *assamica* refers to the area in Western India from which this varietal was first discovered. The leaves of this plant are larger than those of *sinensis*, and it prefers tropical and sub-tropical climates. The leaf length varies from fifteen to thirty-five centimeters, or between six and fourteen inches.

ALERT

The most well known *Camellias*, the *Camellia japonica* varietals, are widely used in landscaping. Though similar in appearance, they cannot safely be brewed into tea. Only *Camellia sinensis* varietals are used for tea. The white flower is one visible distinction of the tea plant, along with the serrated leaf edges, but it cannot be assumed that any *Camellia* with a white flower can be safely consumed.

Five Teas, One Plant

All five main categories of true tea—green, black, oolong, white, and pu'erh—come from the same plant. When one compares the dark teas, heavily flavored and nearly opaque in the cup, to the almost clear liquor of a white tea, the differences that can be created from this plant become intriguing. This also hints at the artisanship of tea masters and skilled workers who attend to every detail, from the early morning picking to the final packaging of a finished tea. And importantly, the differences in appearance and flavor also create variations in tea's healthful benefits.

From the Leaf to the Cup

Tea is a complex agricultural product to bring to market as it requires precise timing at every step. Slight variations can make significant differences in taste and quality. And the quality also determines its usefulness as a medicinal supplement. Beginning in the field, the variables include soil, temperature, season, rainfall, pests, and pesticides (or the lack thereof). Farmers evaluate these conditions in order to make choices about how and when the tea should be harvested and then processed. Fine teas are usually plucked by hand and bulk teas are almost always machine cut, because hand plucking makes the tea much more expensive. Of course, there are variations in the wide range between the two methods. In some countries, like Japan, even very high-quality leaves are machine cut because the criteria for assessing value are less about maintaining the whole leaf and more about the flavor. Once the fresh leaves are delivered to the factory, processing for each type of tea begins a series of unique variations.

Understanding the basics of growing, harvesting, exporting, and selling teas can help one select the best quality and value. The care with which your tea is handled, beginning at the source, ultimately determines its benefits and your best choice.

A Select Harvest

Whether the tea is hand plucked or machine cut, only the bright green flush of new growth is harvested. The amount selected can range from snapping off a single bud (the unopened leaf at the tip of the stem) to about five inches of tender stem with the bud and two newly opened leaves. If the leaves are not picked at this early stage, they begin to thicken, the stem stiffens and darkens, and the chemical composition changes so that the leaves become bitter and undesirable for tea.

ALERT

Concerns about the amount of heavy metals in agricultural products prompted studies in tea leaves. Findings tend to show that, if there are trace accumulations drawn from the soil, they tend to be stored in the surface cells of the leaves with higher concentrations in older, more mature tea leaves selected for less expensive teas and less in the younger, tender leaves reserved for artisan teas.

The growing seasons for different geographic areas vary greatly. In a few locations with prime conditions, particularly at latitudes near the equator, tea can be harvested year-round. At higher elevations in areas farther from the equator, the productive season may be limited to only one or two flushes of new growth. For example, Kenya, which straddles the equator, is one of the countries with the potential of year-round harvests, while farmers in areas of Shandong Province, the most northern tea farms in China, begin harvest in April and end in September. Throughout the more than forty countries that grow tea commercially, there is a wide range in conditions that lead to the great variations of harvest times and in the flavors of the teas they produce.

Picked by Hand

When harvested by hand, pickers snap off either a leaf set of two leaves and a single bud or, for some very fine teas, just the single bud. Depending on the size of the leaf and the amount of each stem being picked, there can be between 7,000 and 70,000 plucks required to make a single pound of dry tea. The pickers, usually women, begin early in the morning and end their work by midday.

Some of the finest teas grow in high elevations and on hillsides where large harvesting machines cannot navigate the slope. These fields are usually considered to produce some of the finest and, therefore, the most valuable teas, which must be harvested by hand. In many areas, the pickers take great pride in their work, knowing that this is a skill developed with great patience and practice and is essential to the quality of the finished product. It is not uncommon that a family will have generations of women picking the same bushes.

ALERT

"Monkey Picked" is a phrase used to describe some rare Tie Guan Yin oolongs. Uneducated or unscrupulous retailers may market this deceptively. Monkeys are not trained to harvest tea. This was an eighteenth-century way of referring to the fact that the plants grew on such a high, steep slope that it was of exceptional quality. Today it is usually the name given to the highest-quality Tie Guan Yin available.

Harvested by Machine

Only slightly more mechanized than hand picking is a simple tool used for cutting some teas that looks like a pair of hedge clippers with a bag attached. The blade of the clippers snaps a swath of dozens of shoots, which then fall into the attached collection bag. It is the most basic form of machine harvest and is certainly a more rapid method than breaking each stem one by one. Another simple version of the machine harvester operated by a single person has a small gasoline-powered blade. Increasingly larger versions exist, such as a wheeled one that moves through the rows of plants, operated by four to five workers, replacing the work of fifty people.

Those larger machines may be used to harvest level fields for commercial production of bulk tea. But even when machines are used, timing of the harvest is critical. Preparation for machine harvest requires that the fields be pruned just before the new growth begins, so that the fresh shoots are available at a uniform level for the height of the cutting blades. Without these modern methods of both harvest and production, tea would probably be unaffordable for most people.

Some large farms practice multiple harvest techniques. Large, open areas will be harvested by machine for a profitable high-yield crop while sections of specialty teas are plucked by hand. These latter products may be entered in competitions, bringing great honor to the grower as well as higher prices.

In the Factory

As soon as the leaves are picked and dropped into a basket or sack, they begin to soften and wither. This withering continues at the factory where the leaves are spread out on white sheets to be heated either in direct sunlight or on interior tables with controlled heat and airflow. Withering is one of two stages of production that all tea categories have in common. The additional stages that may take place at this point involve controlling how much the leaf will be allowed to oxidize and turn brown, how it will be shaped and then dried or aged, and at what point the tea is considered finished before a final drying so that it can be packaged and shipped. After withering, this final drying is one of the processes similar to all categories of tea. In order to be shipped around the world, the moisture content in the finished tea must be less than 5 percent or there is the possibility of mold developing.

FACT

Variables during the growing and processing of tea that affect both the health benefits and the flavor include: where it grows, what time of year it is harvested, rainfall, processing, packaging, storage at the factory or in a distributor's warehouse, and finally, time on the market shelf.

Tea En Route

When the tea is finished and dry it is packed into waterproof and airtight bags, and sometimes crated in large wooden boxes to ensure that it will not be contaminated in transit. Crates and pallets of tea are loaded into cargo containers and shipped from the country of origin to major ports around the world. Brokers and wholesalers deliver the orders to companies who blend, flavor, and package it in their own facilities. Importers specializing in wholesaling to small tea shops repackage into one-, five-, or ten-pound quantities, usually vacuum sealing it to further protect the tea from being compromised by light, moisture, and other aromas.

A relatively recent innovation is for companies in the countries of origin to package and ship products directly to stores, tea shops, or directly to the consumer. Some of these companies have developed brands recognized worldwide and are creating their own channels of distribution, emphasizing freshness since the products are sealed at the factory as soon as the tea is finished.

Choosing a Tea Purveyor

Have you noticed more brands and flavors of tea filling more shelf space in grocery stores? Does your local health food store now stock loose-leaf tea in the bulk food section? Have you visited a tea specialty shop with a menu of dozens of flavors, or surfed the online sellers who may offer more than a hundred teas? There are now many ways to buy tea, and a wide range of price and quality. Whether you're looking for premium loose-leaf teas or basic teabag blends, it is important to find a source you can trust.

Knowing the factors that can affect the quality of the tea—light, moisture, aromas—will inform your choices, both in the tea you buy and whom you trust as a seller. For example, is the packaging an airtight foil wrap or simple paper? You may be pleasantly surprised when you find that many value-priced teas are packaged in such a way that the health benefits, as well as the flavors, are managed with care and consideration. On the other hand, when you see tea carelessly displayed and poorly packaged you may opt to shop elsewhere.

Tea Is Medicine and Promotes a Healthy Lifestyle

Tea has a 5,000-year history as a potent medicinal herb. Long before the flavor was developed, transforming it into a palatable beverage, the bitter tonic from boiled tea leaves was recommended for treating specific ailments. Noted in ancient Chinese texts on medical practices, tea had many accepted healing qualities including aiding digestion, increasing mental focus, dispelling heat and dampness, dispelling toxins, and maintaining a healthy balance in the body. In the last few decades, it has become one of the most researched foods and, consequently, there are now thousands of studies by reputable medical institutions to support the validity of the old beliefs. For example, it has been widely accepted that tea keeps the mind alert into old age and increases longevity. A recent 2013 study on Alzheimer's disease shows that drinking green tea can help protect brain cells from developing an accumulation of amyloid plaques associated with brain deterioration.

Many Studies Show Positive Benefits

There are hundreds of new studies being published every year, but a few recent notables help build an important body of evidence so that the following assumptions can be made:

- Tea is a powerful neurological stimulator that invigorates the mind and may help protect the cells of the brain.
- Tea contains significant amounts of antioxidants that may help disrupt the growth of certain kinds of cancer cells.
- Tea's antioxidants help lower levels of undesirable cholesterols and may reduce the threat of clogged arteries.
- Tea helps maintain stable blood sugar.
- Tea is 99 percent water and assists with hydration.

Tea Is Used for Relaxation and Spiritual Practices

Buddhism's emphasis on meditation and the invigorating properties of tea are closely associated. Monks helped spread the usefulness of tea in their practice, and it became an important part of rituals and spiritual traditions throughout China, Japan, and Korea. Tea's association with the practice of clearing one's mind to relieve the stress of the day is especially valued today.

- Tea preparation is a form of meditation in many different cultures. The way it is brewed and served requires focus and practice to ensure unwavering attention to detail.
- Tea inspired a philosophy called Teaism, closely associated with Taoism.
- Tea was served ceremonially to samurai warriors preparing for battle.

- Tea preparation and consumption is a ceremony and a performance art. In addition to formal rituals, it is also part of weddings and business meetings.

Tea Brings People Together

Tea has woven itself into the fabric of life for many cultures around the world. A simple cup can be the focal point of large and small gatherings.

- Tea is a social event. From royal garden parties to wartime dances to contemporary fundraisers, tea sets a standard for group gatherings.
- Tea offers a time of day to rest and pause, to take a break from work. Many factories in Great Britain provide teacarts for break times in offices and factories, realizing that the stimulation of the tea and a small snack increases productivity.
- Tea is a light afternoon meal introduced to the British court in the 1840s by Anna Maria Russell, the Duchess of Bedford, which quickly gained popularity in many social classes. This afternoon repast is now popular around the world today. In Britain, "high tea" refers to the hearty evening meal eaten by workers home from work, served at the "high" table rather than a "low" table in a parlor or drawing room.
- Tea is a way in which guests are welcomed. Hospitality in many societies—both Eastern and Western—is demonstrated by immediately offering tea to the guest.
- Tea can be a moment of comfort shared with a friend in crisis.

ESSENTIAL

Tea is so often thought of as a beverage that people forget that it has always been a food as well. As a food, tea leaves are cooked as a leafy green vegetable in many countries where it grows. Brewed tea is also used in cooking.

Tea Is Communication

The image of a round-bellied teapot with steam wafting from the spout, a delicate cup and saucer waiting to be filled, a child pretend-pouring plastic cups for teddy bears, and even a tall glass of the brown liquid embellished with a sprig of mint are strong visual gestures. Serving and sharing tea has an almost universal implication of peacefulness, generosity, and relaxation. Teatime immediately suggests that respect is being shared between host and guest and that it will most likely loosen the lips and inspire conversation. As varied as the practices may be, there are some common denominators that make tea a global language.

- Tea is a transmission of culture and history through which much can be learned by sharing the way it is prepared and served.
- Tea is a symbol of elegance and beauty. Painters pose models gracefully musing over a teacup. The media portrays a character sipping from a porcelain cup to indicate their sophistication.
- When we invite someone to share a cup of tea, it usually suggests that we wish to enjoy relaxed and peaceful conversation.
- In some cultures, the tea selection and way it is served communicates whether the guest is held in high esteem or with less respect.
- Tea forms a bridge between East and West. Though not a comfortable history, tea was one of the commodities that opened the door to an exchange between the two worlds, and helped the two populations both understand their differences and discover many of the ways in which they are all the same.

FACT

In his 2006 book, *Three Cups of Tea*, coauthor Greg Mortenson explained the Pakistani tea tradition of hospitality and business. With the first cup you are only a stranger. Sharing a second cup makes you a friend. With a third cup you become family. However much the author has fallen out of respect, the custom of tea being used for hospitality and to further business relationships is not unusual in many cultures and countries.

Tea Around the World

A recent invitation to attend the 2013 Korean Tea Forum was sent to tea people around the world with a beautifully stated sentiment that many tea people share: "One cup of tea makes everyone in the world friends and family regardless of their cultural differences. Within a cup of tea, there is love, culture, and a life of human kind. Therefore, tea is a beverage of the globe."

In today's world, as we struggle to survive amid radical change and tumultuous conflict, it may be that recognizing a common bond in a simple cup of tea might offer a sense of well-being. The following sections explore tea throughout the world.

China

China has many different "cultures" of tea, with enormous differences in the way it is consumed and celebrated. From a simple bowl of hot water on which fresh leaves float, sometimes called grandpa-style tea, to a formal *gongfu* ceremony, tea is an important part of everyday life, of social events, of business transactions, and of the entire Chinese economy. Some of the ethnic minorities within China have their own holidays during which tea plays a symbolic role. One example is the Bai three-course tea of bitter, sweet, and then pungent to represent different stages of life.

An important difference in the Chinese way of tea from most other tea cultures is their focus on the whole, unbroken leaf as a measure of quality. Extraordinary care is taken with specialty tea to bring the fresh leaf from the field without breaking it. And in the production of fine teas, what may be dozens of steps are expertly coordinated so that the end result is a perfect, unbroken leaf.

FACT

Emperor Huizong of the Song Dynasty (C.E. 1082–1135) was famous as a poet, musician, and artist. But he is also known for his passion for tea and for writing a famous book on tea, *Treatise on Tea* (second only to Lu Yu's book, *The Classic of Tea*). It is said that his love of tea and the arts distracted him from ruling the country, and he was thus unable to withstand the invasion of the Manchurian armies.

Japan

Monks introduced Chinese tea to Japan in the ninth century. They began to develop their own production after the Zen priest Eisai returned in 1191 with seeds and information about the medicinal properties. His book, *How to Stay Healthy Drinking Tea*, includes preparations and dosages for treating various ailments.

Japanese tea culture is known for *chanoyu*, the ceremony also known as the Way of Tea, and for the matcha tea that is essential to the ceremony. Matcha tea is also now popular in modern frothy beverages and as an ingredient in cooking.

The Japanese tea growers focus less on preserving the whole leaf and more on the consistency of flavors, even with their green sencha, bancha, and gyokuro teas. There are two basic categories of Japanese teas: sun-grown and shade-grown. Shade-grown teas require more attention in the field and are therefore more rare and more expensive. They also develop different leaf chemistry with distinctive flavors and health benefits.

Korea

Paralleling tea's introduction in Japan, it was Korean Buddhist monks studying in China who returned home with the knowledge of tea and plants and seeds to begin their own tea farming. Tea drinking in Korea became popular with both royalty and common people. Teahouses and pavilions in public parks became places where tea was shared, and ceramic artisans began to develop specialized utensils for brewing and serving tea. The thousand-year-old Korean tea ceremony is called *darye*, which is sometimes translated as "day tea ritual," and emphasizes beauty, harmony, naturalness, and relaxation. Popular Korean teas include three different styles of green tea grown on farms as well as wild tea plucked from older trees.

Vietnam

It may be surprising to know that Vietnam has a 3,000-year-old tea tradition. While the Chinese, Japanese, and Korean cultures use tea in spiritual ceremony, the Vietnamese ceremonial tea service is usually part of a wedding celebration. But the Vietnamese also recognize its medicinal properties and practice the social aspect of showing hospitality. One of the unique and romantic customs in Vietnam is for tea lovers to set out in their boats on lakes covered with blooming lotus and fill the open blossoms with their fresh tea leaves before the flowers close overnight. The next morning the tea will have absorbed the scent of the lotus. The people then gather the scented tea and collect the dew, brewing the two together for a rare experience.

India

It was the British who were primarily responsible for the first cultivation of tea in India, and therefore influenced the first commercial processing and the way in which it was brewed and served there. As part of the British Empire in the 1800s, India, especially the Himalayan regions, appeared to be the best place for England to begin growing its own tea, gaining independence from their sources in China. With great difficulty, The East India Company of England surreptitiously gathered plants, seeds, and workers from China and brought them to the Darjeeling area of India in an attempt to replicate Chinese tea.

Unknown at the time, an indigenous version of the Chinese tea plant, the *Camellia sinensis* var. *assamica*, was growing wild in the Assam region of northeastern India. Cultivating this variety ultimately became a very profitable venture for the British. Ultimately, three different important tea regions were established in India—Assam, Darjeeling, and Nilgiri.

As tea became a significant industry for India, it was integrated into India's culture as well, establishing new westernized customs. One distinctive way that tea is enjoyed in India is *masala chai*, or "spiced tea": black tea boiled into a strong infusion (or brewed directly in milk), mixed with hand-ground spices like ginger, cardamom, pepper, and cinnamon, and milk added if not used earlier. Western tea drinkers often shorten this to simply "chai," which is the Hindi word for tea.

ESSENTIAL

The modern tea industry in India is organized under the Tea Board of India, which works on behalf of all regions to maintain quality control, to ensure good treatment of workers, and to educate the rest of the world on the quality and unique flavors of Indian tea.

Sri Lanka/Ceylon

In the early 1800s, what was then known as Ceylon was enjoying a successful coffee industry until the 1869 coffee blight devastated their economy. A Scottish farmer named James Taylor is credited with transforming abandoned coffee fields into a thriving tea plantation, establishing a tea culture that was strongly influenced by European tastes. It was in Ceylon that Sir Thomas Johnstone Lipton, founder of Lipton Tea, met James Taylor in the 1890s, and soon after purchased quantities of Ceylon tea for distribution throughout Europe and the United States.

Sri Lankans take great pride in their tea industry, knowing that it saved their devastated economy and today is still largely responsible for the country's continued well-being. They consume a great deal of tea on a daily basis, but it has also become an important part of festivals and family celebrations.

Taiwan

Taiwan currently grows some of the most famous and prized oolong teas. Farming began more than two hundred years ago with plants and production skills brought from the mainland area of the Fujian Province of China, known for its oolong teas. Along with the plants, a vibrant and artistic tea-drinking culture developed.

Their traditional tea ceremony is similar to the Chinese gongfu presentation but in the 1980s a new practice called the Wu-wo ceremony was created. Also referred to as the "selfless" tea ceremony, participants bring their own tea and equipage to a scheduled event, take their places in a large circle, and then silently prepare their own tea. There is no leader, but there is an established pattern of sharing tea around the circle so that everyone is equally a server and guest.

The Taiwanese are also credited with one of the most modern formulas for tea, called bubble tea, pearl milk tea, or boba milk tea. It is a blend of strongly brewed tea, rich milk, optional flavorings, and large tapioca balls. Bubble tea shops have gained popularity around the world.

Iran

Iran began developing tea trade with China along the famous Silk Road. Tea quickly gained popularity and surpassed coffee to become their national drink. While early attempts to grow their own tea failed, an Iranian prince, Mohammad Mirza (also known as Kashef Al Saltaneh), started the first tea farm in 1899. While an Iranian ambassador to British-ruled India, Kashef had become fascinated with tea production. Disguising himself as a French laborer, he worked in the fields and factories to glean the secrets of tea production and to covertly collect saplings.

Teahouses called *chāikhānes* are important social gathering places where the strongly brewed tea is sipped from a saucer so that the warm liquid flows over a lump of sugar already in the mouth or held between the teeth.

Myanmar/Burma

Tea is grown mainly in the Shan State and Kachin State of Myanmar and is considered a national drink, usually served with sweetened milk. Tea shops are part of the social network as well as daily meeting places for family and friends.

One of the unique uses for tea is as a food. Tea leaves are pickled and served as a dish called *lahpet*, with a selection of other foods like garlic, peanuts, dried shrimp, fresh ginger, and coconut or dried peas. Another version is where the pickled tea leaves are added to a salad that includes other vegetables and may be dressed with fish sauce and lime or sesame oil.

Kenya

Kenya is currently one of the world's largest exporters of tea, yet they do not have a large tea-consuming culture. Most of Kenyan tea is manufactured as black tea, grown by both large companies and small landowning farmers. Being on the equator with rich, volcanic soil allows for constant, year-round production and full-time jobs for workers.

Tea seeds were first planted in Kenya in 1904 and commercial production began in 1925. In 1980, the Kenyan Tea Development Agency created their own tea research foundation, focusing partly on developing more productive varietals. One of the interesting developments from this research is the recent creation of purple tea. It is reported to be higher in antioxidants and is currently gaining popularity, reputed to have a higher antioxidant value with similar properties to regular green tea.

Germany

The Dutch were the first to import tea to Germany, as well as the rest of Europe, in the early 1600s, promoting its medicinal qualities. Within a hundred years, the popularity of tea in Germany grew to the point where it competed with beer consumption.

An interesting way of drinking tea developed in the East Frisia region of northern Germany that is still popular today. Using a strong black Indian tea from Assam or Darjeeling, or sometimes a Ceylon tea, a three-layered cup is served. The first layer is a foundation of a rock sugar lump, over which hot black tea is poured. The sugar slowly melts, but remains thick and heavy on the bottom of the un-stirred cup. Next the heavy cream layer is added, pouring it into the glass gently so that the sugar layer is barely disturbed. The brew is not stirred, so that more tea and cream can be poured in alternating layers over the sugar for additional rounds.

England and the British Isles

Tea rapidly became the national drink after it was introduced by the Dutch in the 1600s and is consumed in many different ways by almost all economic classes. But it was originally popularized by sellers who promoted its medicinal qualities with some of the first advertising for tea, publishing and distributing broadsheets with extraordinary claims.

Tea drinking spread to Ireland and Scotland at roughly the same time. In Ireland, the preference for strongly brewed tea is that "a spoon can stand up in it." The Scots also developed a preference for strongly brewed black tea. It was Scottish farmers who helped expand the tea industry in Ceylon following the coffee blight. The British Empire played a large role in the spread of tea farming and the development of tea culture around the world, and finally succeeded in developing a varietal for its own terroir. The first local tea plantation began limited production in 2005 on the Tregothnan Estate in Cornwall.

France

Tea was actually imported into France several decades before it arrived in England. It became a treasured beverage of the nobility, even attracting the attention of French physicians. Louis XIV drank tea in 1665, both as a treatment for his gout and protection against heart disease. He had heard, and believed, the tales that the Chinese and Japanese did not suffer heart conditions due to their consumption of tea. French physicians published papers describing it as both mentally and physically stimulating, with the potential to cure headaches and improve digestion.

Because tea was so strongly identified with the upper classes and high taxes, it was shunned as a symbol of nobility by the general populace and rapidly fell out of fashion and availability until the mid-1800s. Tea drinking is now very popular in all of French culture, with a focus on high-quality teas and careful preparation, but without ritual.

Russia

The first tea was delivered to the Russian Tsar Michael I (Mikhail Fyodorovich Romanov) in the 1630s by a Mongolian ruler. A second gift of tea was made around 1680 to Alexis I (Aleksey Mikhailovich) by a Chinese ambassador negotiating trade relationships. On a treacherous route more than 10,000 miles long that required more than a year to transport goods, tea became a highly valued trade product. Tea was then a luxury item, but today is an essential beverage in Russia, served in its own unique teaware. The image of the silver samovar with its stacked-teapot design is distinctly Russian. Preferences are that the tea be strong and sweet, sometimes served with mint or lemon, or sweetened with fruit jam. The leaves or the tea bags are boiled with the water, usually for five minutes or more, the resulting decoction then diluted with freshly boiled water. Teatime, tea served with cakes and sweets, is both an intimate family event and an expression of hospitality.

Argentina

Argentina is one of the largest tea producers in the world. Almost everyone has tasted their teas without knowing it, because they are most often cut and blended into bulk tea sold under major brand names. Very little whole-leaf, artisan tea is exported from there. Within Argentina, the culture of drinking tea is more associated with a different beverage, a tisane called maté, made from the *yerba maté* plant (*Ilex paraguariensis*), an evergreen in the holly family. The beverage is traditionally served warm in a gourd, and drunk through a metal straw called a *bomba* or *bombilla*.

QUESTION

Does maté contain caffeine?
Maté does contain small amounts of caffeine comparable to the rates in some of the lower caffeine-rich teas, but much less than coffee.

United States

The Dutch imported tea to the colonies in the 1600s, around the same time that it was introduced to Europe. When it became controlled by the British and highly taxed, it also became a symbol of British rule, fueling protest events like the Boston Tea Party uprising. Less well known were similar protests in other port cities. Colonists turned away and destroyed shipments from British companies, and there was a strong movement to boycott all tea consumption. It is said by some that this led to the United States becoming more of a coffee culture, and also necessitated substitutes of herbal infusions to brew in the traditional teapot.

Tea farming was first attempted in the American colonies in 1744. Experimental gardens surfaced throughout the south but were only successfully harvested in South Carolina in the mid-1800s. While never profitable, efforts continued. The most successful to date is the Charleston Tea Plantation, established in the latter half of the twentieth century as a research project by the Lipton Company, and now owned and operated by the Bigelow Company.

In recent years, commercial tea gardens have also been planted in Hawaii and Washington. In June 2013, the United States League of Tea Growers was launched at the annual tea trade show World Tea Expo, with interest from growers in many additional states.

CHAPTER 2

Tea's History as a Medicine

The passion for tea that spread around the world, transformed economies, inspired trading wars, and ignited powder kegs of political protest was fueled by the conviction that it was a healthy beverage, a life-changing experience, and supported a better way of life. Even now, the buzz of new tea trends almost always yields evidence of this with documentation from new medical studies. Our modern science is substantiating on a cellular level what has been part of medical history for 5,000 years, and tea is luring newcomers to explore its ancient wisdom and mythology.

Legends, Myths, and Tall Tales

There are three frequently told legends about the origin of tea and appreciation of its healthful qualities. The first two are of Chinese origin: the legend of Emperor Shen Nong, and a story of a Chinese herbalist. The third is the legend of the Indian Buddhist monk, Bodhidharma.

Emperor Shen Nong, the Great Emperor of Medicine

One of tea's most endearing legends is that of the mythical Emperor Shen Nong (sometimes spelled Shen Nung or Shennong), who is said to have brewed the first cup of tea. He is revered as the second of three ancient San Huang Emperors, mythical emperors who are considered the founders of Chinese civilization. The three are sometimes thought of as having divine powers to help mankind. Each of them brought helpful gifts to mankind during their reign.

Shen Nong is also referred to as the Divine Husbandman (or the Divine Farmer), the Divine Healer, the Father of Chinese Agriculture, the Emperor of Five Grains, and the God of the Fields due to his life's work researching beneficial plants and developing farming tools such as the hoe and plow. As a healer he is credited with developing hundreds of herbal remedies, and is considered the author of the Chinese book, *The Divine Farmer's Herb-Root Classic,* a compendium of medicinal compounds said to be developed or discovered by him, though it was not written until centuries later.

QUESTION

What other medicinal herbs are also credited with being discovered by the legendary emperor Shen Nong?
Cannabis sativa and *Cannabis indica* are also attributed to Shen Nong. These herbs are the source of hemp and marijuana.

In temples built to honor him, he is called the Great Emperor of Medicine, and there are lists of hundreds of health treatments he is believed to have developed. One is the practice of taking the patient's pulse to diagnose weakness, which is associated with the beginning of acupuncture. But his greatest and most life-saving health lesson for the ancient Chinese people and, ultimately, the rest of the world, is that of boiling water to make it safe to drink. Before the awareness of dangerous microscopic organisms living in water, Shen Nong promoted the importance of purifying water.

It is said that Shen Nong spent much of his time as emperor traveling the countryside examining the leaves and fruit of various plants and demonstrating his health innovations. The story of the first cup of tea begins with the emperor traveling to teach his people methods of hygiene and how to boil water to purify it. In most versions of the story, his cauldron was set in the shade of a tea tree where leaves fell from the tree and landed in the boiling water, releasing a sweet aroma and beautiful green color. Inspired to taste the brew, Shen Nong is said to have experienced the invigorating effect from what must have been a very bitter tonic, and immediately added the tea plant to his collection of medicinal herbs.

Stories of the Emperor's ancient research describe him collecting leaves, roots, and fruit of newly discovered plants and testing the effects on his own body. In some instances, he poisoned himself and fell ill. It is said that Shen Nong used tea as an antidote to the effects of other toxic plants, and that tea saved his life on at least six occasions.

FACT

The Bronze Age in China is considered 3100–2700 B.C.E. (Before Common Era) when the technology of metal pots made it easier to boil water. Since Shen Nong is said to have boiled the first tea leaf in 2737 B.C.E., it is possible that he was also traveling the countryside introducing this new technology to his people.

The significance of the legend of Emperor Shen Nong is debated in tea circles. Though usually found to be less than historical, it is nonetheless a pleasant legacy that honors tea. Even Lu Yu, the respected author of *Ch'a Ching* (*The Classic of Tea*), written between C.E. 760 and 780, mentions the legend of Emperor Shen Nong.

The Legend of the 22,000 Virtues of Tea

An ancient Taoist legend speaks of an elderly Chinese herbalist said to have collected 84,000 benefits (virtues) of medicinal herbs. Nearing the end of his life, the healer began teaching his son to take his place, but died before the training was complete. The son recorded only 62,000 treatments. He was said to have been devastated by both the loss of his father and for the loss of the other 22,000 methods of healing. Then during a dream one night the spirit of his father visited and told the son to visit his grave to receive the remaining plant virtues. The son went the next day expecting to find 22,000 plants. Instead, he found only one—a single tea plant. The son is said to have instantly realized that the wondrous plant contained all the remaining virtues.

The Legend of Bodhidharma

In the fifth or sixth century C.E. Bodhidharma, a Buddhist monk from southern India, traveled to China to share the Buddha's doctrine of enlightenment through meditation. Two versions of his experience with tea and meditation are told.

The more dramatic and slightly gruesome version begins with Bodhidharma visiting a Shaolin Temple in Henan Province, demonstrating the intense devotion of his practice by sitting in meditation without closing his eyes for nine years. When attempting to repeat this feat, he unintentionally fell asleep after he had been sitting in meditation for only seven years. When he awoke, he was so angry at his failure to reach nine years that he cut off his eyelids and threw them to the ground. It is said that a tea bush sprang from the soil where his eyelids fell.

ALERT

One of the popular Chinese green teas, Chun Mee or Lu Mei, is translated as Precious Eyebrow Tea. Some have mistakenly connected this name to the Bodhidharma story. The name actually refers to the long, rolled shape of the dried leaf looking like the eyebrow of a beautiful woman—not the famous monk.

The other variation on Bodhidharma's "failure" during his long meditation is that, when he felt himself growing drowsy and falling asleep, he reached out and grabbed a handful of green leaves from a nearby bush. Of course, the leaves were those of the true tea plant, *Camellia sinensis*, and it was in that moment that the famous monk was said to have discovered how tea can aid in staying awake and maintaining focus during meditation.

It is possible that Bodhidharma was actually introduced to tea by Chinese Taoist monks who had already been using it for centuries. But the stories of Bodhidharma, now considered the father of Zen Buddhism, illustrate the strong connection between spiritual meditation practices and tea. It was legends like this one that expanded the use of tea from being just a medicinal treatment to part of a daily spiritual practice.

ESSENTIAL

A Simple Tea Meditation: Choose a quiet environment with the intention to "unplug" for a few minutes. Focus all five senses on the experience: the sound of the boiling water, the aroma rising from the cup, the color of the tea liquor, the flavor of the warm tea as it rests on your tongue, and the warmth of the cup nestled in your hands. Set other thoughts aside and try to relax more with each sip.

Spreading the Influence of Tea

Beginning in the sixth century C.E., the spread of tea throughout Asian countries is easily tracked by following the teachings of monks who traveled to China to study both Buddhism and Taoism, and then returned home with the practice of brewing tea to aid in alertness during meditation. They also brought back seeds and cuttings to grow the teas in local soils. Tea's route to Japan is well known, but tea farming and tea culture found their way to other countries, such as Korea, Vietnam, and Tibet, in the same way. In many cases, the monasteries were also schools and places of worship for the communities, so it is easy to imagine that the beverage found its way into local gardens and into the lives of people who discovered its other benefits. Eventually, art and literature discovered tea, transmitting the wonders of the herb to the aristocrats.

Recognized as the first book on tea, Lu Yu's *The Classic of Tea* or *Ch'a Ching*, was written between C.E. 760 and 780. In addition to advice on the way tea should be grown, picked, manufactured, brewed, and consumed, he includes poems, stories, and the known health benefits already recorded in Chinese medical books by that time. He focused attention on tea as a medicinal herb, providing recipes to prepare elixirs for cures. In one passage, he compares the medicinal value of tea to that of ginseng, and suggests that properly prepared tea would help with headaches, joint pain, chest congestion, and some forms of weakness.

ESSENTIAL

Lu Yu was an orphan adopted by a monk and raised in a monastery who chose to devote his life to the study of tea. He is referred to as the Saint of Tea and the Sage of Tea. Early in his studies, he discovered the importance of using fresh water of fine quality, which is one of the first lessons in making healthful and flavorful tea.

Popular Trade on the Silk Road

The Silk Road and its three main routes connected China and its tea to the rest of the world. Yunnan Province, the birthplace of tea cultivation, was linked to the main route via another famous path called the Tea Horse Road. As information about the wonderful qualities of tea spread, so did the demand. With so many stories of tea's value as a stimulant and its potential as an antidote for poisons and toxins, it is no small wonder that traders from around the world wanted to return with this miraculous prize. However, delivering green tea from the fields to points of sale without it developing mold was a challenge. Finding solutions to overcome the problem is actually what created the various categories of tea, and ultimately made it possible for tea to travel great distances.

Originally, baskets of tea were transported on horseback, taking as long as a year to reach their destinations. Over that amount of time, green leaves would oxidize and turn black. One of the first innovations in tea manufacture was to compress the leaves into dense blocks of tea, called tea bricks, which made it easier to carry more tea while reducing the air between the leaves that caused mold. Techniques of drying and preparing the bricks for travel became an art form. The compressed bricks became so valuable that they were eventually traded like money, so much so that it threatened the government control of trade and the Honwu emperor Zhu

Yuanzhang banned their production in the mid-fourteenth century in order to stop the threat to the official Chinese currency of the time. This prompted greater production of loose-leaf tea.

ESSENTIAL

Emperor Zhu Yuanzhang's son, Zhu Quan, contributed greatly to modern tea production by publishing his *Tea Manual* in C.E. 1439, advocating the superiority of loose-leaf tea and suggesting ways to grow, manufacture, and brew it.

Chinese Tea Dynasties

What we now know of the gradual spread of the use of tea and the tea arts further validates its importance in the history of healthcare.

- From prehistoric times tea was used as a ceremonial gift and recognized as a beneficial medicinal herb, but was not widely brewed as a beverage until about C.E. 221. Traditional Chinese medicine recognizes many authors of ancient medical publications who mention tea's healing properties.
- Tea farms were first planted in the Yunnan and Sichuan Provinces as early as 1000 B.C.E. It was during this time that tea leaves were also harvested and cooked as a fresh green.
- Tea as a medicine gained prominence during the Han Dynasty (206 B.C.E.–C.E. 220) and was also recognized as the official imperial beverage that eventually established the practice of tribute teas being sent to the court.
- During the Jin and Sui Dynasties (C.E. 265–618), tea was considered both a medicinal herb and a beverage. Its use spread throughout China to a much larger population, as did the cultivation of tea on farms.
- During the Tang Dynasty (C.E. 618–907), tea became recommended as one of the seven essentials of daily life for all people. Bowls of tea were shared in teahouses, and Lu Yu wrote *The Classic of Tea* in C.E. 760–780.

- In the Song Dynasty (C.E. 960–1279), tea became an important commodity traded via the Silk Road on land and sea to Arab countries and Africa. The spread of tea by monks to other Asian countries practicing Buddhism flourished.
- In the Yuan Dynasty (C.E. 1271–1368), there was disruption in the evolution of fine tea appreciation during the time of Kubla Khan and the Mongolian influence.
- The Ming Dynasty (C.E. 1368–1644) saw the proliferation of loose-leaf tea production throughout China, and the innovation of teaware for infusing, serving, and drinking fine teas. Teaware made from Yixing clay became popular.
- The Qing Dynasty (C.E. 1644–1911) marks the time when tea gained popularity in Europe, both as a medicinal herb and as a healthful beverage, and then spread around the rest of the world by land and sea.

Europe Imports the New Health Rage

Portuguese missionaries and traders may have been the first Westerners who tasted tea, and returned with the first exports of tea via caravan from China, but it was the Dutch traders in the early 1600s who first dominated tea trade to Western Europe and North American colonies like New Amsterdam. Rumors of its stimulating properties proved to be true and were enough to make the drink quickly popular, although expensive.

In the early days of trade, tea was sold in coffeehouses and apothecary shops (pharmacies). Being a stimulating beverage similar to coffee, sales in coffeehouses made sense. However, it was not considered proper for women during this time to be seen in coffeehouses. One way that women were able to partake of the wondrous new Chinese elixir was to purchase it from the apothecaries as a "dose" of tea. Taking this dose home to brew may have inspired private gatherings of women to share the precious commodity even before the custom of afternoon tea parties that usually included cakes and sweets became famous.

Early Health Advertising

In the year 1657, for the first time in thousands of years, information about the drinking of tea to improve health was shared in a way that was not direct, person-to-person communication: It was advertised in print. A London coffeehouse owner, Thomas Garway, presented his version of the remarkable properties of tea on a famous broadside (a large printed poster, an original of which is preserved in the British Museum, London). He described the leaf and drink that had previously been available only "as a Regalia in high Treatments and Entertainments, and Presents made thereof to Princes and Grandees." In the famous ad, Garway listed the following among his "virtues" (partial list).

- Purifies the blood
- Vanquishes heavy dreams
- Eases pain and giddiness in the head
- Eases breathing and helps cure fevers and colds
- Clears the sight
- Vanquishes superfluous sleep and prevents sleepiness
- Drives away dizziness and makes one more nimble
- Drives away fear
- Eases the pain of colic
- Strengthens memory
- Sharpens the will and quickens understanding

With such staggering promises, who would not be curious enough to try a sip? The result was a rapid rise in the number of coffeehouses serving brewed tea and the number of shops selling packets of tea to be prepared at home. England was quickly on its way to selecting the *C. sinensis* brew as their national beverage.

Claims as astounding as these in any form of advertising by a tea company today would not only be stopped by the U.S. Food and Drug Administration, but would raise the suspicions of consumers as well. However, interestingly enough, in recent years science has substantiated most of Garway's claims.

FACT

Thomas Twining, founder of Twinings Tea in London, originally owned coffeehouses. In the early 1700s, competition between coffeehouses was stiff, and Twining decided to offer brewed tea as a new way to attract clientele. It was such a success that he soon established The Golden Lyon shop next door to his coffeehouse to sell dry tea, which enabled ladies to purchase it as well.

Modern Tea Health Marketing

Businesses and organizations wanting to promote tea for increased sales continue to use the "health" message, similar to Garway's first broadside. But they are now able to use modern medical research to substantiate their claims in ways that Thomas Garway wasn't able to do in the 1600s, and as a result, the list of tea's "virtues" is growing. Modern marketing also takes place in different forums and media.

- **Calm-A-Sutra Tea Scholarship, USA.** In 2008, the United States Tea Association launched a campaign to educate and entertain the public about tea's health benefits. The challenge was to create a YouTube video presenting the health benefits of four main tea categories: green, black, white, and oolong. The grand prize was a $20,000 scholarship.
- **Tea Industry News, Magazines, and Bloggers.** News sources addressing the thirst of a tea-committed niche fill their print and virtual real estate with updates on new research and trends. Every study that reaffirms health claims with a significant number of percentage points over the placebo test group reminds tea drinkers that they have made a wise choice.
- **TV Personalities.** Some of the most notable talk show hosts and guests such as Oprah, Dr. Oz, and Dr. Weil have all found opportunities to address new tea research and make recommendations about adding the brew to a healthy lifestyle.
- **Tea Lovers' Festivals.** Conventions and festivals for tea lovers are becoming increasingly popular, with events in several states at different times of the year. Some are beginning to refer to these shows

as tea tourism, and attendees arrive thirsting for tastings and educational workshops.

- **Tea Business Trade Shows.** Industrial trade shows for tea are becoming popular events around the world. Growers and manufacturers of tea-related products exhibit directly to retailers. The World Tea Expo in Las Vegas, NV, recently hosted its eleventh year, bringing tea people from around the world together for trade and education. A similar annual event in Xiamen, China, recently brought together a panel of experts from Hong Kong, Mainland China, India, Taiwan, and the United States.

- **Symposium on Tea Health.** Every five years the Scientific Symposium on Tea and Human Health convenes, inviting prominent scientists to present their research. The most recent gathering in 2012 was sponsored by the American Cancer Society, the American Institute for Cancer Research, the American Society for Nutrition, the American College of Nutrition, the Linus Pauling Institute, the American Medical Women's Association, the Food and Agriculture Organization of the United Nations, and the Tea Council of the USA. The event featured eleven scientific presentations about tea effects on cancer, heart disease, weight loss, and cognitive performance, as well as new observations regarding how tea works on the cellular level in the body.

CHAPTER 3

What Is Healthy about Tea?

The wisdom of the age-old expression, "If it sounds too good to be true . . . it probably is," may echo in your mind as tea-touting articles proliferate in the daily newspapers, dominate magazine articles, and temper talk show topics, TV ads, and general health advice chatter. Indeed, it seems that there is some new health issue every day. How much can be believed, and what are the most trustworthy sources?

The Growing Body of Evidence

Most people develop beliefs and make personal decisions based on their life experiences and most trusted sources of information: family, friends, experts, their own research, and reliable media. In this information age, the sources are massive, but often the information can be filled with conflicting opinions and recommendations, particularly with nutritional claims. What's fad and what's fact? Does something going viral on the Internet make it true? In the case of tea, the current media darling of the beverage world, you may easily accept the basic claim that it is one of the healthiest drink choices and that it's vastly better for you to drink than canned sodas. But, can you trust the enormous list of benefits inspiring the buzz? In the last few years, health research on tea has inspired the media. From TV talk shows to grocery store tabloids, tea continues to steal headlines. But it's difficult to consider a respected medicinal with a 5,000-year history as just a fad.

On a journey circling the globe and spanning millennia, tea has arrived in this modern age almost unchanged, even now surviving scientific scrutiny. Scientists are matching the observations of ancient Asian healers and the theories of traditional Chinese medicine with results of experiments in controlled laboratory environments. Medical science is not only explaining the historic beliefs but is adding more to the list of ways in which *Camellia sinensis* supports the human body.

As the evidence builds with the publication of each new research project, the recommendation to drink tea every day does not change. The recent Fifth Annual Symposium on Tea and Health (2012) put forward the vetted research of almost 100 papers. The chairman, Jeffrey Blumberg, PhD, a research professor from Tufts University in Boston, said, "The many bioactive compounds in tea appear to impact virtually every cell in the body to help improve health outcomes, which is why the consensus emerging from this symposium is that drinking at least a cup of green, black, white, or oolong tea a day can contribute significantly to the promotion of public health."

Very few people become daily tea drinkers because of the bioactive compounds or the way tea extracts are helping annihilate cancer cells in test tubes. Studies on groups of humans who have been lifelong tea drinkers tell more about why people choose tea as a favorite beverage. They may be following cultural or family traditions established generations before they were born. If you ask someone from an historic tea culture why they choose the drink, they may not have an answer since the practice is so deeply embedded in their lifestyle that to them the science is irrelevant.

But for anyone living in a coffee, soda, fast-food, take-out, and convenience food culture, the merry-go-round of dietary recommendations can sound faddish—even if it is only the advice to drink a single cup of tea every day. Any tea will provide similar health benefits: green, black, oolong, white, pu'erh. As much as the magazine covers catch our eye with the powerful "proofs," there may be a lingering concern that it may be too much of a good thing to be true. And, even if it is true, is it really worth the trouble?

Wading through the science and statistics can be almost as intimidating as wading through some of the fashionable new flavors and brewing devices. But by scanning a sampling of recent research, comparing their observations and conclusions using varied populations and methods, we begin to see some interesting patterns. And we are also gathering evidence with our own bodies, inspiring changes in old eating and drinking habits. Do we sleep better, or weigh less, or feel happier? Is it because of the tea?

The Science of the Leaf

There are some basic chemical compounds that occur naturally in the tea plant, which generate most of the positive benefits. They conduct important "work" for the plant body as well as for the human body. This "work" tea can do includes helping feed, nourish, and protect cells throughout the body in ways we are just beginning to understand.

- Antioxidants in tea, as in many other foods, are compounds that reduce the effects of the pollutants that attack your body on a cellular level by neutralizing free radical molecules. Free radicals have only unpaired, single electrons, which search for a missing electron to pair with. This results in oxidation, deposits of unhealthy byproducts, and damage to other healthy cells. By providing the missing electron, antioxidants restore the natural and healthy pair. But antioxidants do not have a long lifespan after they are ingested, so it is critical to replenish them throughout the day, maintaining resistance to infection and a support for healthy cell reproduction.

- Polyphenols are some of the antioxidant compounds that are available naturally in many plants that you eat. Tea has unique polyphenols, and the research is now proving much of the ancient folklore about tea's benefits based on these compounds. Some of these benefits are protection against cancer and coronary heart disease, protection against stroke, reduced risk of osteoporosis, protection against liver disease, and protection against damage caused by inflammation.

- Catechins are one category of polyphenols unique to green tea that has not oxidized (turned brown). Within the category of polyphenols, there are several unique catechins. The one currently the most discussed and researched is epigallocatechin gallate (EGCG). In addition to the more general benefits of other polyphenols, the catechins in tea are showing benefits to Alzheimer's and other forms of dementia and neurological decline, a balancing of cholesterol between the healthful and harmful types, and maintaining balanced blood sugar. EGCG is one of green tea's five main catechins. It is called a super-antioxidant, proving to be much more powerful than other common antioxidants.

- Flavonoids function in plants to produce color and to protect the plant from microbes, fungi, and insects, and to filter UV rays. Research is studying some of their properties in the human body, including their functions as anti-inflammatories, antibacterials, antivirals, antifungals, and antioxidants.

- Thearubigins are polyphenols that are formed during tea's oxidation process, and therefore are more numerous in black tea. Thearubigins are reddish substances, one of the ways in which black tea develops its dark, reddish-brown color. Their discovery as accounting for up to 70 percent of the dry weight in black tea is relatively recent and much of the research on thearubigins points to the compound's role as an antioxidant and its ability to reduce oxidative stress, reduce the volume of destructive free radicals, and help reduce the effects of irritable bowel syndrome. Once ingested, the body has the ability to convert thearubigins back to catechins, the beneficial polyphenols more abundant in nonoxidized green teas.

- Theanine is an amino acid almost exclusively found in tea. It has been shown to have psychoactive properties, and to easily pass through the blood-brain barrier where it can bind to receptors and transporters involved in neurotransmission. It can also increase alpha brain activity when the body is at rest. Some animal studies have shown that it also provides neuroprotective properties.
- Caffeine is a naturally occurring stimulant. Tea is relatively low in caffeine. A cup of black tea, for example, contains about forty milligrams of caffeine, or about half as much as a cup of coffee. Caffeine is known to affect physiological, psychomotor, and cognitive performance, as well as mood. The caffeine in most tea creates what is frequently described as a "state of calm alertness."

Cancer

Some of the most abundant research into the health benefits of tea relates to cancer. While the work is still in the early stages, many studies over the last ten years are building a body of data while moving from laboratory to clinical trials. Clinical studies on the ways in which tea polyphenols may inhibit the growth of tumor cells and encourage their demise have shown positive results on several kinds of cancers. These include cancers of the bladder, breast, lungs, ovaries, esophagus, pancreas, prostate, and skin.

Evidence indicates that the catechins in tea help reduce the invasiveness of some tumor cells, and have demonstrably shown to reduce angiogenesis, preventing blood vessels from supporting tumor cells. The problem with cancer cells is that they continue proliferating, overriding the natural cycle of growth and death. In cancer cells, the switch that regulates the natural death of the cell is damaged or nonfunctioning, and apoptosis (cell death) doesn't occur. Drinking tea appears to help maintain the integrity and functionality of those switches, preserving the natural process of apoptosis.

ALERT

Considering that some of these studies were conducted in the controlled environment of the laboratory with concentrated tea extracts, it should not be assumed that the same effect could be recreated at home. There is an unpredictable variation in the quality and concentration of brewed tea. Population studies on habitual tea drinkers may, in many ways, be more relevant.

Breast Cancer

The National Institute of Health's Cancer Institute released a 2010 report, based on sixty-six different studies, stating that the biochemicals in green tea changed the way in which women metabolized estrogen, which is thought to reduce the risk of developing breast cancer.

Another interesting study of 472 Japanese-American women with varying stages of breast cancer found that the women in early stages of the disease who had been lifelong tea drinkers of approximately five cups a day before diagnosis were less likely to have a recurrence after they had finished their normal medical treatments.

In another U.S. study of 5,082 women between the ages of twenty and seventy-four, it was found that drinking three to five cups of tea per day was beneficial, especially in those women for whom tea drinking had been a practice for more than five years prior to diagnosis of the disease.

Ovarian Cancer

A 2002 study conducted in China included 906 total women, 254 of whom were diagnosed with ovarian cancer plus 652 control subjects. Factors considered included the frequency, type, and duration of tea consumption along with other lifestyle and predisposition factors. It was concluded that a daily habit of drinking green tea reduced the risk of developing ovarian cancer. Authors of the study noted that their work focused on green tea and recommended that similar studies be conducted for black and oolong tea.

A sizeable study of 61,000 Swedish women, followed for fifteen years, demonstrated a 46 percent reduced risk of developing ovarian cancer. This observational study is of great significance because of the large number of women followed over such an extended period of time, and because it included consumption of both green and black tea.

Prostate Cancer

In 2011, U.S. researchers at the School of Medicine in Los Angeles, CA, concluded that, "human population studies provide some supportive evidence for a decrease in risk of CaP [prostate cancer] associated with increased consumption of tea. Evidence is stronger for GT [green tea] compared to BT [black tea]." Their research included both animals and humans, and encouraged that more work be done.

Skin Cancer

One of the interesting findings announced at the Fifth Annual Tea Health Symposium in 2012 is that tea provides the body with a mild SPF benefit (SPF of 4), both when applied topically and when ingested. Therefore, drinking a cup or glass of tea regularly also maintains that slight protection consistently for cells.

Research by Santosh Katiyar in 2011 also found that green tea helps prevent non-melanoma skin cancer. In his 2011 article, "Green tea prevents non-melanoma skin cancer by enhancing DNA repair," Dr. Katiyar stated: "The outcome of the studies therefore suggests that regular consumption of green tea or green tea polyphenols may be considered as an effective strategy for the prevention of inflammation-associated skin diseases including UV irradiation-caused skin tumor development."

Another report comparing sixty-nine different studies on tea relative to skin cancer concluded that: "From these findings it can be seen that orally consumed EGCG has two different mechanisms of action and can act as both a chemopreventive and photochemopreventive drug; it can protect the body by suppressing, slowing down, and reversing the process of carcinogenesis, as well as protecting the skin from damaging radiation caused by harmful UVB rays."

Lung Cancer

The effects of smoking and inhaling other contaminants have shown to increase the risk of lung cancer. Some studies now demonstrate that tea, particularly green tea, may play an important role in improved health with regard to lung cancer, particularly for smokers. In 2010, I-Hsin Lin reported results from his study of more than 500 subjects, noting the benefits of drinking green tea: "Tea, particularly green tea, has received a great deal of attention because tea polyphenols are strong antioxidants, and tea preparations have shown inhibitory activity against tumorigenesis."

A new 2013 laboratory study on rats concluded that it was the tea polyphenols that significantly alleviated bronchial lesions in treatment of animals with the disease. This suggests that tea polyphenols may eventually assist in the prevention of lung cancer, and may inspire further study.

Liver Disease

Several animal studies indicate that drinking tea frequently throughout the day can help protect the liver from the damage by toxic substances such as alcohol, reducing inflammation of the liver. After extensive review of scientific studies conducted between 1989 and 2007, a 2008 report was published stating that the general findings suggested increasing the consumption of green tea may reduce the risk of developing liver disease.

Increased Bone Density

Measurable benefits of tea drinking have been found in older women but not in pre-menopausal women, though much of the available work suggests that it is the long-term and habitual use of tea that provides the greatest benefits. Several reliable studies have published results showing improved bone mineral density may be associated with drinking tea. An *American Journal of Clinical Nutrition* study found that older women who drink tea had stronger bones than non-tea-drinkers. Additionally, a 2002 study published in *Archives of Internal Medicine* found significant improvement in bone quality of older women who had been daily tea drinkers for more than six years.

Fighting Super-Bugs

At a 2008 meeting of the Society of General Microbiology, research was presented by Dr. Mervat Kassem from Alexandria University in Egypt showing that green tea enhanced the bacteria-killing potential of many antibiotics. It also showed that green tea rendered 20 percent of drug-resistant bacteria vulnerable to at least one of the new cephalosporin antibiotics, designed to treat more resistant strains of bacteria.

FACT

To be sure, medical science has no actual cure for the common cold or other respiratory infections like influenza. But medical recommendations infused with good common sense remind us that maintaining healthy bodies is a wise defensive strategy. It is known that antioxidants, like those abundant in tea, help keep cells strong and better able to resist disease, including colds and flu.

Heart Disease

In general, studies have shown that tea drinkers who consume at least three cups a day enjoy a reduced risk of heart disease and stroke. Some observations note improved functions in the blood vessels, better circulation, and healthier cholesterol levels.

A Taiwanese study on 1,500 subjects discovered that those participants who drank between two and three cups of tea per day reduced their risk of developing high blood pressure by 65 percent, compared to those who did not drink tea. And a Harvard study followed 1,900 post–heart attack patients and reported that those who had drunk tea regularly prior to their heart attack had a better survival rate in the three to four years following the event than the non-tea-drinkers did.

One hypothesis put forward states that tea functions as a vasodilator, opening the blood vessel walls, thereby reducing the risk of atherosclerosis, which is a high-risk indicator of cardiovascular disease. Ability to keep flexibility in arteries is an important factor in heart health.

In 1994, one of the largest studies to date, following more than 40,000 middle-aged Japanese subjects for seven years who drank more than two cups of green tea daily, found that they had a 22 to 33 percent reduced rate of death from cardiovascular disease as compared to participants who drank a half-cup or less per day. They concluded that "green tea consumption is associated with reduced mortality due to all causes and due to cardiovascular disease but not with reduced mortality due to cancer."

Controlling Cholesterol

The polyphenols in tea have been shown to help block the LDL, low-density lipoprotein (the "bad" cholesterol), from being absorbed into the intestine, thereby reducing the levels in the blood. Increasing its benefit, tea also raises the HDL, high-density lipoprotein (the "good" cholesterol). In a study conducted by the U.S. Department of Agriculture on people with mildly elevated LDL cholesterol levels, the LDL Rate in participants drinking five servings of black tea per day was reduced 11 percent over those consuming a placebo beverage.

ALERT

Research continues to find that drinking tea daily can help maintain healthy cholesterol levels, but not to the extent that someone currently under a doctor's supervision can substitute tea drinking for prescribed medication.

Mental Function and Neurological Health

Most tea drinkers are aware of mental clarity and focus when drinking tea, or the lack of it when they have not enjoyed their daily dose. But tea research is proving that it has additional benefits for neurological function. It appears that the L-theanine in tea increases alpha waves and cognitive function, and tea is one of few beverages that naturally contains L-theanine.

ESSENTIAL

Drinking green tea could mitigate the development amyloid plaques that many scientists believe may contribute to the deterioration of the brain, causing Alzheimer's disease. The flavonoid EGCG is showing promise at providing protection for the brain.

Diabetes

People with high levels of glucose or insulin in their blood are at greater risk for diabetes, cardiovascular disease, obesity, and more rapid aging. Studies on people with type 2 diabetes have shown that drinking an average of six cups a day for eight weeks lowered blood sugar by 15 percent. Additional studies suggest that drinking tea daily can slow the development of both type 1 and type 2 diabetes. Studies are also being done using tea extracts.

Because people with diabetes learn to be aware of the subtle changes in their blood sugar and must regularly test the precise measurement of their blood sugar levels, they can determine which foods and beverages have the most value in their diet. Unsweetened tea, especially one that has a natural sweetness without additives, is an excellent beverage option.

Weight Loss and Weight Management

Weight loss is such a hot topic these days that any new product with a pleasant turn of phrase inspires many to hit the "buy now" button. Tea is no exception. There is no shortage of ads and articles touting the pounds that can be shed if you tip a cup. In tea circles, among those who drink copious amounts of the brew, there is a bit of humor regarding claims to weight loss. A rather rotund tea lover being challenged about the slimming claims will respond, "Imagine what I would look like if I didn't drink tea."

The more responsible recommendation for using tea to shed pounds is to add it to a complete program that includes diet and exercise. There are several ways in which drinking tea helps maintain a healthy weight.

Tea Can Speed Up Metabolism

The assumption that drinking one or two cups per day will quickly strip off the pounds is not accurate. On the other hand, it is well established that brewed tea does slightly increase the metabolic rate by about 4 percent, giving you a small energy boost. This added energy may encourage more frequent exercise or increase the length of a workout. Additional activity can significantly help with weight loss, especially when it is part of an overall healthy lifestyle. Tea concentrates, especially those in over-the-counter energy drinks and pills, may have a more rapid and more predictable effect, but be cautious about selecting quality products and using them properly.

As a Replacement for High-Calorie Beverages

When you substitute unsweetened tea for several calorie-laden sodas or juice drinks, especially ones containing high-fructose corn syrup, you can reduce your daily intake by hundreds of calories. Developing an appreciation for the naturally sweet flavors of tea, or even those blended with dried fruit and herbs, can help conquer your demanding sweet tooth.

If you learn to recognize the danger zones during the day when you experience cravings, you can transform these moments into teatime—without the baked goods. Flavored teas are now available in both green and black formulations, with added concentrates that replicate the taste of chocolate, fruit, and cream to the extent that you might find teas that taste similar to famous candy bars, but with little to no calories. Give your metabolism a little boost while you overpower your seductive cravings.

Tea and Oral Hygiene

Tea contributes to good oral health in multiple ways. It does contain a measurable amount of fluoride that maintains healthy tooth enamel, although this varies greatly cup to cup. The flavonoids reduce the ability of bacteria present in the mouth to form plaque. And green tea helps with factors related to gum disease.

Unsweetened tea is shown to help control bacteria, unlike heavily sweetened drinks that increase bacterial growth. A reduction in bacteria and acid can be measured after a five-minute rinse with tea. This also indicates that it may help prevent tooth decay. The anti-inflammatory properties of tea may also help fight against gum disease and tooth loss. By killing the microbes that cause bad breath, tea can help fight halitosis. In addition, studies have shown the effectiveness of green tea antioxidants in slowing the growth of precancerous lesions in the mouth.

Hydration

Suggestions for how much you need to drink every day vary, especially considering an individual's age, activity level, and body weight. Good quality water is probably the most important source for hydration, but a British study found tea to be equally effective as water and enhanced sports beverages for cellular hydration. And considering the many other benefits of daily tea drinking, it is both a flavorful and healthful option to keep tissue well hydrated.

The Harvard School of Public Health created a visual aid for recommended beverage consumption, similar to the food pyramid. The infographic they produced is a pitcher indicating that total daily fluids be approximately ninety-eight fluid ounces. Half of this should be water; then twenty-eight ounces could be unsweetened tea or coffee. Of the remaining 22 percent, sixteen ounces should be low-fat milk and no more than four ounces of fruit juice. Alcohol and beverages with artificial sweeteners or high-fructose corn syrup were not recommended.

ESSENTIAL

The development of kidney stones is associated with lack of hydration, and studies show that tea drinkers have a slightly reduced risk of developing kidney stones, perhaps in part due to increased and more stable levels of hydration.

Benefits Beyond the Leaf

Even though the focus is on the beneficial properties of the tea leaf itself, it is important to recognize a few of the ways in which a tea lifestyle and the ways you drink tea can also contribute to improved health.

Subdue Stress

Stress has been shown to cause or to contribute to many health issues, including heart disease, digestive problems, sleep problems, headaches and migraines, asthma, PTSD, depression and anxiety, Alzheimer's and other forms of dementia, diabetes, obesity, autoimmune diseases, skin conditions, accelerated aging, and premature death. Setting aside a daily de-stressing time in which to enjoy a simple cup of tea, either alone or with family and friends, may support treatment of many stress-related health conditions and can encourage an overall sense of well-being.

Encourage Sensory Awareness and Stimulation

Tea drinking, especially a more dedicated appreciation of artisan teas and ceremonial experiences, encourages focused attention on the sensory experience, enlivening the whole body. All five senses are engaged in the experience of sipping tea. Beyond the taste and comforting warmth in the mouth, you can appreciate the aroma and the visual transition of the leaves as they swirl in the cup, and feel the warmth radiating from the cup in your hands. Sometimes just the sound of the whistling kettle can change a mood and signal relaxation. You can be comforted by conversation or favorite music while you enjoy your tea. There are many aspects of tea drinking that connect with art and beauty, and can provide a sense of elegance, peace, and contemplation.

Meditation and Mindfulness

Using tea in simple meditation practices does not require elaborate settings, expensive tea, or complicated routines. A few minutes of focusing complete attention on preparing and sipping tea while quieting your racing thoughts can be a very effective form of meditation. Sen no Rikyu, the renowned sixteenth-century Japanese tea master, said, "Tea is nothing but boiling water and making tea. This is the only rule you should know." The Japanese tea ceremony to which he devoted his life, however intricate and complicated it may seem, is an exercise in the elegance of simplicity and practiced mindfulness.

A Healthy Lifestyle

The Japanese priest Myoe (1173–1232) summarized his thoughts about the overall benefits of tea and inscribed them onto the surface of a ceramic teakettle in which he warmed water for tea preparation. They included the observations that tea has the blessing of deities, promotes filial piety, drives away evil spirits, banishes drowsiness, keeps internal organs in harmony, wards off disease, strengthens friendship, disciplines the body and mind, and grants a peaceful death. As exaggerated as this may sound, it reminds us that hundreds of years ago there existed a strong belief in the simple power of tea, the use of which was already a rather ancient tradition.

Current Medical Research

The tea industry has joined with a number of medical and research associations to sponsor an International Scientific Symposium on Tea and Human Health every five years since 1991, inviting respected researchers from around the world. At the symposium, selected research is vetted and reviewed by other scientists, then published and made available to the industry and to the media, supporting quality without the hype. At the 2012 symposium, held at the U.S. Department of Agriculture Headquarters in Washington, DC, keynote speaker and chairman Jeffrey Blumberg from Tufts University presented a summary that there was an overwhelming body of evidence to support the recommendation that drinking at least one cup of tea per day is likely to improve overall health.

Who Is Conducting the Research?

Hundreds of new studies on tea's benefits associated with specific diseases are being published in medical journals every year. The researchers represent the fields of biology, botany, nutrition, cardiology, and neuroscience, to name a few. Health organizations, universities, and hospitals in countries around the world have been sharing their work, continuously adding new scientific data to the growing understanding of the interaction of *Camellia sinensis* with the human body. Tea associations from many different countries also promote these findings and support the work in their own regions.

Where Is Scientific Research Being Published?

Reputable scientists and scientific organizations publish their work in several different professional journals, such as the *Journal of the American Medical Association (JAMA)*, the *New England Journal of Medicine*, *Lancet*, the *Journal of Experimental Medicine*, the *American Journal of Clinical Nutrition*, and the *Journal of Clinical Investigation*, to name only a few out of hundreds. The complete articles are available to subscribers, but summaries and abstracts can be accessed by the public through online sources like PubMed (*www.ncbi.nlm.nih.gov/pubmed*).

PubMed is an entity of the U.S. government known as the U.S. National Library of Medicine, part of the National Institutes of Health. This resource provides a database of more than twenty-three million citations for biomedical literature from MEDLINE, science journals, and books.

Stay Informed but Avoid the Hype

The U.S. Food and Drug Administration (FDA) and related health organizations in other countries control health claims that can be made about the efficacy of products by granting or denying their approval. They set standards for the wording of claims for health benefits that can be used on labeling and in promotional material. Anyone trying to sell tea with claims of health benefits—such as "guaranteed to help you lose weight"—would be irresponsibly stretching FDA limits. As most reputable retailers know, it is critically important to know the language that can be used, and caution must be exercised to not to exceed what is allowed. At this time, retailers are not even allowed to quote the conclusions of health researchers on product labels or on their websites. The consequences of doing so may result in the product being removed from store shelves and websites ordered to be taken down. Failure to comply can result in fines.

CHAPTER 4

The Caffeine Question

The arguments about caffeine in tea, coffee, chocolate, and other products are like the cartoon images of the two conflicting spirits, the devil and the angel, sitting on the shoulders of the tea drinker. The little angel offers benefits for those suffering with Parkinson's, diabetes, dementia, liver disease, and some cancers. The devil, on the other hand, dispenses unpleasant side effects for those with caffeine sensitivities, and also the potential for abuse.

What Is Caffeine?

Caffeine is a naturally occurring plant alkaloid that is found in coffee beans, tea leaves, cocoa beans, kola nuts, maté, yaupon leaves and berries, guarana seeds, yoco bark, and in some other beans and leafy plants. When consumed, the caffeine in these plants is a natural stimulant. When it is extracted from the plant and concentrated, caffeine is a bitter, white crystalline powder used as an additive by food, pharmaceutical, and cosmetic manufacturers.

In addition to bottled sodas and energy-boosting drinks, caffeine extract is also added to candy, gum, hot sauce, ice cream, instant breakfast foods, and even some bottled waters. Over-the-counter weight loss products, pain relievers, and cold medicines frequently add caffeine. Caffeine is added to hundreds of beauty products from soaps and facial scrubs to eye creams and lipstick. Some of the newest caffeine-infused products are electronic cigarettes, toothpaste, toothbrushes, and pantyhose.

It was the stimulating quality of caffeine in tea that is alleged to have caught the attention of Emperor Shen Nong 5,000 years ago, who was invigorated when tea leaves accidentally floated down into his kettle of boiling water. The caffeine "buzz" continues to make products like tea, coffee, and chocolate as popular as they are.

Caffeine, the Pharmaceutical

Caffeine is frequently labeled "the most consumed psychoactive drug," since approximately 90 percent of adults in North America *intentionally* consume it daily in coffee, tea, and bottled drinks. Because it is also common in many other goods, there can also be significant *unintentional* consumption by consumers who are unaware that the stimulant has been added. The stimulating effect on the central nervous system produces an alert state with increased energy and focus when used in appropriate amounts. Added to other medications, it helps reduce pain from certain types of headaches and can improve airway function slightly for those suffering with asthma. Scientific and medical studies associate caffeine with reduced risk of several diseases as well as improved cognitive ability. However, used in excessive amounts or for those with increased sensitivity, caffeine can have adverse effects.

Caffeine Pros and Cons

The balance between the positive benefits and the potential side effects is largely one of individual sensitivity. For those who are ultra-sensitive to caffeine, even small amounts can produce undesirable reactions. Even for those who tolerate caffeine, there are limits to the amounts that can be considered beneficial. For example, drinking between two and five caffeinated beverages per day is considered relatively safe for most adults. Consuming ten or more beverages in a single day usually indicates abuse that can lead to significant side effects. If this consumption is then combined with super-charged energy drinks or diet medications, it can become dangerous.

One of the most hazardous uses of caffeine occurs when it is mixed with alcohol. Several years ago, some commercially produced alcoholic beverages began adding caffeine. In 2010 the U.S. Food and Drug Administration described these products as a public heath concern, and required that manufacturers remove their products from the market. The products were cited as a health and safety problem, especially among young adults and teens. The beverages containing high amounts of caffeine mixed with alcohol prevented sleepiness, which in turn increased the potential for excessive drinking and often contributed to risky behaviors.

Undesirable Caffeine Side Effects

While reports of reactions to caffeine consumption are rare enough that the U.S. Food and Drug Administration categorizes caffeine as GRAS ("generally recognized as safe"), it is not without consequences if abused. The tolerances for every individual vary with body weight, age, amount of physical activity, and whether or not the caffeine is consumed with food or on an empty stomach. Some adverse reactions are: irritability, insomnia, increased heart rate or blood pressure, heartburn, dizziness, changes in breathing, nervous jitters, or blurred vision. Of course, any one of these may also indicate other health issues.

How much is too much caffeine?
Moderate amounts of caffeine are generally considered to be up to 250 milligrams per day, which is between two and four caffeinated beverages. High consumption would be 1,000 mg per day, an average of ten caffeinated beverages. But because caffeine varies greatly in each product, it is difficult to calculate precise daily intake. In 2010, the American Congress of Obstetricians and Gynecologists recommended that pregnant women limit their overall caffeine consumption to 200 mg per day. Caffeine is one of the substances that passes through the placenta, and could possibly affect the baby.

Caffeine Withdrawal

Some habitual caffeine users experience headaches when abruptly stopping. This is referred to as *withdrawal*, and for this reason caffeine is sometimes considered addictive. It is on these grounds that there are religious groups who ban the consumption of tea, coffee, and cocoa or the consumption of any product containing caffeine.

Abruptly discontinuing caffeine generates headaches in approximately 50 percent of the subjects participating in research projects within twelve hours. Additional changes in mood and irritability, distraction and inability to focus on work, nausea, and muscle pain were also reported. The duration of these symptoms vary between one and nine days. Roland Griffiths, PhD, professor of psychiatry and neuroscience at Johns Hopkins University and director of their study on caffeine withdrawal, concluded that unpleasant symptoms do encourage continued use, and recommended a gradual reduction rather than suddenly stopping caffeine consumption. "We teach a systematic method of gradually reducing caffeine consumption over time by substituting decaffeinated or noncaffeinated products. Using such a method allows people to reduce or eliminate withdrawal symptoms," says Griffiths.

ESSENTIAL

Habitual coffee drinkers experiencing the "jitters" from excessive caffeine consumption find that substituting tea can be a first step in their plan to reduce total daily consumption of the stimulant and still sip a comforting, warm beverage throughout the day. With a lower caffeine level and the additional L-theanine to soothe the experience, withdrawal may be more pleasant.

Caffeine Toxicity

Reports of extreme caffeine toxicity have been associated with products other than regular coffee and tea. For example, toxicity levels may be reached by an average-sized adult consuming more than eighty cups of regular coffee or about twice as many cups of tea. Of course, this also assumes no other conflicting health issues, and that cumulative caffeine is calculated. It is difficult to imagine anyone drinking enough coffee or tea to be toxic, but there is greater potential for abuse with products containing concentrated doses of caffeine. One recently reported case of caffeine toxicity identified a lethal overdose in a forty-year-old male who ingested hundreds of mints infused with 80 milligrams of caffeine per mint.

Benefits of Caffeine

The other side of the caffeine coin is the growing list of benefits, both anecdotal and scientific. The "buzz" that jump-starts the day seems essential for many. Taking the edge off afternoon hunger pangs may help reduce snacking and shave extra calories from the day's meal plan. A runner might log a faster time after a cup of tea, or a student may feel more focused to study for the next day's big test.

ESSENTIAL

"It has a strange influence over mood, a strange power of changing the look of things, and changing it for the better, so that we can believe and hope and do under the influence of tea what we should otherwise give up in discouragement and despair." (*The Lancet*, London, June 6, 1863.)

Some of the more interesting studies on benefits of caffeine show a slower decline in cognitive ability among older women who habitually ingest moderate amounts of caffeine, slightly improved clarity for some dementia patients and those with Alzheimer's, reduced respiratory symptoms for people with asthma, improved management of liver disease, benefits to the management of type 2 diabetes, and reduced incidence of colorectal cancer. Anecdotal reports from those suffering with attention deficit disorders frequently name caffeine as one of the products with which they self-medicate to improve focus and increase attention span.

FACT

French and German chemists first isolated and studied pure caffeine derived from coffee in 1819 and 1820. Seven years later, French chemist M. Oudry isolated the compound "theine" in tea that was later acknowledged as a form of caffeine. This is different than the amino acid L-theanine, even though the similar names can be confusing.

L-theanine and Caffeine in Tea

Balancing the stimulation of caffeine in tea is the amino acid L-theanine. This is the component within the tea leaf that provides relaxation and a sense of calm focus, sometimes called relaxed alertness. Some techniques of tea growing have proven to increase the amount of L-theanine in tea. Studies have shown that the consumption of L-theanine leads to:

- Increased brain levels of dopamine (and possibly serotonin) that increase an overall sense of well-being
- Reduced blood pressure (animal study)
- Increased alpha waves in the brain
- Neuro-protective effects that have shown to reduce neurological damage in animal studies
- Reduced psychotic symptoms in schizophrenic patients when added to antipsychotic medication

While there are no conclusive studies as yet, research in the worldwide scientific community continues to add new data to a growing body of evidence that L-theanine will prove to have value, both in daily consumption of brewed tea as well as being incorporated into some prescription medications.

FACT

The first synthesized caffeine was successfully generated from the raw material in 1895 by a German chemist, Hermann Emil Fischer. His work was awarded the Nobel Prize in 1902. When Fischer was presented with the award, Professor Hj. Theel, president of the Swedish Royal Academy, remarked, "As certain representatives of the group—caffeine and theobromine—are not solely esteemed in beverage form but have also been used medicinally down the ages, it is reasonable to expect that several of the new purine derivatives will prove to have a *medicinal value.*"

The Tea Plant's Need for Caffeine

Theanine, the caffeine in the tea plant, also assumes a role as part of the plant's survival system by acting as Mother Nature's own insect repellant. Production increases with new growth and surges in much higher concentrations to the new shoots and buds, effectively protecting the tender new leaves and buds from attack by predators. It is this new growth that is harvested for tea. In addition to its bitter taste that repels pests, caffeine is actually toxic to some insects. It also defends the young tea leaves and buds against some bacteria and fungi.

Caffeine's Natural Concentrations

This concentration of caffeine in the tea plant becomes part of a frequent discussion about which tea category contains the most caffeine. The fact that caffeine is higher in new growth also contradicts the myth that the darkness of the leaf or the brewed tea indicates the amount of caffeine delivered to the consumer. In fact, the greatest amount of caffeine in the plant is usually in the newest growth, the unopened leaf bud. Generally speaking, this means that the higher-quality tea with a greater percentage of "tippy" unopened buds will most likely have a higher amount of caffeine.

FACT

In addition to protecting the plant, caffeine is present in some floral nectar and is known to attract pollinators. In one study with bees, caffeine made the insect better able to remember the location of the source, facilitating multiple return visits. The frequency of visits increases the plant's chance for survival.

Unfortunately, there is no easy way to determine the precise amount of caffeine in a brewed cup of tea. The variables determining this begin with the plant varietal itself, the time of day the tea was picked, the processing of the fresh leaf, the storage of the dry leaf, and the way it is brewed. The most significant, and most manageable, factor is the brewing. Using more tea relative to the amount of water and infusing it with hotter water for a longer time will deliver more caffeine to the cup. Of course, the inverse is also true, putting the control of the general level of caffeine into the consumer's hands.

Caffeine in Brewed Tea

Another recently disproved popular tea and caffeine myth is that you can decaffeinate your tea at home by giving it a quick brew, about thirty seconds, and then discarding that first wash. It was assumed that caffeine in the tea leaf was quickly infused into hot water. However, in 1996, Monique Hicks, Peggy Hsieh, and Leonard Bell published their study in the *Canadian Institute of Food Science and Technology Journal* showing that only 9 percent of the caffeine was drawn from the leaf in the first thirty seconds, and that it required fifteen minutes with the leaf submerged in hot water to more fully remove the caffeine. What their work substantiates is that tea infused multiple times will have increasingly less caffeine with each steeping. This is true for both tea bags and loose-leaf tea, even though loose-leaf tea releases caffeine at a slightly slower rate.

Caffeine Changes During Tea Processing

Commercial tea production generally focuses on the flavor and quality of the final product and not on the amount of caffeine. However, the decisions a tea master makes, from the time the plant is first set into the ground until the dry tea is finally packaged and shipped, affect the amount of caffeine present in the final tea product. This is, however, of greater concern to the consumer. Understanding the way in which growing and processing determine caffeine in the plant can help you make more informed choices for the cup. That being said, anticipating the amount of caffeine in a tea can be difficult. For every "rule," there are always additional, perhaps unknown, factors in play.

In the Field

Some of the variables that affect the caffeine in tea while it is still on the plant are:

- Plants grown from seed tend to produce more caffeine than those grown from cuttings or as clones of other plants.
- The *Camellia sinensis assamica* varietals with larger leaves are higher in caffeine than the smaller-leafed varietals.
- Nitrogen fertilizers can add to the plant's production of caffeine.
- The season during which the tea is picked makes a great difference in the amount of caffeine stored in the fresh leaf. Warm weather and rapid growth may produce more caffeine than slower growth in cooler climates.
- Shade-grown tea, in which the bushes are covered for weeks prior to harvest, generally contain more caffeine in the leaves due to a shift in chlorophyll and other chemicals, triggered by less direct sun exposure. This technique is more common with Japanese-grown teas.
- Matcha and other powdered teas are higher in caffeine for two reasons: They tend to be shade-grown and, in grinding the entire leaf, more of the caffeine is retained to be consumed.

In the Factory

Once the leaves reach the factory, every step impacts the final amount of caffeine remaining in the dry leaf and how it is released when brewed.

- Finely cut leaves (like those for tea bags) tend to release the caffeine more rapidly.
- Tightly twisted and rolled leaves that unfurl slowly release caffeine at a slower rate and, with multiple infusions, produce a serving with lower caffeine.
- Blended teas that combine pieces of spice or whole flowers may be lower in caffeine, because there will be less actual tea used to brew the pot or cup.

Decaffeination

As with many discoveries in history, the first decaffeination was discovered by accident in 1903 when a shipment of coffee beans was waterlogged and ruined during shipment. The importer, Ludwig Roselius, tested the beans and discovered that they were lower in caffeine. Further experimentation led to Roselius patenting the first decaffeination process in 1906. Finally, in the 1930s, the Swiss Water process was developed and is still used today for coffee, but not for tea.

QUESTION

Is decaffeinated tea as healthy as regular tea?
Very few studies include decaf tea as a controlled variable, or have compared decaf with caffeinated teas side by side. It is generally thought that the decaffeination process reduces the amount of antioxidants in the leaf, and in this way also reduces the healthful benefits of tea. But more research is needed to support this assumption.

There are three methods of removing the caffeine from fresh tea leaves. Each method uses a different solvent but essentially the same process. The leaves must first be moistened, then rinsed in one of the solvents, and finally dried. Two of the solvents, ethyl acetate and supercritical carbon dioxide, are allowed in the United States, but the U.S. Department of Agriculture prohibits the import of any tea decaffeinated with methylene chloride, which is classified as a carcinogen.

Ethyl Acetate

Ethyl acetate, a liquid with a sweet smell, is a naturally occurring substance and can therefore be described on product labels as "natural," even if the solvent used at the time of caffeine extraction was synthetically produced. After the processing, the tea must be rinsed.

FACT

None of the decaffeination processes remove 100 percent of the caffeine from tea leaves. There is usually 2–5 milligrams remaining in a cup of brewed tea.

Supercritical Carbon Dioxide

This method is also considered to be a fluid extraction. When pressurized, carbon dioxide acts like a liquid and is used to rinse the caffeine out of tea leaves. Once the pressure is normalized, the carbon dioxide returns to its gaseous state, leaving the crystallized caffeine separated out from the tea leaves.

Tea's Caffeine Compared with Other Products

The most frequent comparison between the caffeine in coffee and tea is that a brewed cup of tea has less than a cup of coffee, and that the tea makes you less jittery and better able to focus. Because it is naturally occurring in tea, coffee, and cocoa, and nearly impossible to calculate the actual number of milligrams per cup, there is no government requirement to label the amount of caffeine. Most manufacturers will state that their product either "contains caffeine" or is "decaffeinated." The U.S. Food and Drug Administration does require products containing additional, synthesized caffeine to list the amount per serving. Some brand names also list this on their websites.

Checking Labels

Since both the advantages and cautions about caffeine are based on the total daily consumption, it is important to read labels and to recognize that many additional nonbeverage products also contain caffeine. Some of these are super-charged, containing quantities that could be hazardous.

Brand Name Product	Milligrams of Caffeine	Serving Size (ounces)
Brand Name Sodas		
Coca-Cola	34	12
Pepsi	38	12
Mountain Dew	54	12
Barq's Root Beer	23	12
Brand Name Energy Drinks		
Jolt Energy Drink	280	23.5
Monster Energy	160	16
Rockstar	160	16
Red Bull	80	8.4
Caffeinated Foods		
Jolt Gum	45	per piece
Jelly Belly Extreme Sport Beans	50	1
Perky Jerky	150	1
Bang!! Ice Cream	125	4
Blue Diamond Coffee Flavored Almonds	25	1
Hershey's Kisses	9	1.4
Hershey's Chocolate Bar	9	1.6
Quaker Cocoa Blasts	6.9	1 cup
Over-the-Counter Medications		
Zantrex-3 Weight Loss Supplement	300	2 capsules
Excedrin Migraine	130	2 tablets
Midol Complete	120	2 caplets
Buzz Toothpaste	80–100	per use

Other products jumping on the caffeine trend are popcorn, hot sauce, toothbrushes, pantyhose and other lingerie, deodorant, shampoos, and other soaps.

CHAPTER 5

Can Tea Be Unhealthy?

Tea's introduction to Europe in the 1600s was not without concern about the health claims. Ever since then, a watchfulness within the tea industry as well as the medical communities maintains a checks-and-balances integrity with research. As exciting as it may be to discover hot new topics about tea benefits, there are certain people who probably should not drink tea because of specific health issues. And everyone should use good judgment in the amount they consume per day.

Historic Concerns

Cautionary warnings against tea started in the 1600s when the tea rage first hit Europe. A few European physicians looked askance at the new offering with its claims of health benefits. One of the earliest and most vocal nay-sayers was a Danish physician and naturalist, Dr. Simon Paulli, who published several documents warning that tea might actually "hasten the death" of those who drank it. One of his theories was that the attributes of tea grown and consumed in China did not apply to the European climate. Therefore, its properties were compromised. In his work *Commentarius De Abusu Tabaci Americanorum Veteri, Et Herbœ Thee Asiaticorum in Europe Novo* (1661) he issued warnings against the use of both tea and tobacco. Paulli was very well respected as a botanist, even having the botanical genus *Paullinia* named after him, yet the rapid growth in the consumption of tea continued, despite his warnings.

Other cautions during the same period of time came from an Italian Jesuit, Martino Martini, who had lived in China as a missionary, historian, and cartographer for many years. He returned to Italy as something of an authority on China at the time that tea was first becoming known on the continent, and he is quoted as saying, "Down with tea! Send it back!" Yet despite his dislike for tea, he returned to his work in Hangzhou, China, wrote many books on the country, is credited with building one of the most beautiful churches in Hangzhou, and remained there until his death.

FACT

While Martino Martini did not seem to endorse the practice of drinking tea, other Jesuits in China wrote and published observations as early as 1616 about the plant, with generous descriptions in their writings about the ways in which the plant grew and was used for its health benefits.

In 1648 Guy Patin, a famous and respected French physician, wrote a scathing rebuttal to a tea-supporting 1648 essay called, "Does Tea Increase Mentality?" written by a Dr. Philibert Morisset. Patin presented it publicly to his peers and convinced a gathering at the Collège de France to deny publicly that there was any value to drinking tea. But even this did not discourage its popular use.

Not Respecting the Power of Tea

Today, the cautious wisdom of "everything in moderation" sometimes clashes with the exuberant energy of the "more is better" attitude of the media headlining health news. This is as true with tea as it is with many other things. If three to four cups per day are recommended, that does not mean that ten cups a day would be better. If it is suggested that a black tea be steeped for three minutes, the health benefits do not increase if it is steeped for ten minutes. It may, on the other hand, increase the bitterness. One of the lessons in tea drinking is controlling the variables: quality and amount of the tea selected, temperature of the water, time of steeping, and the vessel in which it is steeped. Learning to control and harness the flavor and the power of the tea is one of the goals of brewing good tasting and healthful tea.

One way that the potency of tea might easily and unknowingly be abused is with tea concentrates. They are showing up as ingredients in many food products, and the degree of concentration varies greatly. Some supplement manufacturers package tea concentrates so that you can enjoy the benefits without the brew: tea in a pill without the fuss and expense. But these also lack some of the sensory benefits. Reading the product labels is always recommended. Some ready-to-drink bottled teas are 100 percent brewed teas, and their caffeine concentration is comparable to a brewed cup.

Sensitivity to Caffeine

While most people experience caffeine in a limited amount as invigorating, others with high sensitivity may find the effects unpleasant. Their reactions can range from a case of restlessness and jitters, insomnia, headaches, and irritability to allergic reactions like rashes, generalized itchiness, and itchy mouth. While the caffeine in tea is different from that in coffee and sodas, and provides most people with a comfortable, calm state of alertness, it can still be problematic for someone with significant caffeine sensitivity.

Anyone suspecting caffeine of causing health issues should begin to monitor their consumption of all caffeine. Check product labels and be aware of the cumulative caffeine exposure from tea, chocolate, coffee, cola, and energy drinks.

ALERT

Abruptly stopping a daily caffeine habit can have unpleasant side effects. For example, if you have been drinking three to four cups of strongly brewed black tea (or coffee or energy drinks) every day for several months and suddenly stop, it may trigger a headache.

Pregnancy and Menopause

Pregnancy and menopause are two significant times of hormonal changes in women's lives when settling down with a steaming cup of Earl Grey may seem like an essential mental health moment. But these are times when women may need to measure their tea consumption relative to their total intake of caffeine. Because this includes not only tea but also coffee and chocolate, women may face the difficult choice between these popular comfort foods.

Pregnancy and Breastfeeding

For years obstetricians have recommended that pregnant women reduce or eliminate caffeine consumption. Current studies support controlling the total amount of caffeine consumed in a single day, and medical guidelines for pregnant women suggest to keep their daily consumption under 200 mg. Caffeine is rapidly absorbed into the body and freely crosses into the placenta, and has been studied in association with low birth weight.

When newly pregnant, it may be a good idea to keep a caffeine journal over a few days. Take careful note of all products that contain caffeine, becoming aware of those you might not suspect. Record the total amount of caffeine for tea, coffee, pain medication, and snacks. Create a "menu" that will keep daily consumption under the recommended 200 mg.

Similar cautions about drinking tea persist throughout breastfeeding, although a breastfeeding mother can usually consume more caffeine than when she was pregnant. When it concerns pregnancy and breastfeeding, young families are always encouraged to be extremely careful about what the mother eats and the surrounding environment to which she and the baby are exposed. The mother shares everything ingested or consumed with her child in utero during the nine months of gestation, and her mental and emotional well-being also impact her baby. Balancing good nutrition and a calm family environment can be a challenge during pregnancy and the baby's first year. As an example, a lightly brewed cup of tea has caffeine, which may affect the baby, but it is probably a better choice than a can of soda, especially if it generates a more relaxed mood and overall sense of well-being.

Menopause

Tea can be helpful with some menopausal symptoms, but hormonal changes during menopause can alter a woman's sensitivity to caffeine. This may necessitate changes in what have previously been lifelong habits. These changes could be as simple as changing the type of tea, changing tea brands, modifying how strongly you brew your tea, or adjusting the time of day you take a tea break.

Anemia and Iron Absorption

The contraindication about tea and iron has to do with tannins (which are not the same as tannic acid, something else that tea contains). Black tea contains the most tannins of the tea categories and, like wine, can interfere with the body's ability to absorb protein from meat sources if they are consumed at the same time. Drinking tea with lower tannins, like green tea, is one choice. Another option is to enjoy tea between meals, not directly before, during, or after eating a meal. It should be said that there have not been enough studies of the interactions between tea tannins and iron absorption to be conclusive.

An additional concern with green tea is that it may inhibit the absorption of folic acid, which is especially important in the first trimester of pregnancy, and even pre-pregnancy. In addition to tea from the *Camellia sinensis* plant (black, green, oolong, white, pu'erh), drinking some herbal teas are also cautioned during pregnancy, although this warning is unrelated to caffeine content.

Drug Interactions

While mild tea drinking—two to three cups per day of a lightly steeped brew—is of little concern, caution is required when taking certain medications. There are potential reactions of tea with particular prescription drugs. These include some antibiotics, beta-blockers like propranolol and metoprolol, benzodiazepine, blood-thinning medications like warfarin, some chemotherapy medications like doxorubicin, tamoxifen, bortezomib, and others. It is always important to consult your pharmacist and your physician and to read the manufacturer's recommendations regarding any concern about your diet and all medication. Birth control pills are another category in which monitoring total caffeine intake from foods and beverages is advised.

Heart Disease

Symptoms that may indicate heart diseases such as high blood pressure and irregular or rapid heart rate could also indicate that you should be mindful about tea (and all caffeine) consumption. The strength of brewed tea and the number of cups per day may need to be reduced. While much of the scientific evidence indicates tea drinking can help prevent heart disease, anyone with an active heart condition needs to consider potential reactions of all foods and beverages relative to their medications and treatment. Two specific concerns for anyone who has suffered a heart attack or stroke are the amount of caffeine consumed, too much of which can elevate blood pressure, and any possible drug interactions with tea.

Tea for Children

Very few scientific studies include children. It is therefore impossible to say that there are age-specific concerns for children and teens drinking tea. However, tea has been a common beverage around the world for all ages, including very young children. The potential concerns would involve serving quality and quantity, and the way in which tea is prepared and served. For anyone considering whether or not tea drinking is appropriate for children, consider the question in comparison with drinking sodas, eating chocolate, and processed or fast food. Researcher Iman Hakim, professor at the

Arizona Cancer Center at the University of Arizona, said that "if tea proves to be good, it might be good to switch the kids to tea," noting that tea has much less caffeine than coffee or colas. Another scientist studying tea's health effects, John Foxe, professor of neuroscience, biology, and psychology at the City College of the City University of New York, reports that he gives his young son six or seven cups of milky tea a day. An additional consideration for children over and above caffeine and sugars would be the temperature at which it is served, so that spills and burning the mouth are not a hazard.

ESSENTIAL

Cambric tea is a traditional way to serve tea to children. Usually a half-and-half mixture of tea and milk, the creamy beverage is served luke-warm, and is very safe for young ones who may still be unsteady when holding a cup.

Teeth Staining

Even though tea can help keep your breath smelling fresh and your teeth and gums healthier, it is one of several foods that can gradually discolor tooth surfaces, much to the dismay of avid tea drinkers. Black teas, which are higher in tannins, are more likely than green tea to stain the teeth. Some dental hygienists recommend drinking tea through a straw to avoid staining the teeth, but that would eliminate the warm glow and taste burst from sipping tea from the cup. (Notice the grimace on the face of any serious tea drinker hearing that suggestion.) Good oral hygiene and professional cleanings help prevent long-term darkening. In addition, chewing crunchy, raw vegetables like carrots and cauliflower will also help scrub the surface of the teeth and neutralize the acid in your mouth.

ALERT

Previous reports that tea was linked to esophageal cancer have been proved incorrect. It is now believed that tea itself is not the actual cause, but the temperature at which it is consumed. In several studies it was observed that people who drank their tea when it was still very hot were twice as likely to develop esophageal cancer as those who allowed it to cool a few minutes until it was warm.

Sweeteners

Tea drinking has been associated with additional calories in two ways: adding sweeteners to the cup, and sipping tea with decadent desserts. It seems important to mention these unnecessary calories, given the obesity epidemic of the last fifteen years. Being overweight factors into so many different health problems that taking every opportunity to address it is important. Choices of sweeteners for tea might be one easy way to begin an effective health improvement regime.

One thing about brewing your own tea is that you select the sweetener, if any, and how much. That opens the door to many choices, some healthier than others. Choices range from processed white sugar and artificial sweeteners to herbal stevia, organic raw sugar, brown sugar, honey, or agave nectar. Whether you're watching calories or measuring your blood sugar, the amount of added sugar is one of the factors you control for your own health. Developing a preference for lightly sweetened or unsweetened tea could be that healthy option.

Becoming Tea Drunk

If you find yourself in the company of deeply committed tea drinkers, you might hear the term "tea drunk." While reports of this experience are only anecdotal, it could be something to watch for if the sense of being in a slightly altered state is not desirable. There are no known medical studies for this affliction.

Becoming tea drunk is not an alcoholic reaction. It is sometimes associated with the buzz or agitation from ingesting too much caffeine causing mild jitters, slight nausea, or dizziness, creating an unpleasant experience. But often people refer to tea drunk as pleasurable, associated with drinking specific kinds or qualities of tea. It is most often described as euphoric with a sense of being grounded and calm. There may be an experience of giddy lightheadedness. Some people report becoming exceptionally introspective. While this may sound pleasant, it can be disorienting if it is unexpected.

ESSENTIAL

Episodes of tea drunkenness are usually associated with some specific artisan teas. High-quality Tie Guan Yin, an oolong from Taiwan and Fujian Province, China, is one of the teas that have been associated with the experience. Shade-grown Japanese teas like the very expensive gyokuro are another.

In his book, *The Spirit of Tea*, Frank Hadley Murphy explains: "Overindulgence in tea does not diminish or impair my faculties as with alcohol; it enhances them. There are sensations that we may equate with being drunk if we have no other language for it, but the altered state produced by tea has an entirely different spin on it."

Irresponsible Hype and Counterfeit Products

Popularity of new products in the media can attract scoundrels and charlatans who want to make a quick and easy profit or steal a moment of fame as a tea guru. As the popularity of tea stepped out of the quiet corner of grandma's pantry and into the spotlight as the hip new thing, tea has suffered some of the same abuses. Tea "gurus" or "masters" abound, selling tea, products, and education packages, often with very little education or experience themselves.

Anyone inspired to pursue a life in tea is wise to look carefully at the many options. Read books and respected blogs, attend focused tastings, sample and compare different teas, join tea groups, attend festivals, and visit tea farms and factories around the world. It is only through first-hand experience that you will achieve your desired measure of mastery and confidence.

In the early 1800s, the demand for tea in England was great and taxes on it were so high that it inspired both the practices of smuggling and the adulteration of the product. The word for contaminated or counterfeit tea was "smouch." There are gruesome tales of how other leaves were made to look like tea with darkening agents, and how real tea was blended with other materials like sawdust, iron filings, and colored with such pigments as Prussian blue, also known as ferric ferrocyanide.

Counterfeit Products

In the United States there are government safeguards in place that provide a certain level of protection against fraudulent and dangerous alteration of foods and beverages. With the case of tea, however, there still is room for deceptive practices. The most common is probably price gouging, misrepresenting a less valuable tea as something rare and high priced. Uneducated and unsuspecting new tea buyers (and some old hands as well) may not have an experienced enough palate to discern the difference. There may not be adverse physical reaction to this bit of fraud, but the experience can create a negative feeling about tea in general.

The remedy for this deception is to become a more educated and prudent buyer. Invest in your own tea education by dealing with reputable sellers with confidence. Maintaining a reputation for quality products and customer service is essential, and should be the top priority for an honest retailer. As communication on the Internet has expanded over the last few years, the threat of suffering customer complaints publicly and uncontrollably breeds caution, and motivates even more careful practices for most tea businesses.

CHAPTER 6

Green Tea

Green tea is currently the most talked-about tea for the associated health benefits. It is the most researched, and therefore the current media darling. There are thousands of flavors from which to choose that have been packaged and prepared and sold in dozens of different ways. But assuming that a scoop of the dry leaves bathed in a teapot of boiling water will produce a sweet cup may be a disappointment. For this reason, green tea is frequently mis-brewed, misunderstood, and thus not the tea of choice that it might otherwise be. The most common complaint regarding green tea is an astringent or bitter taste due to confusion about how to brew to bring out its best qualities. But when prepared properly, most green teas have a fresh sweetness, often compared to fresh vegetables, fruit, or flowers.

What Is Green Tea?

As discussed previously, all tea comes from the same plant, the *Camellia sinensis*. Differences between green, black, oolong, white, and pu'erh categories are created by the choice of a specific varietal, the terroir (the unique environment including soil and climate) in which it grows, the way in which the leaf is harvested from the plant, and the way it is processed in the factory. The basic difference between green and black teas is that the beautiful green color of the fresh tea leaves is preserved by arresting the natural oxidation process. In black teas the dark color is intentionally developed. In oolong teas, the amount of oxidation is controlled. And with white teas, the leaves are allowed to dry and oxidize (darken) naturally.

There are hundreds of green teas with dramatically different appearances and flavors. Two of the most readily available options are the common varieties of green tea in tea bags and matcha, the powdered green tea used in latte beverages, smoothies, and in cooking, as well as in the Japanese tea ceremony. But venture a little further into the world of specialty green teas and you will discover single green leaves rolled tightly into tiny pellets about the size of grains of rice, or a set of leaves on a thin stem rolled into perfect pearl shapes. There are unopened leaf buds that "dance" when they are revitalized in water, long leaves that are flattened between screens to perfectly preserve the leaf, and sculpted spheres of bundled and dried leaves.

QUESTION

Are the health benefits of green tea significant enough to take the additional time and trouble?
The answer is uniquely personal and depends on the reasons you find yourself exploring tea as a health supplement. Like anything new, the difficulty of learning new brewing techniques lessens with experience. With green tea, considering the hundreds of options available, you will find one that fits comfortably into your daily routine. You may even find that the fresh aroma and taste of green tea becomes as important to you as its health benefits.

The liquor, the brewed tea, can range from a pale straw color or pale yellow-green to a brilliant jade green. Flavors can be sweet and creamy, smooth, slightly grassy, or noticeably vegetal. Green tea is frequently compared to the flavor of asparagus or spinach. But green teas can also be bitter and astringent, and it would be a mistake to assume that this is always an error. Some tea drinkers find this very desirable. Brewing to your taste preferences is simply a matter of controlling time, temperature, and the amount of tea used.

Health Benefits of Green Tea

The same variations in processing green tea versus black tea also alter the chemistry of the leaf. By arresting the oxidation that causes the leaf to darken, it is believed that more of the valuable polyphenols are preserved. A compelling body of evidence collected over the last twenty years suggests that green tea is more healthful than other categories. One consideration is that there are not an equal number of studies on other teas, and that very few studies have made comparisons between green, black, oolong, white, and pu'erh. What is now proven to be true about green tea may, in the near future, be found similarly beneficial in others.

Some of the most interesting research concerning the habitual drinking of green tea has drawn the following conclusions:

- It reduces risk for heart disease by lowering LDL (bad cholesterol) while increasing HDL (good cholesterol), thereby improving blood flow.
- It lowers triglyceride levels.
- It reduces the risk of heart disease.
- It helps keep blood sugar stable.
- It blocks DNA damage associated with toxic chemicals.
- It increases activity in the working memory area of the brain.
- It blocks formation of plaques in the brain associated with Alzheimer's disease and may slow other forms of dementia.
- It blocks the attachment of bacteria in the mouth that causes tooth decay.

- It may help prevent various types of cancer, including: bladder, breast, ovarian, colorectal, esophageal, lung, pancreatic, prostate, skin, and stomach cancers.
- It can support a weight loss program of diet and exercise.

Some of the research on other teas duplicates these same results with very little difference between the different types of processing (black, oolong, and white).

Brewing Green Tea

If your tea style is to drop a tea bag into a mug, add water from a whistling kettle, and leave the bag in while you focus your full attention on your work, then green tea might not be your first choice. Brewing it usually requires a little more thought, or at least removing the tea bag from the cup after one to two minutes of steeping. But there is such great diversity among green teas, certainly one will fit into your daily brewing style.

Before tea became a beverage, the characteristic astringency may have been considered a good thing. Astringents are used to shrink pores and mucus membranes, control bleeding, and accelerate wound healing. They reduce swelling and unwanted discharge, and can relieve irritations caused by fungal infections and insect bites. Used cosmetically, they firm and tone the skin.

How Much Tea?

If your green tea preference is packaged in a tea bag, then the contents will most likely weigh between two and three grams (net dry weight). Tea bag manufacturers have spent a great deal of time testing their product for the way it brews in a mug or teapot. They will very likely print suggestions about brewing the tea on the box. But don't be afraid to run your own experiments. If it seems unsatisfyingly weak, use two bags. Too strong? Adjust the other variables: time and temperature.

For loose-leaf teas, there is a ratio of tea to water that will brew the right concentration for you, but this will vary with each tea. Taking time for a little experimentation and practice, making adjustments will become easier—even fun! Recommendations for brewing loose-leaf tea are most often given in grams (by weight) for consistency. But unless you are a professional tea taster or tea sommelier serving high-end teas, the individual gram is not likely to make a noticeable difference. The alternative of measuring the tea by teaspoonful (by volume) is much less accurate. The different sizes and shapes of the leaves change the way the tea rests in a spoon. Finely cut tea leaves fill the space with no significant pockets of air, while curled, whole leaves take up considerably more room because of the air space between the leaves.

ESSENTIAL

If you have a scale that can weigh small amounts, you should try this comparison. Open a tea bag of green tea. Weigh the contents. It should be 2–3 grams. Then weigh the same amount of whole-leaf green tea. Notice the difference between cut and broken leaves versus large whole leaves.

What may seem complex and intimidating at first could become a pleasurable aspect of your green tea preparations and drinking. When you realize that there is no right or wrong, no absolute formula, then the preparations become more relaxed, personal, and intimate. Find your own style. It's all about you and your palate. What tastes good to you? Tea preparation can become an adventure for your taste buds.

How Hot Is Too Hot?

The most common mistake is to brew green tea the same way you brew black tea, with boiling water (212°F). There are very few green teas that tolerate water above 195°F without becoming slightly bitter. If using a beverage thermometer or an electric kettle is inconvenient, you have two simple options. One is to watch the bubbles in the water and brew your tea when they are small, before the turbulent roil of full boil. The other is to put a bit of cold water in your cup with the dry tea while you're waiting for your hot water, then slowly add the boiling water.

ALERT

Controlling the quality, buying the freshest tea, storing it properly, and preparing it carefully, maximizes its healthful qualities. If you are drinking tea because it is a healthy beverage, then choose freshness over high price or the fame of its legendary history. Being one of the most famous or expensive does not necessarily make it healthier.

Controlling the Time

The same green tea can be either sweet and flavorful or bitter and unpleasant, depending on the length of time the leaves sit in the water. If you first explore your new purchase with a very short steep—thirty seconds to one minute—and aren't satisfied with the taste, you can easily correct this by brewing for a longer time. After you and your new tea flavor become better acquainted, the ratio of time to temperature and quantity of tea per cup require less attention.

Selecting a Green Tea

Your two first considerations when buying your tea are what you can comfortably afford and how you want to brew it. If you haven't had a cup since your childhood parties with your grandmother, then keep it simple. Start within your comfort zone. If that means you pick up a colorful box of tea bags in the grocery aisle and dunk them in a mug—not the one you use for coffee—and sip it on your afternoon break when you have that sinking feeling, then that's your place to begin.

Or if you're the adventurous soul who has always wanted to step into the corner shop displaying a wall of shiny stainless steel canisters with a hundred different teas to choose from, then go for it. Remember, there are no rules. There is no right or wrong tea. Ask questions. Ask for a taste. Let your senses guide you.

Green Teas in Tea Bags

Tea in tea bags has been cut into pieces small enough for packing machines to be able to fill the small bags. As you venture into the tea aisle of your local market, you may wish that there were not so many choices. Every brand now features several flavors of green tea. Most of them will be blended with other popular botanicals such as mint, chamomile, or berries. But some large brands are beginning to offer green teas that bear the same names that you see in a gourmet tea shop. An increasing number of specialty green teas like Gunpowder, Dragon Well, and Jasmine Pearl are now being conveniently bagged for the mass market.

The higher-end green teas are more likely to be packaged in the larger, pyramid-shaped bag often described as "silken." The additional space in this bag allows more room for the leaf to open as it rehydrates. Many people believe that the silken bags, whether made of nylon, cornstarch, or plastic, protect the clarity of the tea and are less likely to add the flavor of the paper.

QUESTION

Are tea bags described as "silken" made of silk?
Some manufacturers state that their alternative nonpaper tea bags are made of food-grade nylon or food-grade plastic (polyethylene terephthalate), or a newer corn-based plastic. Unless the packaging states that the bags are made of real silk, which would be rare, the bag is probably one of these, or the more traditional paper.

Green Leaf Teas

Dozens of traditional green teas all have intriguing histories and unique shapes. As you begin to explore these options, you may begin with some well-known Chinese teas. Gunpowder green tea is made from single leaves rolled into tiny pellets about the size of a grain of rice. Jasmine Pearl is made from two to three leaves and a bit of stem, rolled into a perfectly round ball the size of a pearl, then scented with fresh jasmine blossoms. Dragon Well is a single bud only, and is one of the most prized and expensive green teas. Some Japanese greens you are likely to see are sencha and genmaicha. Sencha is the sun-grown tea, harvested in the spring, that is steamed soon after picking to preserve the green color and rolled as it is dried to flatten the dry leaf. Genmaicha is made from a late harvest bancha tea (also sun-grown) but with rice kernels added, giving it a mellow, toasty flavor. Recognizing some the names and being able to sample can make tea shopping more fun and help you make better choices.

ESSENTIAL

One ounce of dry tea is equal to a little more than 28 grams. If you calculate 3 grams per cup, which is comparable to a tea bag, one ounce will brew about nine cups of tea. Your tastes may vary, of course, as will the amount of tea needed to make a satisfying cup for yourself.

Most loose-leaf retailers allow you to examine the dry leaf. If you do, compare the color and aroma of your choices. Taste some that have been brewed, if possible. One advantage of purchasing loose-leaf tea is being able to buy a small amount of tea, enough to brew a few cups in the comfort of your own home, before you invest in larger quantities.

Where Green Tea Grows

Since all tea comes from the same plant, you could say that every tea farm and plantation grows green tea. But in the tea world, production of each type of tea is specialized and even the tea in the fields has been grown with the intention of crafting the final product. Some tea farms and factories only produce green teas; they do not switch to black tea production at the change of season. Varietals have been hybridized to grow in specific locations, and the combination of the varietal, the environment, and the experienced craftsmanship of growers are all necessary in order to produce green teas.

Based on the volume exported, four countries are the best known for growing green teas: China, Japan, Indonesia, and Vietnam. Other countries producing notable green teas are Kenya and Sri Lanka.

How Green Tea Grows

There are two different methods by which green tea plants are grown—
sun-grown and shade-grown. This factor alone affects the price, as shade
growing is slower and more labor intensive. Tea grown in open fields
fully, or sometimes partially, exposed to the sun is certainly much more
common.

Shade-grown tea plants are covered with mats or mesh for a portion
of the growing season just before the leaves are plucked. This intensifies
the sweetness and color of the tea, and reduces the astringency and
polyphenols. The leaves of a shade-grown plant are thinner, as they spread
out their surface area to take in more light, so they are noticeably more
tender when brewed.

How Green Tea Is Processed

In order to understand the processing of green tea, it might be helpful to compare it to other green vegetables, like fresh spinach leaves. Once spinach is
picked, it begins to wilt unless it is chilled or the stems are set in water. Quickly
steaming or blanching them retains and sometimes intensifies the bright
green color. On the other hand, left to dry and wilt and suffer decomposition,
the spinach turns brown. It oxidizes. The same thing happens to tea leaves.

ESSENTIAL

Tea harvesting machines differ in size and complexity. Some are as
small as a hedge clipper with a fine blade and a net bag to catch the
tender trimmings. Others are as large as a tractor and span several
rows so they can cut an amount equal to what fifty pickers can pick in
a day by snapping each stem by hand.

Freshly hand-plucked or machine-cut leaves are allowed to wither in
the sun or on a withering table inside a factory with controlled heat and
airflow until they soften. The moisture in the leaf is reduced, and several
biochemical reactions are activated. The sweetness begins to develop,
replacing some of the natural bitterness. At a point in the processing

determined by the factory's production master, the leaves will be heated or steamed to stop the oxidation. This preserves and enhances the green color and the fresh flavor. Depending on which type and quality of green tea is desired, the leaves may then be rolled, twisted, cut, or ground before the final drying.

Buying Green Teas

Grocery stores and restaurants have been quick to respond to the growing demand for green teas. You may have noticed a doubling in the last five years of boxed teas available on store shelves, with large companies increasing their variety of green tea flavors to be more captivating. What was once an almost generic packet of green tea of undetermined origin and with little information about brewing has been replaced with a wider range of interesting offerings and more descriptive packaging containing helpful suggestions for preparing a tasty cup of tea.

Buying Tea in Grocery Stores

There are also newer, smaller companies with special blends finding places on the shelves next to the familiar big-name brands. Markets are expanding from a basic green tea to flavored green teas and those blended with other herbs and bits of fruit. The choices for all teas, and especially green tea, are constantly changing. Health food stores are also a source for some of the new tea brands, particularly those that are blended with other herbs to produce specific "functional" blends with specialization for various health concerns. In addition to already having more bulk foods and herbs available, health food stores are adding loose-leaf teas that can be purchased by the ounce.

Ordering Tea in Restaurants

Restaurants, most of which are still offering bagged tea, have increased the number of flavors brought to the table in a basket or bowl designed to hold a selection of up to a dozen different flavors including green tea options. And as the demand grows, the green tea options have gained prominence and it is possible that your tea might be served in a teapot instead of a mug. Occasionally there could even be a selection of loose-leaf teas beyond the brand-named, wrapped sachets. Some fine dining restaurants offer a smaller but very-high quality selection of loose-leaf teas brewed in teapots.

Restaurants who want good reviews from tea lovers will even go the extra step to provide hot water that has not been run through the same filter or poured from the same pots that brew coffee. With water being 99 percent of a cup of tea, if it hits the leaf already flavored by the bean, it will brew a very disappointing cup of tea, especially with the more subtle green teas. Some fine restaurants have a tea sommelier on staff to advise on which tea would be best with your entrée and who would then properly prepare and serve your selection.

Specialty Tea Shops

If you want to seriously pursue the world of romantic-sounding green teas, you will ultimately want to visit a specialty tea shop—either a brick and mortar business or a virtual e-shop. The advantage of stepping through the door in person is being able to view and sample a wide variety of teas, and spending time with an owner or trained staff to glean details of when and where the tea was picked. Many shops offer focused tastings and classes where you will also have the opportunity of meeting fellow tea people. Especially important with green teas are the new arrivals from spring harvest and tea shops frequently celebrate with special events such as focused tastings. Your purveyor should be able to tell you if the tea you are buying is from a previous year or if it is the new crop.

But online businesses can now provide many of the same experiences from the convenience of your computer. Samples are often provided upon request or as a small promotion included with an order. Websites now have extensive descriptions that should also provide you with information about when and where it grew. Subscribing to newsletters from these virtual tea vendors can be helpful to learn about their teas and expand your own tea education and adventures.

Popular and Legendary Green Teas

Green tea is grown in almost every country where any category of tea grows, even if it is only on a small scale and consumed locally or only sold domestically. The most famous are from China and Japan. Developing some familiarity with the names you are likely to see in specialty tea shops can help you make some of your first choices.

Chinese Green Teas

Some of the most famous green teas in China are grown in the eastern provinces. There are dozens of beautiful teas with interesting stories, but three of the most popular are:

1. **Longjing (Dragon Well).** Longjing is probably the most famous Chinese green tea, always included on lists of the top ten teas. It grows in the Hangzhou area of Zhejiang Province, south of Shanghai. This is a spring tea: the best quality is picked in early April, and lesser quality picked during the month after the first week of harvest. Only the tiny end shoots are plucked, and the quality is very dependent on which leaves are chosen. The rarest is a bud only, sometimes called "Lotus Heart Dragon Well," and may require more than 40,000 individual plucks to make a pound of finished dry tea. Additional grades have an extra one or two leaves but are still picked and finished by hand. This tea was granted imperial status during the Qing Dynasty as a favorite of the emperor.

2. **Bi Luo Chun (Green Snail Spring).** Bi Luo Chun originated in Jiangsu Province, one of the more northern tea-growing provinces. It was originally called "Astonishingly Fragrant Tea" or even "Scary Fragrance." The legend is that a young tea picker, drawn to the bushes outside her usual area, had run out of room in her basket. Wanting to return with as much as she could carry, she stuffed extra tea leaves into her bodice. As the tea warmed, the exceptional aroma of the tea surprised the girl and astonished the farm's tea master. Bi Luo Chun is usually picked early in the morning, requiring up to 70,000 leaves to produce a finished pound. The tiny leaves are tightly twisted into spirals like snails and the liquor is a light green with the namesake fragrance enlivening the cup.

3. **Zhu Cha (Gunpowder).** Gunpowder is not considered one of the finest green teas, but it is very popular and usually more affordable. Grown in Zhejiang Province, the fresh leaves are tightly rolled into small round bits that look like grains of gunpowder. The aggressive rolling process makes this tea dry much darker than most other green teas and actually helps the leaf retain much of the aroma and flavor. It also makes this a stronger flavored tea that brews darker green liquor. This will not be as expensive, but within this type of tea you will find a wide range of differences in quality. The best choice will be one where the tea has a shiny surface and is more tightly rolled. This tea can become bitter with over-brewing.

Japanese Green Teas

Japanese green teas are also separated into two general categories: sun-grown and shade-grown. The sun-grown gives a less intense "green" flavor and a slight yellowish tinge to the liquor, as compared with the shade-grown. Being covered for a significant period of growth intensifies the shade-grown tea's color and flavor.

1. **Sencha.** A sun-grown tea, sencha is one of the most popular Japanese teas and well known worldwide. Harvest begins at the end of April or early in May and can be picked using simple cutting machines or, for more expensive senchas, they are hand-plucked. The leaves are steamed to "kill green"—to stop the oxidation—and, as is traditional with most Japanese teas, more focus is on controlling the flavor of the leaf and the consistency of the production rather than on preserving the whole leaves. Finally, the leaves are rolled in such a way that they sometimes look cylindrical, like thick needles. The flavors usually tasted in sencha tea tend to be pleasantly grassy and can be mildly astringent, especially if they are over-brewed. However, good-quality sencha is aromatic, brews a brilliant liquor, and is available in a price range to fit every budget, including good-quality bagged tea.

2. **Gyokuro (Jade Dew).** One of the highest grades of Japanese teas, gyokuro is so expensive that not every specialty tea shop carries this tea. It is a shade-grown tea, covered with bamboo mats or dark netting for at least

three weeks prior to harvesting, usually at the end of May. This deepens the green color of the fresh leaf, intensifies the flavors, and makes the leaf thinner as it tries to absorb more light. The name can also mean "Precious Dew," referring to the pale green color of the liquor. Shaded teas like this produce more L-theanine and may have more healthful qualities. Gyokuro is usually brewed with much cooler water than other green teas. One brewing technique is where the leaves are suspended on a screen in a specially designed infuser with one container below and one above. Ice is added to the upper container. It melts and drips slowly through the gyokuro leaves, dropping a very concentrated brew into the lower container. Enthusiasts of this tea are known to intensify the brewing by using more dry tea relative to the amount of water so that the liquor is darker and the flavor surprisingly intense.

3. **Kukicha (Bocha).** Also called twig tea, because it is made from the stems and bits of leaf byproduct from sencha production. And yet, this tea is developing a strong following for the slightly nutty flavor, naturally lower caffeine, and greater tolerance for the temperature of the water and the time it is steeped. One additional level of quality in this type of tea is made by using the stems of the gyokuro that are greener, sweeter, and more tender than those of sencha. This special version is sometimes called karigane to set it apart. Brewing instructions for this tea are similar to other green teas (excepting gyokuro).

4. **Genmaicha (Brown Rice Tea).** Genmaicha is a very popular green tea with a sweet creaminess and mellowness that is distinctive and pleasing. It is a blend of sencha and toasted brown rice, sometimes mixed with a bit of matcha (finely powdered green tea) to give it additional flavor and color. Another name for this tea is "popcorn tea" because some of the rice kernels pop during the roasting and will appear in the dry tea as white, puffy bits. It is also called "people's tea" because it is usually more economical for daily use. Genmaicha enjoys an origin legend unlike most other Japanese teas.

There is a tale of a powerful samurai warrior whose personal servant responsible for serving tea was named Genmai. It was Genmai's practice to store a few kernels of toasted rice in his sleeve to snack on as he performed his duties. On one unfortunate day, a few bits of rice fell out of his sleeve as he was pouring his master's tea. When the warrior noticed the bits of rice polluting his tea, he unsheathed his katana and, in a rage, beheaded his servant. But, as he dipped the tea, he was delighted by the flavor and named the tea in his honor. As colorful as this story may be, there are also tales of tearooms adding toasted rice to the tea to make a more affordable beverage.

Other Forms of Green Tea

In addition to the familiar tea bags and the increasing number of green tea options you can see in your local market now, there are four green tea products that should be mentioned separately, as points of interest: matcha is a powdered Japanese green tea; yellow tea is a green tea that is transformed with one additional step in the processing; purple tea is a new varietal that was developed in Kenya; and green tea extracts are concentrations of the chemical components in the leaf, and can be purchased over the counter in many supplement forms.

ESSENTIAL

Matcha, made from tea leaves and a small section of thin stem that have been ground into a fine powder, originated in China. Even though it is now considered to be a Japanese tea, the practice began in China at least as early as the Tang Dynasty (C.E. 618–907) and was introduced to Japanese Buddhist monasteries in C.E. 1191 by the Japanese Buddhist monk Eisai.

Matcha

Matcha contradicts almost everything this book has said about green tea, beginning with the fact that it is not a leaf from which brewing draws out the essences and soluble extracts with heated water. When you consume matcha, either as a beverage or cooked in food, you are ingesting the entire leaf. Matcha is the pulverized powder that results when the green tea is ground. Because of this, all the catechins, amino acids, proteins, vitamins, minerals, and caffeine are considerably higher. The ORAC score (a standardized measure of antioxidant value in foods) of 1 gram of ceremonial grade matcha is 1,384 units, one of the highest scoring foods.

Matcha is also easier to prepare. Using the same water temperature as for most green teas—just under boiling—the bright green powder can be stirred until the lumps are dissolved or can be whipped until frothy with a whisk. It can be served while still warm or it can also be chilled, and is now a popular item in coffee shops that feature steamed milk lattés and frappés. When sifted into dough, batter, or broth, it enhances breads, cakes, and other recipes. Many grades are available, from an expensive food grade to a higher ceremonial grade.

Chanoyu, the Japanese tea ceremony, is centered on matcha tea. With artful precision, the tea is prepared and served in a setting meant to convey the four principles of harmony, respect, purity, and tranquility, as originally taught by tea master Sen no Rikyu in the late 1500s.

Yellow Tea

The main difference between green teas and a true yellow tea is that the leaves are allowed to dry more slowly, traditionally wrapped in a special kind of paper. They are then stored in wooden boxes for a few days until they are finally roasted. The process is said to reduce the astringency, developing a natural sweetness.

Yellow teas are brewed in water that is just below boiling, like all green teas. In addition, great care should be taken with its storage. You will only find this tea in very high-end tea shops or from online dealers who specialize in rarer teas. Use caution to ensure that you are buying from a reputable dealer.

Purple Tea

Purple tea is a new hybrid from Kenya and is not yet commonly available in many tea shops. It is most similar to green tea in processing and brewing. It is also an example of how the tea industry is evolving. This new varietal is said to have greater medicinal value than green teas, but has not yet been subjected to the rigorous examination of other tea categories. In the next decade or so, it may develop into a category of its own. If you are a newcomer to tea, you may want to watch the developments of present day tea history in the making by following news of purple tea.

Green Tea Extracts

Green tea extracts, a concentration of the solid elements in the tea, are made in four basic ways:

- The leaves are brewed and then the liquid is reduced, concentrating the tea elements.
- Remaining solid materials after infusion are dehydrated and powdered.
- The leaves are infused in an alcohol solution.
- Purified extracts are acquired by solvent extraction or column chromatography.

Tea extracts are used widely in scientific research as they can be studied with greater precision, eliminating many of the variables that cannot be controlled in studies using brewed tea. If the research continues to support the use of tea as a pharmaceutical, it will likely be as measured doses in concentrated form rather than numbers of cups of tea to drink per day. At the same time, the number of supplements, stimulant beverages, and specialty foods using the concentrates has grown to the point that there is also potential for abuse associated with these products, such as consuming unhealthy amounts of caffeine.

CHAPTER 7

Black Tea

Black tea is the boldest and most assertive of all the tea categories. A darker brew in the cup, the liquor has a more intense aroma than green tea. Its strength is bracing and vibrant, brisk and warming, standing up to the slosh of milk without backing down, glistening in partnership with other flavors. The typically larger leaves, blackened from the abuse of processing and handling, unfurl gradually with a calm and dignified power.

What Is Black Tea?

What may have first been exported from China as mistakes (tea that unintentionally turned black), or first sold in the United States as "burnt tea," rather quickly became a popular flavor. And today black tea connoisseurs seek out deeper and more robust notes, rather than the lightness and astringency of green tea. The flavors of black teas are often compared to wines such as Muscatel and Burgundy, and rest on the tongue with spiciness and the suggestions of dark fruit like ripe plum and raisin. The sweetness of black teas is quite often equated to chocolate and honey. The liquor ranges from soft golden amber to garnet red to deep brown. The dry artisan products more often feature a sheen on the surface of the twists of dry leaf than green teas, which usually do not. And they tend to be more tolerant of water temperature and steeping time without developing bitterness.

Like all other true teas, black tea comes from the *Camellia sinensis* plant. While certain varietals are hybridized specifically for black teas, the difference between green, black, oolong, white, and pu'erh teas is more about the method of production than the leaf. Black teas are fully oxidized, turned completely brown with no trace of the original green in the leaf, whereas green teas are prevented from changing color. What manufacturers call the "kill green" stage of green tea means that the potential for the leaf to oxidize is arrested. The oxidized black tea leaves produce a much darker liquor with more robust flavors than other teas, with the exception of pu'erh, a very bold tasting tea that is sometimes (arguably) considered a black tea.

ESSENTIAL

A bit of nitpicking in the argument about oxidation would suggest that as soon as the leaf is picked, it begins to oxidize as the exterior cell walls of the leaf break down and are exposed to air. Even the small amount of time necessary to transport the freshly picked leaves from the field to the factory and the small amount of associated withering (softening) add a bit of oxidation, even if this does not produce a color change.

The History of Black Tea

There is very little recorded history about the origin of loose-leaf black tea. Since Asian tea preferences were for green tea, most of the lore is focused there. It is known that black tea existed during the Ming Dynasty in the late 1500s, probably originating at a factory on Lapu Mountain in the Wuyi Mountains of Fujian Province. Tea people today enjoy conjecture and imagination, sharing folktales that black tea was an accident, or an attempt to rectify a mistake, or a bit of unpleasantness with soldiers passing through the area. That first intentionally produced black tea was probably one that is now called Lapsang Souchong (Zhengshan Xiaozhong), known for its smokiness. Even when the first black tea arrived in the United States in 1828 it was sometimes referred to as "burnt tea" to differentiate it from the green tea that Americans habitually drank.

Popular Preferences Change

While green tea was the first tea to arrive in the West, including Europe and the colonies, the demand for black tea eventually dominated. In his classes, American tea master Roy Fong frequently speaks about how teas from different provinces in China pair with the great differences in styles of cooking. Since black tea rather quickly became the taste of choice in Europe and North America, we might consider that Western cuisine may have found it more complementary. Additionally, the oxidation process of black tea eliminated the astringency that can cause bitterness in green tea if brewed in water that is too hot or for too long. Certainly the British habit of adding milk and sugar to tea tasted better with black teas.

However, it would not be accurate to say that the addition of milk and sugar to black tea originated in England. Boiled brick tea, usually an oxidized black tea highly compressed into easily transported blocks, was known in several of the nomadic regions bordering China, including Tibet and Mongolia. Milk, sugar, and some grains were usually added as the pot boiled, forming a thick, soupy broth. Early explorers and missionaries may have transported the recipes as well as samples that flavored the folklore as tea spread around the world.

Today's cuisine is not limited, and preferences for flavors have become much more individual rather than limited socially since the kinds of foods and beverages now available give us considerable choices. Taste preferences are changing and, even in Asia where green teas have traditionally dominated, a demand for black tea is growing. At the recent 2013 Xiamen International Tea Festival in Fujian Province, China, a panel of international tea experts presented a black tea forum entitled "Crisis and Chance—The Future and Innovation of Black Tea." Speakers focused on the necessity of quality production to meet the expectations of worldwide consumers, improved communication from the field to the cup, and hybridization to increase health benefits and new flavors.

Black Tea Misconceptions

There are two different terms used in describing black tea that can be confusing. The first is when black tea is called fermented tea, and the second is when it is called red tea. You will often see the words fermented and oxidized used interchangeably when describing black tea and, in China, black teas are referred to as red tea and this distinction is beginning to spill over into western tea descriptions.

Oxidized versus Fermented

You may sometimes see black tea referred to as "fermented," but this term is inaccurate and confusing for two different reasons. The first reason is that the reaction causing the tea leaves to turn brown is not a microbial process, like the process of fermenting wine. The second reason for this term causing confusion in discussing black teas is that there is another category, pu'erh tea, which actually *is* fermented.

ESSENTIAL

To better understand oxidation, cut an apple into wedges and allow the cut surfaces to stay exposed to air for several hours. You can observe the white flesh of the apple gradually turn brown as it oxidizes from the exposure to oxygen.

A more visual way to understand what happens to black tea is that it oxidizes during processing. The tea leaf oxidizes in much the same way that a banana peel browns as it ages, or pears darken and shrivel, but it does so in a controlled factory environment under the watchful eye of the tea master.

Black Tea versus Red Tea

Another difference in language between eastern and western cultures that can be confusing exists when black tea is called red tea. In most cases, we are referring to the same tea. The western world's choice of the word *black* refers to the color of the dry leaf. The Chinese choice of the word *red* refers to the color of the liquor. In the worldwide market, you are more likely to experience *black* as the accepted categorical designation.

This becomes even more confusing when you look at a list of teas that includes rooibos, an herbal tea from the rooibos ("red bush") of South Africa. This tea is sometimes listed as a red tea and, in this case, both the short needle-like leaves as well as the brewed liquor are bright red.

Blended, Flavored, and Scented Black Teas

Black teas are often sold in blends, or scented or flavored by additional ingredients. In the last few years, there has been a huge boom in the number of tea flavors filling the store shelves and finding favor with tea lovers. Tea with fruit and spice additives boasting colorful packaging and intriguing names attract new tea drinkers.

ALERT

It would be rare that a high-quality tea would be amended with any additional flavoring techniques. That does not mean that flavored teas are only made with poor-quality products. Certainly, there are many grades and qualities of tea now being prepared to appeal to popular flavor preferences and budgets.

Blends

Most of the recognized big brand names rely on the consistent flavor and aroma of their teas. For example, one company's English Breakfast tea will certainly taste different than another company's English Breakfast, but each brand will strive to maintain their own unique flavor profile from one year to the next. Companies blend teas from dozens of sources in order to maintain the consistent flavor that defines their product and is what their customers expect. Tea blending is both an art and a science. It requires an extremely sensitive palate to be able to evaluate the differences in each season's fresh products and then calculate exactly what percentage from each source will produce the hallmark blend.

As well as blending tea leaves from different sources, tea is also blended with herbs, spices, fruit, and flowers to broaden the number of flavors a company can offer. Some of the most traditional flowers blended with tea are jasmine, rose, and hibiscus. Dried berries, ginger, apple bits, and orange peel blend well with black tea. Popular spices for blending are cinnamon, nutmeg, and clove, which may be familiar to tea drinkers as chai spices. Some of the herbs used are mint, vanilla, lavender, sage, stevia, and rooibos. Blending bits of dried fruit and crushed herbs adds color as well as flavor to loose-leaf teas. Other additives that might be surprising to discover in blended black teas are vegetables. Dehydrated and pulverized bits of tomato, cabbage, and beets have found their way into a few tea combinations.

QUESTION

Do black teas infused with other ingredients provide the same health benefits as those without?
There has been very little research on questions like these. But there is the potential, using good-quality teas and herbs, to create a blend that offers multiple health benefits. However, the blend would reduce the specific benefits of using tea alone, as the amount of actual tea leaves would be reduced.

Flavored

The most famous and popular flavored tea of all time is Earl Grey. There are several versions of the story about how it came to be, but it is generally presumed that the flavor was created in honor of the second Earl Grey, Prime Minister of Great Britain in the 1830s. It is a black tea flavored with the oil of bergamot, a hybridized citrus plant like an orange, grown in Italy.

ESSENTIAL

Earl Grey tea is the basis for a beverage called the "London Fog," made with steamed milk and sweetened with vanilla-infused sugar syrup.

Flavored black teas are extremely popular in North America and account for the boom in sales of black tea. You can easily find dozens of different flavor combinations. Some of the same spices and fruit used in blends are also available to tea companies as oil essences. While there may be an aromatherapy health value, either calming or invigorating, it is impossible to know if the addition of essential oils offers additional health benefits. Some flavoring oils are also very fugitive, and may lose the added flavors quickly. Some tea drinkers shy away from flavored teas because of various food sensitivities.

ESSENTIAL

There are great differences in the quality of essential oils used to flavor tea. One way to distinguish the quality of a flavored tea is by the presence of a slight aftertaste, caused by lesser-quality oils that would not be present in better additives.

Blended and Flavored

It is extremely common for tea companies producing both tea bags and loose-leaf products not only to blend their black tea with other non-tea products to add flavor and color, but also to enliven the experience with essential oils.

Scented

Here are two examples of scented black teas that produce extremely different flavors. One is jasmine tea, when both black and green teas are layered in large piles with fresh jasmine flowers so that the teas absorb the flavor and aroma. The other is Lapsang Souchong, which is stored in baskets above pine fires to absorb the flavor and aroma of the smoke.

Jasmine Tea

The expertise and labor involved in making jasmine tea involves many steps that are rarely appreciated. Contrary to other altered teas, jasmine tea manufacturers usually begin with a high-quality tea harvest, selected to blend well with the flowers. The tea must be carefully finished and stored until the flowers bloom in the summer. The jasmine flowers used are a special variety with large white blooms that have an exceptionally strong smell. They are harvested just before they open so that there is time to layer them with the tea before they release their heaviest scent. The tea and flowers are left together for several hours. Then the two are separated, the flowers being removed from the scented tea. The scenting process can be repeated several times, the highest-quality jasmine tea sometimes being scented with more than seven different batches of fresh flowers.

It is frequently misstated and incorrectly assumed that, because of the dark color, black tea has more caffeine than other types of tea. The oxidation process for black tea can actually reduce the amount of caffeine remaining in the leaf. What may make black tea drinkers feel slightly more invigorated by the caffeine is the fact that black tea is usually steeped longer, using more tea leaves and at hotter temperatures, releasing more caffeine from the leaf.

Lapsang Souchong

The finished black tea chosen for Lapsang Souchong is held in bamboo baskets in a closed room where the floor is open to a furnace below. Fresh pine firewood is consistently fed into the furnace and heavy smoke is funneled up to the room above, where the tea absorbs the smoke's flavor. The amount of smoking is carefully controlled, depending on the buyer's request. Certain markets around the world value the heavy smoky flavor, while others prefer the tea only minimally smoked.

Health Benefits of Black Tea

For many years, people believed that green tea had more health benefits than black tea. This assumption is now being challenged by current scientific research. Because green tea is not allowed significant oxidation, the compounds in the leaves are subjected to less change than in black tea. Generalizations have been made that black tea offers more benefits for heart health and digestion, while green tea does more to protect the body against developing cancer. But these lines are becoming increasingly blurred with the hundreds of new studies every year. Now more of them are considering both tea categories, with additional studies focusing on black tea, pu'erh, oolong, and white teas.

Some of the most often mentioned benefits of black tea are that it:

- Hydrates the body—with less tannins than green tea, black tea is less astringent
- Strengthens the immune system with bacteria-fighting antioxidants

- Has anti-inflammatory qualities
- Balances hormone levels
- Balances cholesterol levels, may reduce incidence of stroke, and generally improves heart health
- Reduces the risk of coronary artery disease
- Promotes blood flow to the brain, and improves mental focus and concentration
- Stimulates metabolism, giving more energy
- Improves oral health, and may reduce the risk of oral cancer
- May reduce the risk of many other cancers
- Aids digestion and the breakdown of fats in the gastrointestinal tract

Brewing Black Tea

Black tea lends itself to many different brewing methods and almost unlimited experimentation. It has a very wide margin for what can be considered "good" taste. From a very quick, light brew to something dark and intense, black teas allow an almost infinite range of appreciation. Guidelines for water temperature usually encourage boiling or near-boiling water, assuming that the greatest majority of black tea lovers want a bold cup. Lowering water temperature will still infuse the flavor from the tea, but it will do so more slowly and with less intensity.

ESSENTIAL

Conduct your own experiment with water temperature. Choose your favorite black tea (either tea bags or loose-leaf tea) and measure equal amounts into three different teacups. Heat your water in an open saucepan so you can watch the developing boil. Fill your first cup when the water starts to simmer, the second before it comes to a full boil, and the third at full boil. When cool enough, taste from each of your three cups with a spoon. Notice differences in the liquor color, aroma, and flavor. Then choose the preferred temperature for your cup of tea.

Your choice of teaware and brewing style may also vary with the tea you select and how much you want to be able to observe the brewing process.

If you are using bagged tea or cut teas, there is less to observe. But most loose-leaf teas, especially quality tea with whole leaves, are interesting to watch as they are restored in the brewing process. Some people use the color of the liquor as a reference to the strength they wish to serve.

Traditional Western-Style Brewing Method

The traditional British style of tea is prepared in a teapot. Whether you're using bags or loose leaves, black tea is much more amenable to the water being in contact with the leaves for a longer time and greater variations in water temperature. Teapots are usually warmed by first filling it with boiling water. The warming water is poured out just prior to adding tea and the brewing water. One variation when serving with a teapot and using loose leaves is to have a second teapot warmed and ready for serving decanted tea. Warm the second teapot while brewing the loose-leaf tea in the first pot. When it is ready to serve, strain the tea into the waiting pot by pouring it through a small sieve or tea strainer, but keep the leaves in the first pot so they can be infused a second time.

Where Black Tea Grows

Britain's colonization of India and Sri Lanka led Britain to develop black tea production in these countries. As growing conflicts with China worsened, England wanted to secure their supply of tea, so they established tea plantations in the areas of the world they controlled, such as India. Englishmen like Robert Fortune and Robert Bruce developed a thriving crop of seeds and plants transported from China, and eventually discovered and developed the Indian native varietal, *Camellia sinensis* var. *assamica*. They focused the tea industry on black tea production to satisfy the English desire for strong black tea that would stand up well to milk and sugar.

FACT

Large British companies developed many areas around the world for black tea production. Unilever (the current parent company of Lipton Teas) even established dozens of test sites around the United States in the twentieth century to evaluate the viability of commercial tea production. The costs were too great in the States, but other countries now produce enormous quantities of black teas. In order to meet the world's demand for black tea, a greater percentage of overall production is manufactured in large operations, harvested, and processed mechanically in bulk for large companies who blend for their signature flavors, create the new and popular flavored teas, and manufacture ready-to-drink beverages.

How Black Tea Grows

As a very general rule of thumb, more black teas are grown at lower elevations and with the larger-leafed *Camellia sinensis assamica* varietal than with the smaller-leafed Chinese varietal. But, of course, there are exceptions. What is necessary to produce good-quality tea, both in flavor and abundance of the cellular compounds, are mineral-rich soils in which the long taproot can draw from abundant groundwater, as well as a very hot and humid environment. Black tea production benefits from a tropical climate and favors areas where there are also heavy mists and fog. Farms and plantations near the equator, as in Kenya, can continue to harvest throughout the year. Other countries, like India, may have an average of four periods of harvest. In higher elevations with shorter growing seasons and less rainfall, the plants grow more slowly, and so there is considerably less tea produced.

How Black Tea Is Processed

The tea is picked and brought to the factory where the withering cycle begins. This first phase is much longer for black tea than for green, oolong, and white teas. The leaves may be stacked in deeper piles, exposing them to less air. They may remain in these piles for as long as eighteen hours. This long, slow withering, the first step in oxidation, is critical to developing the complex flavors of black tea, producing thearubigins and protecting the whole leaves from breakage. Between 5 to 15 percent of the original moisture in the leaf is driven out during this phase and the leaves become soft and pliable. Once the leaves are sufficiently withered, they are then rolled. Being softer allows the leaves to be rolled and manipulated with less breakage. The remaining moisture is gradually released during rolling, shaping, oxidation, firing, and drying until the tea is dry enough to package (3 percent moisture may remain).

The rolling breaks open the cell walls, exposing their inner juices to air, stimulating the activity of the enzymes. Rolling may be repeated several times, as the tea master instructs, in order to fully open the cell walls and prepare the leaf for full oxidation. The rolling also helps shape the leaf, forming its unique character. This method of processing, aimed at preserving the whole leaf, is referred to as orthodox production.

ESSENTIAL

The term "orange pekoe" refers to a grade of tea that includes all fully opened leaves and no buds. Another example in the grading system is FOP (Fine Orange Pekoe) that contains full leaves and some unopened buds.

On the other hand, black teas intended for bulk sales are usually harvested and finished largely by machines, in a process called CTC (Cut-Tear-Curl). The leaves are cut during withering and then shredded into small pieces prior to oxidation. This method is much more economical, as it reduces the labor of lengthy withering, rolling, and processing.

Oxidation is important in developing the full flavor potential of the black tea, regardless of the processing method used. It is not that the duration of oxidation, longer or shorter, determines the quality of the tea, but it does build character and flavor. Controlling the humidity and temperature in the environment is crucial to the oxidation process.

While oxidation removes a lot of moisture from the leaves, there is still water in the leaves that must be removed in the final drying stage. Once they are completely dry, the leaves are sorted, separating the whole leaves from broken bits that are an obvious byproduct of handling, before the tea is finally packaged for shipment.

Grades of Black Tea

The grading of teas is extremely specific in the professional tea trading market, with a complex grading system that defines about thirty levels of cut and quality. It isn't necessary to understand the entire system to make informed choices, but familiarity with some of the general considerations for assessing value can help you decide if a tea you're sampling is worth the asking price. A tea with only whole buds of unopened leaves is considered the highest quality, but whole buds are less frequently seen in black teas. Whole leaves with some buds are becoming more common and still considered to be very high-quality—the greater percentage of bud indicating higher value. Below that, combinations of whole leaf with some broken bits are still very desirable, as they deliver a good flavor, and are more affordable.

Buying Black Tea

Many of us have been buying black teas most of our lives. The names and brands are a little more familiar and the thought of shopping in a specialty tea shop then seems a little less intimidating than considering the options for green, oolong, white, and pu'erh. The aromas and flavors are more anticipated, and therefore may seem less challenging. But there is still considerable diversity among black teas available today. Exploring them can seem like a trip around the world in your teacup. You can begin by comparing teas from some of the recognized countries of origin: India, China, or Sri Lanka. If you visit specialty markets, you will easily find specialty black teas from these countries.

Indian Black Teas

India is famous for black teas from three regions: Darjeeling, Assam, and Nilgiri. They are often identified by the name of the grower or estate, as well as the time of year when the tea was picked. The different times of harvest, from the first flush of spring to the late autumn create distinct flavor characteristics and in some ways, different health benefits.

ESSENTIAL

The Tea Board of India organizes growers throughout the country, ensures good conditions and benefits for all workers in the industry, and controls international sales of its product. They recently implemented a policy to further ensure the quality of tea being exported. By more closely examining shipments and having the power to return unacceptable products to the growers rather than releasing it for sale, they want to assure buyers that Indian teas are safe.

Chinese Black Teas

Teas in China are sold by the name of the tea, usually specific to the varietal, the region in which it is grown, and the way it is produced. The names may refer to geographic origins but in ways that might not be as obvious as with Indian teas. For example, Keemun is one of the most famous Chinese black teas, and it is traditionally grown in Qimen County of Anhui Province. The evolution in the spelling makes the location a little less obvious. However, the names of the growers are seldom stated. Tea is mostly grown and processed on small farms and collectives rather than larger estates, and individuals are not considered as important as regions and legends associated with the origins of the tea.

Sri Lankan Black Teas

It's not uncommon to still see Sri Lankan teas referred to as Ceylon tea, the island country's name before it was changed to Sri Lanka in 1972. The Sri Lanka Tea Board's "Symbol of Quality" logo featuring the Ceylon Lion is attached to every tea product that is 100 percent grown and packed in Sri

Lanka. The words "Pure Ceylon Tea, Packed in Sri Lanka" are also reserved for those teas, though overseas importers may use the term "Ceylon Tea" to designate tea grown in Sri Lanka but packed elsewhere. Famous for black tea, the island nation is also closely associated with tea magnate Sir Thomas Lipton, who was one of Ceylon's largest tea-producing landowners. At one point, he farmed more than three thousand acres of tea. His historic estate has even been reopened to the public for tourism, with access to the original factory and to Lipton's colonial bungalow.

Tea production in Ceylon (later Sri Lanka) was built, rather heroically, on the demise of coffee plantations during the blight first identified in the late 1860s that ravaged the economy of the island nation. Today, the tea is marketed according to elevation, districts, and plantations. The main growing areas are differentiated as high altitude, medium altitude, or low altitude. The high-grown teas are the lightest, and low-grown the darkest.

Popular and Legendary Black Teas

As tea has become more popular, retailers have begun to increase the number of products, increasing specialty teas instead of (or in addition to) bulk teas. Some of the more interesting specialty teas are finding places on grocery shelves alongside bulk teas that have been blended and flavored. As mysterious as the names might sound, information about them is readily available and can add interesting details to your own enjoyment. Filled with both legend and history, every tea tells a different story. The following are a few examples from different origins that may pique your curiosity.

Chinese Black Teas

One difference between Chinese tea production and that of other countries is the many legends about the origins of each tea. Many of them are mythical, and involve spiritual beings. Others are just part of an oral history so ancient that they cannot be proved or disproved. Most tea experts give little credence to the folklore but still enjoy the entertaining tales.

1. **Lapsang Souchong.** Generally thought to be the first black tea, excluding brick tea and compressed teas, Lapsang Souchong is completely

processed and then smoked over pine fires so that the tea absorbs the flavor of the smoke. As with many other Chinese teas, there are variations to the legend associated with Lapsang Souchong's beginning, and most involve a conflict with soldiers.

One version claims that the presence of soldiers in the area prevented the workers from properly finishing their harvest. The fresh green leaves were left to oxidize too long, turned brown, and ruined the day's harvest. The workers quickly dried the tea over a pine fire, trying to salvage some of the tea, and were pleasantly surprised with the accidental result of the smoky black tea.

Another version tells us that a band of soldiers passing through a village made their camp near the factory and slept on the soft piles of withering leaves. In so doing, they bruised them and "ruined" the day's crop. To make up for their lack of consideration, the soldiers dried the tea over their own pine fire for the tea workers, and so inspired the new flavor.

2. **Keemun (Qimen).** Often referred to as the "Burgundy" of black teas, Keemun is one of the most popular Chinese black teas internationally and is currently enjoying a new popularity with Chinese aficionados. It is produced from the leaf set of the bud and top two leaves of the smaller-leafed *Camellia sinensis* varietal. The finished leaves maintain a dark, reddish-brown luster and brew a beautiful golden-brown liquor. The aroma and flavor sometimes include a hint of stone fruit, like ripe plums, or subtle chocolate, and may have delicate honey sweetness. There are many different grades of Keemun, from ones affordable enough to be included in some breakfast blends to ones of such meticulous production as to be considered rare.

3. **Yunnan Black (Dianhong).** Considered the birthplace of tea, Yunnan Province is well known for pu'erh but less known for their distinctive black tea, sometimes listed as Yunnan Red or by the Chinese name, *Dianhong*, whose production is traced to the early 1900s. It is often characterized by a high percentage of golden buds. Both the flavor and aroma in good-quality Yunnan black teas are gentle and sweet. Variations in quality are usually determined by the amount of golden buds, the amount of broken leaf, and the color of the liquor. Higher-quality Yunnan tea leaves are more of a reddish color, while lower-quality leaves may be darker, producing liquor that is not as sweet and may even have a bitterness or astringency.

Indian Black Teas

Of the three major growing areas, it is easiest to find Darjeeling and Assam teas in unblended offerings by which you can experience the true, uncompromised character of the tea. Most specialty retailers offer these Indian teas in many different grades, with widely variable prices. The leaf grades from Orthodox (with full and unbroken leaf) to CTC (cut-tear-curl), as well as variations of the amount of whole bud, will be obvious in the dry loose-leaf tea.

1. **Darjeeling.** Usually referred to as "the Champagne of teas," Darjeeling is sold according to the spurts of new growth called "flushes." The first flush of spring tends to be lighter, is highly valued, and devotees wait with great anticipation for each new year's harvest. Second flush, from the early summer months, is darker and more flavorful, able to deliver a characteristic spicy, Muscatel-like flavor popular with tea lovers. The third flush is from the late summer, early fall months of the monsoon season. The last harvest is collected after the rains of the monsoon season, referred to as the autumnal flush, and brews with more body and a darker liquor. The first flush and second flush teas are usually more expensive than the later flushes.

2. **Assam.** The Assam region in northeastern India straddles the Brahmaputra River, placing it geographically close to Yunnan Province in China. Assam tea is usually described as brisk and malty, offering the potential for a very strong brew. For this reason, it is extremely desirable for blends, and for the same reason it stands up very well to milk and sugar.

Sri Lanka—Ceylon

There is typically a citrus note in many black teas from Sri Lanka with great variation, due to the differing elevations of the fields. Lower elevation teas are much darker, while the highest elevations produce teas that are typically lighter in color and flavor. Price and value are based on the leaf quality and the percentage of broken leaf, with the high-altitude teas considered more valuable.

CHAPTER 8

Oolong Tea

Blending the freshness of green tea and the intensity of black tea, oolong teas are the most complex of the tea categories. Each one is crafted with a unique balance between the extremes of dark and light. Enhanced by beautiful legends, oolong teas charm as they satisfy the craving for the rare and exotic. The flavors are multiplied in the leaf by repeated processes of rolling, shaping, and firing to layer a variety of flavors for repeated infusions. This complexity fascinates tea lovers and has made them some of today's most popular teas.

What Is Oolong Tea?

The manufacture of oolong tea is the most intricate. Simply explained, it is a partially oxidized tea with characteristics of both green and black tea. But this simplicity is almost misleading, because it suggests that there is a scale between the two extremes with a selected stopping point somewhere in the middle. While there is actually a specific degree of oxidation that the tea master targets in the manufacturing process, there can be between twenty and thirty steps in the process.

ESSENTIAL

Combining black and green tea may provide an interesting brew, but it is not the same as an oolong and will taste nothing like it. The flavor in oolong is created in the processing of fresh leaves. It is not an added artificial flavoring.

The amount of oxidation varies with each different oolong tea. Some are very green (as low as 8 percent oxidation), while others are nearly black (75–85 percent oxidation). These differences are obvious on the dry leaf but even more apparent when the leaf is fully opened after multiple infusions. The edges of the leaf will be brown where it was tumbled and bruised, even on a lightly oxidized green oolong. There may be obvious places where the leaf was cracked during processing and the cell walls broke open, the amount of oxidation showing up in lines on the leaves.

Other differences in oolong teas are in the way the leaves are finished. Some long leaves are tightly twisted, while others are rolled into balls the size of pearls. The elevations at which the tea grows and the time of year it is harvested also contribute to many subtle flavor differences. Tea shops that sell a variety of oolongs will usually mention these characteristics.

FACT

Oolong is frequently referred to as the Black Dragon; in Chinese *wu* means black and *long* means dragon. The original oolongs were long, dark, twisted leaves that inspired an association with the dragon's tail. The dragon is the Chinese symbol of strength, power, and good fortune, making it a fine name for this remarkable tea. Misunderstandings between the sound of "oo" and "wu" can account for the difference, and it is not uncommon to see the name written as "wulong."

Oolong Flavors

The complexity of possible flavors includes combinations from a list of descriptive terms like honey sweetness combined with a rich body, creamy, flowery, fruity, spicy, roasty, chocolaty, buttery, nutty, and more. Oolongs can unveil the essence of dark stone fruit, or freshly picked flowers. Overall, they tend to have flavors reminiscent of florals and fruits, and tea lovers seldom limit themselves to a single favorite, enjoying the adventure of tasting a variety. The liquor also changes with the amount of oxidation. The lightest, about 8 percent, produces a very pale yellow-green tea; moderately oxidized gives a glowing jade green; and the most highly oxidized oolongs, at about 85 percent, brew a cup almost as dark as black teas.

The History of Oolong Tea

Long before the first techniques of controlling the oxidation of tea were used, various methods of tea processing had been developed. While there is not a definitive date, it is widely believed that oolongs originated in Fujian Province—possibly in the late 1500s. But it was certainly known by the early 1600s, then referred to as Yan Cha (rock or cliff tea). Some stories tell of monks keeping tea gardens, using oolong as a healing herb and to help their meditation practices.

The origin legends of oolong tea, like many other ancient Chinese legends, are told with variations. An entertaining story is that a farmer named Wu Long was distracted by a deer leaping through his garden while he was harvesting his tea. Forgetting his work, he chased the deer and did not return until his tea had already withered too long, and the edges of the leaves had turned brown. Instead of abandoning his day's work, he finished the tea and was pleased with the flavor. It is said by some that the tea method was then named in his honor.

Where Oolong Grows

There are three provinces famous for growing and manufacturing oolong tea. In mainland China, this includes Guangdong and Fujian Provinces. The third area is Taiwan. Looking at the diversity of these optimal growing regions, the microclimates that impact the flavors become distinct. From shrubs clinging to ledges on rocky cliffs to high mountain peaks to fields blanketing rolling hills, the growers in the different provinces work in an intimate partnership with the environment.

Fujian Province

The mountainous coastal province of Fujian has two areas where oolong teas are the primary harvest. One is Anxi, in the southern part of the province, and the other is the more northern Wuyi Mountain region. Both areas have growers specializing in very notable teas. It is in the Wuyi Mountains where oolong tea is thought to have originated, but there is also a legendary tea from Anxi that is one of the most popular of all time. The tales about teas from these areas are some of the most popular with tea lovers around the world. Names like Tie Guan Yin (Iron Goddess of Mercy), Da Hong Pao (Great Red Robe), Jade Oolong, Rougui, Phoenix Dan Cong, and Shui Jin Gui (Golden Water Turtle) are only a few of the dozens of oolongs that now populate the menus in tea shops and are becoming increasingly familiar in fine grocery markets.

Guangdong Province

On the southern coast, the Phoenix Mountain region of the Guangdong Province has been known for tea production and is often referred to as the origin of the gongfu tea ceremony. Farms are sometimes called groves that range up the mountainsides. Phoenix oolongs, also known as Dan Cong, are prized for their flowery notes and lingering flavors. They have been honored as tribute teas, reserved for the imperial court.

Taiwan

Known for lighter teas and a fresh green fragrance, Taiwanese oolongs are characterized by their light oxidation. They are sold in three categories by elevation, as low, medium, or high mountain teas.

Commercial tea farming was started by the Dutch during a period of colonial rule in the 1600s, but the oolong tea varietals were not introduced until 1855 when a Fujian tea grower, Ke Chao, transplanted tea plants from the Wuyi area of Fujian to Tung Ting Mountain. His experiment was immediately successful, but it was necessary to return partially processed tea to the factories in Fujian to manufacture quality oolong. These original bushes that inspired the production of oolong tea in Taiwan are still growing in the township of Lu Gu.

Shipping the tea leaves back to Fujian for processing was considered a very inefficient production method by British tea merchant John Dodd. He recognized an opportunity and set up the first oolong factory so that the tea could be completely processed at the origin. He established Dodd and Company in 1868, and one year later he sold his entire production of 140 tons to the United States. He called his tea Formosa Oolong, using the colonial Dutch name for Taiwan. Today, oolong teas in Taiwan are largely produced by family-run farms and are in great demand around the world.

How Oolong Is Processed

What makes the manufacture of oolong so intricate is that some of the basic steps are repeated many times before the desired amount of bruising and browning of the leaves is achieved. Withering, rolling, shaping, and firing are similar to black tea, but much more attention to timing and temperature is necessary. One last step, baking or roasting, is exclusive to oolong and is referred to as the real art in making this tea.

Withering

Tea experts may argue about the best withering techniques but no one discounts the importance of what happens to the tea when it enters the factory. Oolong teas are generally handled with special care and are withered outside in the full sun when possible. The direct sunlight is considered optimal. Moisture is drawn to the surface and gradually evaporates, softening the remaining leaf. The enzymes become active and, as part of the oxidation, begin to reduce the tendency for astringency.

Shaking, Tossing, Turning, and Bruising

The second step is to manipulate the leaves so that the cell walls gradually rupture. This may be done by repeatedly shaking and tossing them in flat wicker baskets. Modern machines assist by repeatedly turning the stacks and roughing up the edges. These steps also help to remove bitterness.

Oxidation

The tortured leaves are allowed to rest during the oxidation phase while the color darkens to the desired shade of green to red or brown. It is by oxidation that the tea takes on the flavor characteristics that later become the flowery or fruity notes.

Fixing Green/"Kill Green"

When the master of operations in the factory feels that the desired degree of oxidation has been achieved, the leaves are heated to stop the enzymatic action (the browning of the leaf). At this stage, the green color and flavors will be preserved at the designated "kill green" point determining that the oolong will be considered more green or more black. Sources of heat may be either moist steam or dry baking.

Rolling and Shaping

In a step that may be repeated many times, the softened leaves are further manipulated to develop the most complex layers of flavor, "massaged" with techniques that result in the final shape. This step was once performed by hand. There are now rolling machines; however, this process is still labor intensive.

Drying

The oxidized and rolled leaf is finally dried, removing most of the remaining moisture. Some methods of drying include air-drying, sun drying, or being heated in a pan.

Firing

Different than drying, firing and roasting are techniques that add a bit of smoky flavor or further develop the other final flavor characteristics.

Roasting

It is in the final roasting that some of the subtler flavors of an oolong are developed. The tea is usually separated into small batches, spread in shallow baskets with a low heat. It can take anywhere from a few hours to more than a day.

Health Benefits of Oolong Tea

The health benefits of drinking oolong teas are known to be very similar to those of green teas and black teas, depending on the degree of oxidation. This is an easy assumption, since all three categories are created from the same *Camellia sinensis* and their processing shares some of the same methods. Traditional Chinese medicine lists specific oolong consumption benefits of maintaining healthy skin, relieving bronchial tightness, lowering cholesterol, and maintaining a healthy weight. Much of the research in recent years on oolong teas has focused on weight control, with several studies affirming the long-held belief that oolong tea specifically helps with weight management. These studies have even begun to help explain the biochemical properties that make it so.

ALERT

Radical and somewhat irresponsible promises of easy and rapid weight loss launched oolong tea's popularity in the early 2000s. Exaggerations of the potential benefits have created a climate of mistrust regarding many of the health claims and information about tea in general over these last ten years.

Weight Loss

Oolong tea is usually associated with weight control. The mechanism that appears to contribute to this is an improved lipid metabolism. Conclusions are generally that long-term and habitual consumption of oolong tea may help prevent obesity.

A 1998 Chinese study demonstrated that drinking oolong tea for six weeks resulted in measurable weight reduction. Later, in 2001, the U.S. Agriculture Research Services performed more detailed investigation and released results that oolong tea increased the energy levels in their subjects, allowing them to increase their physical exercise and burn more calories than when they drank only water. In a 2003 Japanese oolong and green tea study, it was shown that oolong tea had measurable benefits in energy levels over green tea within a two-hour time frame. A conservative conclusion is that drinking oolong tea can help someone have more energy to participate in active physical exercise resulting in weight loss. It has also been credited with suppressing appetite.

It may be found that the relationship between the bioactive components, caffeine, catechins, and polymerized polyphenols is a factor in weight loss, suppressing pancreatic lipase and inhibiting the absorption of lipids into the intestines.

Diabetes

Several studies have focused on oolong tea and its relationship with controlling blood sugar. Conclusions are that drinking six cups of oolong daily can lower blood sugar by approximately 15 percent.

Brewing Oolong Tea

Brewing oolong tea is easier than brewing green teas, with less likelihood of bitterness in the final cup. But it is also the category of tea often selected for a regular gongfu-style preparation or even an elaborate gongfu tea ceremony. The preferred brewing vessels are the three-piece gaiwan set with bowl, lid, and saucer, a Yishing teapot, or another small teapot made with a fine-quality clay and glaze. Oolong teas are often described (and valued) for the number of infusions that can be brewed from a single measure of dry leaf. Using a gaiwan or teapot, the server will calculate the amount of tea relative to the amount of water and anticipate a number of infusions by varying the water temperature and the length of steeping time. It can certainly be prepared in a western-style teapot but, because the leaves have a tendency to expand greatly as they rehydrate, it is not recommended that oolong teas be brewed in restricted tea balls or bags that limit the way in which the water flows over the entire surface of the leaf.

FACT

Gongfu tea ceremony or gongfu cha is literally translated to mean "preparing tea with effort." The effort demonstrates respect for a fine tea, giving full attention to careful preparation, and respect for the guest, applying focus and skill to providing them with the finest tea experience.

Popular and Legendary Oolong Teas

An education in oolong tea is filled with storytelling and history that reveal the importance of tea in the physical and spiritual life of the Chinese people. We are fortunate that the lovely tales filled with the mythology of tea's healing properties have survived along with the teas.

Chinese Oolongs

Rounding the southern China coast, Fujian Province and Guangdong Province have a long tradition of growing some of the world's finest teas. Oolongs from both provinces are legendary and highly prized.

1. **Da Hong Pao (Great Red Robe).** Da Hong Pao is one of the dark oolongs, a Yan Cha or "rock tea" with twisted full leaves from the Wuyi Mountains of northern Fujian Province, and claims one of the most famous tea legends. The story is most often told that a scholar, who had achieved such recognition that he was allowed to sit for the imperial exams, was on his way to the palace in Peking (now Beijing) when he took ill. Monks in the area are said to have cured him with a remarkable healing tea from sacred bushes growing in a crevice on the steep wall of a canyon.

When the scholar passed his exams and was awarded the Great Red Robe from the Emperor, he returned, wrapped it around the plants, and bowed before them.

The same ancient bushes are protected in a park that is open to the public. Tea made from the original bushes is so rare that it is almost never sold. However, clones from the plants, the children, grandchildren, and great-grandchildren bushes growing in the area, continue to produce this treasured tea. The cuttings have survived many different generations, and they now grow in other areas. Some merchants show respect for the original healing bushes by renaming the tea harvested from the plants grown from cuttings Wuyi Yancha, or Xiao Hong Pao (Small Red Robe), instead of Da Hong Pao.

FACT

Tea from the original tea bushes is only harvested every two years, resulting in just a few grams of dry tea. It has rarely been offered publicly but, the last time there was an international auction, a single gram sold for hundreds of thousands of U.S. dollars.

2. **Tie Guan Yin (Iron Goddess of Mercy).** Named for the mythical Chinese goddess or bodhisattva of compassion (a spiritual being in the Buddhist tradition), the story of this tea is told with very little variation. As the story goes, there was a very poor but devout farmer, Wei, who visited the small shrine to Guan Yin every day. One night, Guan Yin appeared to Wei in his dream and told him where to find a gift that he was to share with generosity. The next day Wei went to the location and found a small tea plant like he had never seen before. He nurtured it and discovered that it produced the finest tea he had ever tasted. Following the bodhisattva's instructions, he shared the seeds and cuttings with his fellow farmers, and eventually with the world as a perpetual blessing from Guan Yin.

Tie Guan Yin is one of the most commonly available oolong teas today, especially popular because of its famous legend, but also because of the extraordinary flavor. It is one of the oolongs where the bud and new leaves, still attached to the stem, are rolled into a tight ball the size of a large pearl. Tie Guan Yin typically brews the flavors of peaches and honey.

Phoenix Mountain Oolongs (Fenghuang Dancong)

This is the representative tea from the third oolong growing region, Phoenix Mountain on the coast of China's southern Guangdong Province. Teas from this area are some of the favorites of oolong connoisseurs due to the great variety in the flavor, yet all are sweet and flavorful. A high-quality Phoenix oolong will have a clear, yellow-orange color and there will be a very sweet aftertaste that lingers in the mouth. The trunks of this varietal grow taller and tend to have a more umbrella-like canopy of leaves, traditionally allowed to grow taller.

You might read that Phoenix Mountain is the true birthplace of oolong tea, and it is certainly one of the oldest oolong varietals and areas of production. It was once a tribute tea, is highly ranked in oolong tea competitions, and has been selected for many tea awards over the last twenty years.

Taiwanese Oolongs

While Taiwan is known for producing lighter teas, this is by no means a rigid rule. In fact, they have developed many of the most diverse oolong teas. The range of elevation and growing techniques continues to develop new hybrids, explore new manufacturing techniques, and produce new flavors of their fine tea.

1. **Bai Hao Oolong (Oriental Beauty, White Tip Oolong).** Bai Hao oolong is grown without pesticides to encourage a tiny insect, the tea leafhopper (like a grasshopper), to visit the garden. The insects snacking on the leaves and sipping the juice from the stems increases the plant's production of monoterpene diols (small molecule compounds) and hotrienols that give the finished tea its uniquely sweet, floral flavor. The intrusion of the insects actually begins the oxidation process in the leaf before it has been picked, and adds additional sweetness to the tea.

   Folklore tells that one of this tea's alternate names was Braggart's Tea. The story is that Beipu, a small farmer, realized one day that his tea crop had been damaged by the leafhoppers, but he decided to go ahead and harvest and finish the leaves, and take them to market anyway. At the market, the local tea shop owner was so impressed with the tea that he doubled the normal price. When Beipu returned to his community of fellow farmers and explained what happened, they didn't believe him, giving his tea the nickname and Beipu a memorable reputation.

Because Oriental Beauty is a very lightly oxidized oolong tea, it should be brewed like a green tea with water that is slightly lower than boiling. It can then be infused multiple times.

FACT

In the early nineteenth century, the British ambassador to China presented a gift of fine Bai Hao oolong tea to the queen of England. The queen was very taken with the unique taste and aroma, as well as its distinctive appearance—quite different to any teas seen before in England—and gave it the name "Oriental Beauty."

2. **Tung Ting.** The first oolong varietals that were transplanted from Fujian Province to Taiwan found their new home in Tung Ting. The name means "frozen summit," and in the 1800s it was the highest elevation where tea was being grown in Taiwan. This tea is treasured as part of tea history, and some of the original plants are still growing in the area.

It is usually sold as a very lightly oxidized green oolong with beautiful, flowery notes and a fresh sweetness. But it is also one of the oolong teas that collectors and connoisseurs select for aging. Like fine wines, some teas lend themselves to being carefully stored in a controlled environment and monitored over time. While the leaves may lose some of the more fragile biochemical compounds, they develop flavors and an unmatched sipping experience that dedicated tea lovers enjoy.

CHAPTER 9

Pu'erh—Dark Tea

It could be said that one of the most healthful and fascinating teas is also the most mysterious. Modern pu'erh is still similar to what was once traded on the ancient Tea Horse Road: bold and earthy, sometimes musky but with complex and lingering aftertastes. It is, however, the allure of pu'erh's legendary healing qualities that draws many to their first taste and encourages them to seek out other dark teas.

The Mysterious Tea

Pu'erh tea has inspired a lengthy and fascinating history. It is an art form in sculpture, design, and craftsmanship. The growing and manufacture require a minimum of two years of diligent control over storage temperature, humidity, and all other possible variations in the atmosphere of the storage facility. When brewed, it has a flavor that is so complex that it almost defies simple description. But the mystery is heightened, because details of production are carefully guarded secrets that make aficionados ravenously curious.

In his book, *New Tea Lover's Treasury,* James Norwood Pratt tempted his readers with this statement: "It was already ancient when the troops of Kublai Kahn spread the use of it from Yunnan throughout China. The secret of its manufacture is as closely guarded today as it was under the Ming, when death was the penalty for even trespassing in the mountain gardens where it was produced." And pu'erh experts in Yunnan are quick to remind those who pester them with questions that their plants and their expertise were once stolen, so they will be even more careful with their remaining treasure.

It is both the mystery and anecdotal health reports of pu'erh drinkers feeling noticeably better that draw even more newcomers for a first cautious sip. Like most categories of tea, you may feel that calm alertness when you drink it, and sippers with digestive problems often notice an improvement within a few days. But there is one cure in tea folklore almost exclusive to pu'erh; it helps one recover from a hangover. It is considered the tea tonic for overindulgence in alcohol that also helps calm the stomach.

However, even pu'erh lovers would be quick to caution that appreciation of its flavor is an acquired taste, and those who seek understanding how to buy it are well served by some background education. For someone who has never tasted anything other than tea brewed from a basic big-brand tea bag, or flavored teas that fill your mouth with the essence of raspberries or gingerbread, pu'erh may seem as if it is from an entirely different realm. It is definitely considered in a category all its own.

Dark Teas

The same confusion that exists with describing black tea also becomes an issue with pu'erh so it is becoming increasingly common to see them categorized as "dark teas." Sometimes people categorize pu'erh as a black tea because of the dark color of the dry leaf, and because the brewed tea can become extremely dark brown and opaque. But because the processing of dark teas is so different than black tea—the dark teas actually fermented and the black teas only oxidized—it is more accurate to consider them separately. There are only a few other teas processed with similar methods as dark teas that are not pu'erhs, so it is a rather small tea category. Another point of confusion can be that pu'erh is often thought of as just a compressed tea. But with loose-leaf and now teabag-cut options available, this must be reconsidered. For these reasons, you will see tea sellers with large and diverse menus use dark tea as a separate category that includes pu'erh as one option. In Chinese, this group is also called *heicha*, which literally translates as "dark tea." For purposes of this discussion, brick tea will be included as a dark tea rather than a black tea.

What Is Pu'erh?

The most authentic pu'erh is the fermented tea that originates in the city for which it is named and where it was first made. But it has long been accepted that teas crafted in the same style from nearby mountain gardens in the Yunnan Province can also be called pu'erh. Nestled in the most southwestern tip of China, this region shares borders and a subtropical climate with Vietnam, Laos, and Myanmar (Burma). From some of the tea fields you can look across the imaginary lines dividing the countries as the jungle descends steep slopes. Only a few hundred miles of mountainous terrain in Northern Myanmar separate Yunnan from the Assam tea region in India. But like fine wines vary between microclimates, the tea grown and manufactured in this region thrives on its terroir: the morning mists, the mineral-rich soils, the constant heat, the precious waters, and the ancient family recipes that have been guarded by generations that stretch back farther into history than is recorded.

Pu'erh is made from the same *Camellia sinensis* as all other true teas. But rather than fully developing the flavors solely with oxidation, pu'erh is aged like wine—fermented. It is actually put into controlled conditions so that, as it ages, it will ferment and develop beneficial microbes. Then it is most often compressed into cakes, blocks, or sculptural forms. The sizes and designs vary greatly: from small spheres with just the amount of tea needed to brew a small teapot's worth of tea, to large, solid forms that look like pumpkins, to large flat forms that are displayed like paintings. Pu'erh manufacturers demonstrate amazing skill and creativity with their designs, the most elaborate and unusual of which will seldom be seen outside of China, and even then only in shops specializing in very high-end pu'erh tea.

Pu'erh Recipes—The Secrets

When the word *recipe* is used in the context of pu'erh manufacture, it refers specifically to a codification that was put in place to identify the grade and factory. It tracks the batch of tea and the variables of processing as it ages. But it also refers to the closely guarded steps of a given factory's processing as their secret recipe. Every factory has its own formula that actually begins when the tea is being grown. Tea selection is critical. Tea masters carefully watch the conditions to schedule harvest, and then follow the process step by step. Considering that it will be a minimum of two years before the tea will be sold—even as a young pu'erh—tea masters are keenly aware that many variables must be controlled to maximize the quality of the tea. Pu'erh manufacture requires great skill, attention, and patience.

ALERT

An unpleasant earthiness without the pleasant notes of fruit and honey usually indicates a lower-quality tea. Good pu'erh tea should not be bitter or moldy. Whether or not it is a "good" tea always depends on how satisfying it is to you, and not on the price, the way in which the cake has been sculpted, or the sales pitch.

Flavors of Pu'erh

The aromatic notes of pu'erh instantly suggest an old growth forest or a barn full of fresh hay. There is a musty earthiness, like finding a clear spring inside an old cave. This is the flavor of quality for pu'erh. It can yield a very dark brew, as dark and opaque as coffee, but without any bitterness, usually finishing with a lingering sweetness that does not come from added sugar or other sweetener. Many tea drinkers seek out pu'erh tea with subtle notes of coffee and chocolate. On the sweeter side, there can be hints of peaches and plums or black raisins, molasses, and honey. When coffee drinkers find themselves in a tea shop for the first time, the intense, dark flavors of pu'erh are some of the most appealing to them.

The History of Pu'erh

More than two thousand years ago, the city of Pu'erh in southwestern China was probably the birthplace of tea commerce. It was also one of the points of origin for one of the most active branches of the Tea Horse Road, on which caravans connected with traders on the Silk Road. As interest in tea grew and trade increased, loose leaves were compressed so that more could be carried in baskets strapped on the backs of the horses that navigated the treacherous mountain roads and endured the long journey. The route eventually connected Yunnan Province with the eastern provinces, requiring as much as a year by horseback to deliver goods to the coast.

Warmed by the heat of the horses' bodies, dampened by rain, and compressed as the leaves naturally fermented over time, the transformed tea eventually brewed desirable and highly sought-after results. Tea growers soon realized they could pack even more tea onto the horses if it was compressed before it was loaded. This ultimately inspired standardized molds holding a specific weight of tea that also became a currency. At one point, the exchange of compressed tea threatened the official Chinese currency, and for this reason, there was a time when compressed teas were outlawed and only loose-leaf tea could be legally traded.

Health Benefits of Pu'erh Tea

As the city of origin of commercially traded tea, Pu'erh was also the tea that inspired the first legends of tea's healing properties, making it famous and such an important part of history. Traditional Chinese medicine considers some of the most important benefits of pu'erh to be a reduction of internal heat and dampness, balance between the stomach and the spleen, and a detoxification of the entire body along with improved circulation. Other health folklore includes improved vision, slower aging, and a cure for headaches, hangovers, and gout. The modern list being scrutinized by western medicine looks very similar today.

FACT

One proponent of pu'erh was the mother of Aisin-Gioro Puyi, the last Chinese emperor. She considered it the treatment of choice for her gout. Puyi, the subject of the movie *The Last Emperor,* abdicated in 1912.

While most of the current medical research involving tea uses green tea, the existing studies on pu'erh tea include cancer and the suppression of fatty acid synthase, the benefits in combating obesity, and observations on antimicrobial activities.

One of the most interesting new studies discovered that small amounts of lovastatin, the most beneficial statin for controlling cholesterol, are naturally present in pu'erh tea. A 2013 study published in the *International Journal of Food Microbiology* also discovered that the concentration of lovastatin increased as the pu'erh aged, although certainly not in an amount comparable to the prescription usage. However, the presence of the statin does explain the long-held belief that pu'erh controls harmful cholesterol and is beneficial for heart and circulatory health.

ALERT

A common mistake is to assume that, the darker the tea, the more caffeine. So many people pass up dark teas like pu'erh believing that they are avoiding caffeine. The fermentation process actually reduces caffeine the longer it is allowed to age.

Pu'erh has also been found to have probiotic properties and digestive enzymes that help with the reduction of gas, bloating, and heartburn.

Where Pu'erh Grows

Like fine wine regions, true pu'erh grows in specific geographic areas of Yunnan Province along the Lancang River. Straddling the Tropic of Capricorn, with a humid, subtropical climate and heavy monsoon season, this area is not only conducive to tea but also known as a source for many other medicinal plants.

Four of the best-known areas for pu'erh production are Pu'erh (Siamo), Baoshan, Lincang, and Xishuangbanna. The region around Pu'erh City is revered as the origin of this great tea, and known for having a large number of the ancient wild tea trees; tea from this region is usually very popular in the marketplace. The Xishuangbanna region is famous for its legendary "six famous tea mountains," and teas from there are also prized. Other tea mountains in Yunnan Province are also known for their pu'erh, and the specific location where the tea was grown and which factory processed and stored it are important factors to serious collectors who buy pu'erh with an eye to its future value.

ESSENTIAL

Yunnan Province is the most botanically and culturally diverse province in all of China. There are more than 17,000 plant species, half of the birds and mammal species in China, including some of the rarest and most endangered, as well as twenty-five of the fifty-eight ethnic minorities in China. Many of the ethnic minorities have their own unique tea traditions and tea legends.

How Pu'erh Is Made

There are two basic methods of creating pu'erh: Sheng Cha (raw) and Shou Cha (ripe). Another differentiation between these two is that they are referred to as green and black pu'erh. One is based on a gradual fermentation formula and the other an accelerated process. However, both begin with the careful selection of fresh tea leaves by the tea master of the garden or estate, and then an extended withering in the sun until the tea reaches a stage called Mao Cha. From this point on, the tea master will supervise and protect variations in the recipes.

Raw Pu'erh, Green Pu'erh, Sheng Cha

In Sheng Cha production, fermented with a more traditional method, the Mao Cha (sun-withered tea) is pan-fried to halt the minimal oxidation in the leaves. This "kills green," and keeps the leaves from further oxidation at this stage. The Mao Cha is then rolled and bruised, further opening the surface cell walls of the tea leaves, before storing the tea in shallow baskets to further dry in the sun. When the leaves reach the desired dryness, they are sent to the factory. They may be kept as loose leaves during the actual fermentation process, or pressed into molds and shaped into their final presentation. Then they are stored for controlled fermentation. Pu'erh tea was traditionally stored in caves or stone warehouses that were considered favorable to developing the healthful bacteria. It takes approximately two years to age until the characteristic flavors and colors begin to develop. The longer it ages, unless there is a flaw or accident, the more valuable it becomes.

Ripe Pu'erh, Cooked Pu'erh, Shou Cha

Shou Cha is produced with an accelerated method. The uncompressed, loose Mao Cha is piled in a cave or factory storage room in stacks deep enough to generate heat but manageable enough to turn so that it ferments evenly. Leaving the tea leaves loose and exposed to air and moisture speeds up the growth of the healthful bacteria. The temperature and humidity are controlled during fermentation, and the piles are frequently moistened with a fine mist when they are turned. The generated heat "cooks" or ripens the leaves more rapidly than it does without being piled together. When the factory's tea master determines that the optimal fermentation has been reached, it will be pressed into molds. The aging and fermentation continues for several more months before it might be sold, or the molds may be moved into storage where the aging may continue for many years.

Buying Pu'erh Teas

Pu'erh comes in many shapes, sizes, and qualities. The compressed cakes shaped like round discs, called *bingcha*, are the most common. However, many more options, including unmolded, loose leaves, are now available as both the green Sheng Cha and in the ripe Shou Cha. Prices can vary greatly with the quality of the original leaves and with the amount of time it has been aged. Collectors and speculators usually invest in teas that they believe will increase in value and then store them under controlled conditions for ten or more years. A single disc of well-aged pu'erh, perhaps as much as fifty years old, can sell for thousands of dollars to connoisseurs.

ALERT

There is a great potential for fraud with pu'erh tea. For someone who has not developed the palate to discern defects, it can be difficult to evaluate quality. It is always better to deal with reputable retailers. Most tea shops will sample teas, explain the value of the particular tea choices, recommend some that might be particularly appealing to you, and suggest ways to brew so that you will enjoy your experience.

Compressed Pu'erh Forms

Some of the more commonly available shapes are:

- Mini Toucha are small spheres (shaped like toucha, see following) weighing 3–5 grams that will brew a single small pot or mug.
- Toucha are shaped like a ball with one side flattened and a small indentation. The weight is usually between 200–500 grams.
- Bingcha are flattened cakes or discs with a slightly rounded top and flat bottom, weighing between 200–500 grams.
- Zhuancha are pressed in the traditional rectangular shape as they had been on the ancient Tea Horse Road. They may be much larger than bingcha or toucha.
- Jingua is shaped like a melon, a form originally created as a tribute tea for the emperor.

Pu'erh Packaging

Manufacturers of compressed tea take great pride in the design of their printed tissue paper wrappers and the way finished tea cakes are presented. A high-quality pure fiber tissue that will not add contaminating flavors to the tea is printed with the name of the factory and its location plus a colorful logo. Small slips of white paper actually embedded into the surface of the cake give even more information (in Chinese) about the processing. Part of that information is a numbering system created by Yunnan producers to help identify the tea quality. It designates the factory, the grade of leaves used, the origin of the recipe, and the batch.

The wrappers have become collectible items, and in order for a pu'erh cake to be authenticated, it must have these identifiers. A cake without the original wrapper is worth much less. Wrappers are sometimes saved after the tea is gone, with cupping notes about the vintage. Rare tea wrappers are even framed and displayed as pieces of art.

Loose-Leaf Pu'erh

As interest in this tea grows, so do the available choices. Having it available as a loose-leaf tea makes it easier to buy a specific quantity. The loose tea is more likely to be cut by manufacturers to fill tea bags, and can also be blended and flavored, which may be more appealing to a broader audience.

Brewing Pu'erh and Dark Teas

With so many different options of this tea, there are also many ways to brew it. In general, a good-quality pu'erh can be steeped at high temperatures (boiling water) for a long time without becoming bitter, and will almost always yield multiple satisfying infusions. It can be prepared in a western-style teapot as well as the smaller gongfu-style teapot or gaiwan. Because it is less likely to become bitter with extended steeping, it is a good tea to brew in one of the double-walled thermos bottles. If you enjoy "playing" with your tea, experimenting with time and temperatures, pu'erh offers comfortable latitude. Its characteristic intensity can be tamed by heating the water to a simmer instead of a full boil and keeping the water on the leaves for only 1–2 minutes per infusion. The liquor color and flavor will be lighter, and you can brew additional infusions after the first steep, as with oolongs.

Brewing Loose-Leaf Pu'erh

Consider the pu'erh loose-leaf options similar to brewing black tea. Make sure that you brew in a vessel that has room for the expansion of the hydrated leaves. It is recommended that all leaf surfaces come in contact with water.

Brewing Compressed Pu'erh

There are two tricks to brewing compressed pu'erh. The first trick is that you shouldn't just flake off the surface leaves without breaking into the interior of the cake, because the layers have different flavors that should be blended for optimal flavor. The second trick is how you break open the cake. One reason a bingcha disc is popular is that it is easier to break apart by hand. On the other hand, the tightly compressed rounded cakes have greater density, aging the interior more slowly, and producing what some feel is a deeper, better flavor.

Breaking the Cake

One of the most important tools with compressed pu'erh is a tray or shallow bowl, ideally one that is used only for tea and not contaminated with other fragrances or oils. A popular choice is a small bamboo tray with shallow sides. It should be slightly larger than your cake. The bowl or tray may also be used to show the quality of tea to your guests in a more formal style, like the gongfu cha Chinese tea ceremony.

Most cakes are easy to break apart with a pu'erh knife, something like a flat-bladed letter opener, where the tip is used like a wedge to flake the tea leaves apart. These are often made of bamboo, sometimes decorated with colored thread wrapped around the handle. A third useful tool is a brush used to sweep the bits of tea from the tray into your pot, and then anything extra back into the tissue wrapper or canister.

For thicker cakes, it might be necessary to make the first break with a hammer. Loosely wrap the tea in a clean, unscented towel or simple muslin cloth so that the broken pieces are contained. Only break the amount you will use for a single use, and leave the rest of the cake intact.

A less aggressive technique (but a more questionable practice) is to lightly steam the dense cake, softening it and heating it enough to allow you to fragment it by hand or with your flat-bladed knife. Tea should never be stored in a jar or canister if there could be additional moisture trapped in the leaves.

Popular and Legendary Pu'erh Teas

Yunnan pu'erhs are sometimes distinguished by the age of the trees. Tea retailers may offer products from antique trees more than a hundred years old, or from old trees that are between fifty and one hundred years old.

There are also differences in flavor between the wild trees and cultivated trees, even if they have been allowed to grow to full height. New trees are usually pruned for more efficient kinds of harvest. Additionally, teas are chosen because of the prominence of and respect for the factory. Menghai Tea Factory and Xiaguan Tea Factory are two of the oldest and most respected factories making pu'erh. Both were founded in the 1940s, have maintained their standards of production for more than sixty years, and have many renowned "recipes" of highly valued, collectible teas.

Brick Tea or Tibetan Tea

One rather rare form of black tea that is not commonly found for sale in the west has an interesting historic background. It is usually called Tibetan Tea or Brick Tea. Its history and importance as a health beverage begs to have it included here with the dark teas. From a health and nutrition aspect, brick tea provides important vitamins and minerals where it is difficult to grow fresh vegetables. For remote, nomadic tribes, the convenience of tea in this form made it an important staple in their diet.

During the Tang Dynasty (C.E. 618–907), long before the more recognized production of black tea in Fujian Province, this tea was traded to bordering countries of Tibet and Mongolia. Trade for tea became so significant that at one point, thousands of Tibetan war horses were exchanged every year for huge quantities of tea from Yunnan Province in southern China.

Tibetan-style brick tea is traditionally made with lower-quality leaves than other teas, using more of the plant than just the two leaves and single bud. It is still a staple of nomadic Tibetan people. When the tea has dried completely, usually fully oxidized as a dark black, it is ground into a fine powder, blended with a binding material such as flour, and then compressed into dense bricks using molds. Some of these are artistically carved to produce beautiful results. Standardization of the size and weight of tea bricks also allowed it to be used as an ancient currency.

Brick tea is usually prepared by breaking off a chunk of the tea, sometimes toasting it first to soften it before grinding it back into a powder. The powder is then boiled in milk (usually yak milk) for several hours. Grains and sugars can also be added to the pot to make it thicker and heartier. It was sometimes considered a food rather than a beverage.

ESSENTIAL

Unusual Compressed Forms

The creative ingenuity of presentations for pu'erh tea cannot be exaggerated. Even though this tea has not become as popular outside of Asia and retailers do not yet market the more exotic presentations, this is changing with the advent of Internet sales. As international online shopping becomes more convenient and affordable, the rest of the world may be able to appreciate the diversity in pu'erhs. These tea sculptures can be as beautiful as fine art and larger than a single person could comfortable carry.

Pu'erh Orange

Rarely seen for sale, but sometimes displayed by people who have traveled to China and visited some of the large tea markets and festivals, are unusual forms of compressed dark tea. One of these is a scented, compressed pu'erh where the tea has been tightly packed into the hollowed-out skin of an orange or tangerine. Wires are wrapped around the outside of the orange to further compress the tea and to mold it into a melon shape. These are usually aged between two and twelve years, during which the tea is infused with the essence contained within the fruit peel.

Bamboo Pu'erh

Another filled-form pu'erh is a bamboo pu'erh. Sections of fresh bamboo are packed full of the fermented leaves. Like the orange peel, fresh bamboo scents the tea while it ages longer and naturally compresses, shrinking into a cylindrical shape. This is another style rarely seen outside of Yunnan

Province. But as the interest in this mysterious tea grows, collectors wanting to expand their collections may build a market for these variations.

Pu'erh Teapot

More artistic and entertaining than regular compressed forms, an actual teapot made of pu'erh with a capacity of about four cups of water can actually serve tea. This shape is not of the highest-quality tea, to be sure, but forms like this are interesting display pieces, sure to spark lively conversation. These are usually purchased as display items and not actually used to brew tea.

CHAPTER 10

White Tea

There is innocence to white tea. It is the most natural and least processed, subject to the least interference by humankind. Between the plant and the cup, the essential processing is the picking of the fresh leaf. After that, there is only drying and packaging. For the majority of tea drinkers, it is the most direct relationship they have with a fresh *Camellia sinensis* plant. And appreciation for it is growing.

What Is White Tea?

Legends of young, virgin women wearing white gloves as they plucked single fuzzy buds at dawn before the dew had time to dry, populate the stories of white tea. And similar legends of virgins, fairy tea pickers, and gentle spirits bestowing tea gifts entertain white tea lovers and promote tea sales. The ancient tales recently inspired a contemporary marketing program, and in the spring of 2011 a grower in Henan Province of central China decided to update the popular lore. He advertised jobs for "inexperienced" young women to pick a very special tea. What grabbed the headlines was that the young women would pluck white tea buds with their lips, never touching it with their hands. As was certainly the grower's intention, the media far beyond China picked up the tale of the "lip-plucked" white tea.

The true nature of white tea is that it is grown from the specific varietal, Bai Hao, or one of a select few hybrids. The characteristic flavor is creamy and sweet with hints of nuttiness in a pale yellow liquor. The buds from white tea varietals are exceptionally long and thick, and are covered with soft, downy fuzz when they first emerge; the same covering remains on the underside of the top two open leaves. To capture this fragile essence, they are picked very early in the morning while the light green buds are still tightly closed and the fuzzy covering is still fresh. From this point on, there is very little handling of the tea. It is spread out to dry in the sun for as long as possible and then stored indoors on bamboo trays so that air can flow through for slow drying. Oxidation is not stopped as it is in green tea, but it is not controlled as it is with oolong and black tea. The leaves oxidize and turn colors naturally. As much as possible, growers treat the leaves as if they fell naturally from the plant and dried on their own. In this way, there is great variation in dry leaf color from the white buds, from bits of gray-green to darker reddish-brown.

Brewing White Tea

White teas are now available in bagged and flavored options as well as bottled in ready-to-drink products. Bagged tea is likely to have brewing recommendations on the box, and those will be similar to brewing green tea, using lower-than-boiling water temperatures (185–195°F). As there is a high percentage of bud, some of the flavor is not released as quickly, and because the flavor is so light, it may be preferable to use more tea and steep longer. Most white teas lack the astringency of green tea, so they are actually more tolerant of near-boiling water temperature. Higher temperatures and longer steeping can bring out more of the flavors.

ESSENTIAL

A properly brewed cup of white tea may, on first experience, be surprisingly light and provoke the question, "What's the point?" For anyone expecting a hearty cup and robust flavor, white tea might be unsettling. Appreciation of this tea requires the various senses to explore its much gentler flavor profile.

Is White Tea a Healthier Tea?

The problem with making a broad statement that any one kind of tea is healthier than another is that many variables can ultimately affect what is in the cup. However, in general, keeping the white tea leaf intact, without disturbing it by rolling, shaping, or the application of heat, helps preserve the antioxidants. Beneficial compounds in the leaf remain uncompromised and make it a slightly healthier brewed tea. Studies of the fresh leaf do show that the varietals used to make white teas tend to be naturally lower in caffeine, which is preferred by some tea drinkers. As for the caffeine, however, the actual amount of caffeine in a brewed cup may be equal to, or even higher than, other teas due to the larger percentage of bud.

Healthier Brewing Temperature

Since one of the few health cautions about habitually drinking exceptionally hot beverages, including tea, is that there is a higher incidence of esophageal cancer, drinking teas that brew at lower temperatures is healthier and safer. White tea can be a gentle reminder that lower brewing temps are better for the tea and for you. Many people notice that they taste more nuance of the tea after it cools slightly. Since the flavors of white tea are already so subtle, sipping at the temperature where your taste buds don't cringe away from the heat enables exploration of many more layers of taste as the buds gradually open.

ESSENTIAL

Emperor Huizong (c.e. 1100–1126) wrote that one of his favorite teas was a white tea. This has been misunderstood and assumed that white tea, the varietal and the method of production, must have originated in that era. A more correct translation of the statement in his book, *Treatise on Tea*, is that his favorite tea was a very soft green, and when it was ground and whisked and frothed, it became the color of creamy, white jade. The reference to the color of the liquor, rather than the color of the leaf, has caused confusion.

The History of White Tea

The actual origin of white tea came about half a century after the reign of the famous "Tea Emperor" Huizong, who in tea-loving circles is known as the emperor who sacrificed his power because of his love of tea. But even the more currently accepted accounts of white tea's history have an element of magic. Like many tea origins, tales of the first white tea plant are associated with spiritual gifts as well as an almost magical healing quality.

Legendary White Tea

It is said that a single tea bush from a new varietal was found growing in a cave on Taimu Mountain in Fujian Province in the 1200s. A mythical being, Tai Mu Niang Niang, told the people of that region that a tea brewed from the plant would cure a disease in children that was causing high fever. Some people associate Tai Mu Niang Niang with the bodhisattva Guan Yin, the goddess of mercy and compassion.

Interestingly enough, there is a similarity in this legend with that of the oolong tea, Tie Guan Yin; a single tea plant is a gift for the benefit of a great many people. Other interpretations of the story consider Tai Mu Niang Niang a mortal, but a respected healer or a devoted mother who discovered a treatment for the children of the community. In fact, Niang Niang translates

154

to "mother." In this case, the varietal for white tea was first used for healing fever and skin rash in children.

Historic White Tea

Commercial production of white tea is likely to have originated in the late 1700s in the Fuding area of Fujian Province. Developed as a process that would be less labor intensive, the local tea master who created the technique dispensed with various production steps. Considering the complexity of other methods of tea manufacture, it is easy to understand why growers would appreciate this innovation. But this creates an interesting contradiction in that a tea process developed as a shortcut has become treasured as something rare and fragile, and now is found to provide even more of the plant's natural healing qualities.

This northern region of Fujian Province was also one of the areas required to provide tribute tea to the emperor. The demand for their other extraordinary green tea was so great that the system of tribute being paid to the emperor (a precursor of tea taxation) created hardships for farmers. Even though they were honored by the recognition, the necessity of producing large quantities of their fine tea impacted how their fields were used, and reduced the time and labor available to produce other tea and crops for income. It is possible that this demand may have incentivized the search for a less labor-intensive white tea method of production.

Where White Tea Grows

Sharing the Bai Hao varietals has made it possible for white tea to be produced around the world. Hybridization for other climates has evolved unique nuances in the tea from each new environment. But this also means that a package label stating only that it is a white tea does not always mean that the contents are from the original, historic province in China. It may now come from many different tea-producing countries. In addition to Fujian Province, white tea is also produced in Zhejiang Province, China. Other countries developing their own white teas include Taiwan, India, Sri Lanka, Japan, Vietnam, Northern Thailand, Nepal, Kenya, South Korea, and Hawaii in the United States.

ESSENTIAL

While there is no single tea council that assesses the quality of world-wide production, there are international tea competitions where respected tea professionals compare the dry leaf, wet leaf, liquor, and aroma in side-by-side blind tastings, and publish the findings. Consumers can use the results as a benchmark for developing their own palates for fine tea. In North America, one such event is the North American Tea Championship: *www.teachampionship.com*.

Some factories are adhering to the established methods for white tea production, and the results certainly provide a similar look to the leaf and taste in the liquor. Other growers are experimenting with efficient methods of harvesting and drying their product. Some of these new techniques are making the tea more affordable, allowing for a wide range in quality. There are still artisan growers who manufacture product for the gourmet tea lover, but also growers who effectively provide a grade of white tea that can be used in cosmetics.

Extracts from white tea have been found to be particularly effective in boosting immune function of skin cells and protecting the skin from oxidative stress, an important element in preventing skin cancer. White tea extracts are now being added to some moisturizing creams, cleansers, and cosmetics.

How White Tea Is Processed

The essential difference between white tea and all others is that its production is *not* complicated. It is not heated to control the enzymatic processes, rolled, shaped, fluffed, roasted, or subjected to any of the manipulations that generate flavor and leaf presentation of other teas. Eliminating most of the steps from fresh tea to dry tea, the factory's tea master focuses on the picking and the drying.

Picking White Tea

Picking is best done on a sunny day so that the tea can, as much as possible, dry naturally. For bud-only harvest to make Bai Hao Yin Zhen

(Silver Needle), pickers work in the early morning hours to collect the large, unopened buds while they are still tightly wrapped and the downy, white fuzz is fresh and shiny. The season is limited to just a few weeks, usually beginning the last week of March or the first week of April. Other white teas, like Bai Mu Dan (White Peony), have a slightly longer season, and pickers collect not only the bud but also the first two leaves and the tender stem to which they are attached. When selecting only the buds, the plucking must be done by hand. When selecting the top one to two inches of stem with the leaves and bud, pickers can use some of the newly developed machines, like small hedge clippers that snip with sharp blades but then catch the tea in an attached bag.

FACT

The word *pekoe* is one factor in tea grading and quality. It refers to the amount of bud and leaf still having the white down. When Thomas Lipton began labeling his tea as "Orange Pekoe" there was some confusion that his teas had been flavored with orange oils rather than the actual fact that this referred to quality.

Finishing White Tea

After harvest and a short withering, the leaves are allowed to rest undisturbed in piles in the direct sun for several hours. During this time, moisture from within the leaves and buds is drawn to the surface. Complete sun drying is sometimes preferred but, because it takes two days of controlled drying, much of the process is now more efficiently completed inside. It is spread thinly on bamboo trays and then layered in the drying racks with 10–12 inches of air space between them for the remainder of this drying phase. Temperature and humidity are closely monitored, and fans are positioned around the drying room to keep the air moving. The tea in this interior drying room is handled very little, if at all. The leaves oxidize slightly as the moisture evaporates, turning the leaves different shades of red and brown. One final phase in modern production is an optional mechanical drying phase, which uses heat in the final phase to drive the remaining moisture from the leaf, preparing it for packing and shipping.

White Tea and Caffeine

Caffeine comparisons between the categories are difficult because of the many variables: the way the plant grows, when it was picked, how it was processed, the age of the dry tea, how the leaf was cut, and how the tea was brewed. Using white tea as an example may help people understand some of the differences, beginning with the fact that all *Camellia sinensis* plants contain caffeine. The amount varies in each different varietal, and it is generally true that the varietals used to make white tea have less caffeine in the fresh, new leaves than many others. For this reason, it is often said that white tea is lower in caffeine than other teas. Consumers may be led to think that there is also less caffeine in their teacup than with green, black, or oolong tea. But, there are at least three ways in which white tea can sometimes brew an even higher amount of caffeine.

- Most significantly, the buds store the highest amount of caffeine in the plant, and teas with more of these buds deliver more caffeine to the brewed cup.
- Manipulation of the leaf, oxidation to make black tea, and fermentation to make pu'erh tea can lower the amount of caffeine in the finished tea. Less manipulation of the leaf with white tea production does not reduce the caffeine content during manufacture as much as it does with other teas.
- The white tea in a home tea cupboard may be served fresher, and therefore the resulting brew many be slightly higher in caffeine. Because white teas are slightly rarer and more expensive, consumers tend to buy smaller quantities at a time, store it more carefully, and not keep it as long. Therefore, it is less likely to be one that loses some of its effectiveness while it sits on the shelf.

ESSENTIAL

Anyone sensitive to caffeine should not categorically trust a general statement that a cup of white tea contains less of it. In fact, a cup of bud-only Bai Hao Yin Zhen (Silver Needle) that was harvested in April and then sold to the consumer in June, then brewed for a longer time to infuse a stronger liquor, could contain more caffeine than a green tea of the same season steeped in cooler water for a shorter and lighter infusion.

On the other hand, because it is more often brewed with lower-temperature water for shorter periods of time, less caffeine is drawn from the leaf with each infusion. In short, even starting with more caffeine in the bud, a tea drinker can control the amount of caffeine in the cup by timing the infusion.

Health Benefits of White Tea

There is a generally accepted belief that less processing or oxidation will retain higher amounts of polyphenol antioxidants. This includes the catechins that are proving to be tea's most active compound for the promotion of good health. Some studies are showing that white tea may have a higher concentration of EGCG than green tea and other tea categories, and that it produces measurably different effects in fighting cancer and helping with weight loss. Research on all kinds of tea is still in the relatively early stages, but the scientific community is releasing more data every year. In the next decade, there may be more definitive comparisons between teas and their particular benefits.

Traditional Chinese Medicine (TCM)

TCM is based on a body of knowledge dating back more than 2,000 years but is still widely practiced today. It incorporates various forms of herbal treatments, diet, exercise, massage, and acupuncture to harmonize the function of the whole individual. Teas are often recommended for specific conditions and overall health maintenance. White tea is one of the treatments recommended by TCM practitioners to reduce inflammation of rheumatoid arthritis, to control insulin secretion, to prevent dry eyes and night blindness, and as a source of vitamin A.

Scientific Studies

Research on white tea, like many of the other teas, has focused on the polyphenol (antioxidant) potential to reduce the development of cancerous cells, oxidative stress, and immune system damage that slows the evidence of aging and improves cardiovascular function. White tea has shown a slightly greater potential than some of the other teas as an antimicrobial to fight infection, and supports good oral hygiene and skin care.

Some of the more interesting studies specifically using white tea include:

- A 2004 study at Pace University (New York) demonstrated that extracts from white tea slowed the growth of both viruses and bacteria, reducing growth of staphylococcus, fungus, dental plaque, and pneumonia.
- White tea was used in a 2012 study conducted at the University of Murcia in Spain that demonstrated its ability in high doses to reverse the oxidative damage done by Adriamycin (doxorubicin), an anticancer agent.
- In 2009, researchers at Kingston University (London, England) measured the high anti-inflammatory, antioxidant, anticollagenase, and anti-elastase properties of white tea, which suggests a potential for reduced risk of developing rheumatoid arthritis, some cancer, and some heart disease with white tea consumption.
- A study by the Linus Pauling Institute (Portland, Oregon) showed that both green and white teas, when used together with prescription medications for prevention of colon cancer, made a slight improvement in the efficacy of those medications.
- A study published in a 2009 issue of *Experimental Dermatology* investigated the topical application of both white and green tea extracts. Both teas showed some benefits in protecting the skin, but to the same degree.

Popular and Legendary White Teas

In contrast to the other tea categories, there are very few unique and unblended white teas sold in specialty tea shops. It is also interesting, due to more affordable methods of production, to find white tea extracts now being added to bottled, ready-to-drink teas and beauty products.

Bai Hao Yin Shen (Silver Needle)

Silver Needle is considered the highest-quality white tea. As the "needle" of the name suggests, it is entirely buds without any stem or leaf, covered in the fine hair that makes it look silvery-white. This varietal was first developed by farms on Tianmushan (Tianmu Mountain) in the Fuding area of Fujian Province in 1857. Crafted from a varietal with the advantage of larger, thicker buds, it also produces a stronger flavor. When brewed, the soft hair is freed from the bud and floats on the surface of the tea. The liquor is a pale yellow with a delicate, creamy flavor. Long buds are considered better quality, while shorter or yellowish color buds are slightly less desirable and usually less expensive.

Bai Mu Dan (White Peony)

Originally from Shuiji in Fujian Province and first developed in the 1870s, the Bai Mu Dan varietal has a larger leaf. Still covered with fuzz, the buds are plucked along with a bit of tender stem and very tender top two leaves just below the bud. These leaves also have their undersides covered with fuzz. An indicator of quality is the unbroken leaf, still attached to the stem and picked fresh enough to have been covered with hair. The dry leaf of White Peony will show variation in color from the white hair to green, red, and brown. These color differences are due to the degree of water content of the leaf, stem, or bud when picked and the way this moisture was gradually released as the leaf dried naturally. The brewed liquor should be yellow with a slightly nutty flavor.

Shou Mei

An additional but lower grade of white tea is manufactured by processing a later harvest of the Bai Mu Dan varietal that has larger, darker leaves and a lower percentage of bud. This tends to produce darker liquor and a stronger flavor. This tea is frequently picked and produced with more mechanized techniques and processed in bulk, making it more affordable.

Jade Lily

The long buds of white tea varietals allow for an additional creative step in the processing to further intrigue tea lovers. Jade Lily is one of these artistic expressions of tea. While still supple after being softened during the first withering, each bud is individually tied into a knot by hand and then allowed to dry. The liquor is very pale with a sweet, pear-like flavor. Because of the fine handcrafting, this is a rather rare tea and not commonly available. But it is an example of the artisan nature of tea and the creative skill that is still important to tea lovers.

White Darjeeling

In the 1990s, growers in the Darjeeling area of India on the slopes of the Himalayas began experimenting with white tea, and have recently begun offering a product that is sometimes referred to as a White Darjeeling. With a much different flavor from Chinese-grown white teas of Fujian, they typically brew a stronger, slightly darker cup.

White Pu'erh

Combining the techniques of white tea and pu'erh tea production in Yunnan Province, long buds are selected and fashioned into the compressed forms traditional to pu'erh tea, like a bingcha disc. The brewed liquor has the subtle characteristics of white tea, light color and subtle flavors, rather than the characteristics of pu'erh.

CHAPTER 11

Functional Teas—Herbal Blends

The renaissance of interest in real tea, *Camellia sinensis* in its classic forms and flavors, has also prompted discussions about the difference between this and herbal tea. Finding creative ways to draw the distinctions between products that contain only herbs, only tea, or a blend of the two has been both a challenge and an opportunity for tea merchants. One of the newest terms to surface is *functional tea*.

What Are Functional Teas?

The origins of boiled tonics and teas thousands of years ago were primarily for their healthful benefits: their *functions* as they support the body. Concoctions were brewed for medicinal reasons rather than for flavors. Today there are creative marketers packaging and promoting beverages that are solution-driven to consumers who are looking for ways to have more energy or better digestion or some other functionality. Tea companies seem to be taking the advice of Hippocrates: *Let food be your medicine and medicine be your food.*

Functional teas are those that are blended and promoted for possible health benefits rather than their flavor. Unlike "real" tea, where the flavor is the most significant part of the drink experience, functional teas are purposeful combinations of botanicals based on the healing folklore of traditional herbs and marketed for the health-related needs of the consumer. Having a pleasant flavor is usually a byproduct, but is not the driving message.

More traditionally referred to as *herbal teas*, functional tea blends are often marketed with names that suggest their potential usefulness. Tea shelves in food markets are starting to look a little like a pharmacy, and a kitchen tea cupboard at home might take on the appearance of a bathroom medicine cabinet. Tea consumers can brew a cup to improve sleep, to calm an upset stomach, to soothe a sore throat, to clear sinus congestion, to quell a headache, to calm an anxious moment, to take the edge off of PMS symptoms, or to support issues with pregnancy and lactation.

Everything Old Becomes New Again

If you believe this trend is something new, then you are failing to appreciate the wealth and abundance of ancient medical history, one of the most precious legacies of our ancestors. From oral traditions practiced by tribal shamans to formulas recorded on papyrus scrolls, through thousands of years of humans caring for the ills of other humans, plants have been prepared as healing teas. Some of these herbal treatments eventually became the active ingredients in pharmaceutical medications.

ESSENTIAL

Pharmacologists continue to study ancient medical texts, comparing the herbs and treatments with contemporary products and methods. One group of researchers at the School of Pharmacology at Shanghai Jiao Tong University concluded that: "Combination formulas may hold the potential to become the therapeutics of choice in the future due to the synergistic effect and dynamic adjustment achieved by the multiple ingredients that will restore the balance of an imbalanced or diseased human body."

Ancient Chinese Functional Teas

Emperor Shen Nong is not only credited with accidentally brewing the first cup of tea in 2737 B.C.E. and realizing its invigorating properties, but also cataloging as many as 365 medical treatments derived from plants, minerals, and parts of animals. His discoveries were collected posthumously in the *Shennong Bencao Jing* (Emperor Shen Nong's book, *The Divine Farmer's Herb-Root Classic*). His original contribution has grown within the current practice of traditional Chinese medicine to more than 12,000 plants combined in almost 100,000 treatments. One way in which these formulas are delivered today are as *teapills*. Teas are brewed and the liquor concentrated until they are reduced to powder, which is then rolled into small pills.

The Art of Tea

There is, of course, an important function to the art of beautiful tea.

It is the function of art to renew our perception. What we are familiar with we cease to see. The writer shakes up the familiar scene, and, as if by magic, we see a new meaning in it. —Anais Nin

Like all fine art, tea serves that function on the palate by enlivening the senses. The attention and skill necessary to perfect the rolling of a fresh leaf into a perfect pearl-sized ball and then scenting it so that the flavor of a fresh jasmine flower feels alive on the tongue is no less rigorous than the art of music, painting, sculpture, or poetry. Tea has been revered in the arts for thousands of years, from the ancient poets to contemporary ceramists, musicians, and filmmakers.

ESSENTIAL

Much of the appreciation for fine teas is derived from the artistic way in which the presentation of the leaves is crafted. The technique by which the leaves are rolled and oxidized does alter the chemical composition of the leaf and accounts for slightly different health benefits, but the labor and skill involved in crafting tea adds another opportunity for pleasure.

Form versus Function

Identifying specialty tea production as an art invites comparison with other creative forms. You can appreciate fine art for its intrinsic loveliness, having no other purpose than to explore its meaning and beauty. On the other hand, many functional items also exhibit great beauty. A chair, a table, a kitchen water faucet, a garden fountain, a car, a house; the design complements the item's purpose. It is the same with fine teas. The more tea is studied in populations where it is widely used, and in laboratories where extracts are studied in carefully controlled settings, the more you find that the beauty of tea is also functional; in short, the experience of tea is a beautiful blend of the two.

Tea and Herb Blends

Blending tea with herbs can be for both flavor and function, even for fun. One of the most famous blends of tea and herbs is the flavored tea Constant Comment, created by Ruth Campbell Bigelow in 1945. Inspired by an historic colonial recipe, she blended bits of dried orange peel with cinnamon and other sweet spices, creating a popular tea formula that is still on tea shelves almost seventy years later. Thousands of blends now add flower petals and bits of dried fruit and spices, creatively expanding the opportunities to find a perfect personal favorite. Many tea shop blenders have created their own signature blends using techniques of combining flavors with black or green tea as a base. This provides the best of both worlds, the stimulating and flavorful experience of tea along with the diversity of herbals.

Non-Tea Herbal Blends

It is traditional for teas not containing *Camellia sinensis* to be called herbal teas, usually inferring that there is no caffeine. Some of the most common herbs, flowers, and dried fruits are mint, cinnamon bark, clove, chamomile, jasmine, hibiscus, chrysanthemum, orange and lemon peel, cranberry, blueberry, ginger, lemon grass, ginseng, and licorice. Many of these ingredients are naturally sweet and are excellent options for children or anyone sensitive to caffeine that want a tasty beverage. These herbals tend to be very flavorful as well as useful for various health issues. They may soothe a scratchy throat or an upset stomach while being enjoyed for their taste.

ESSENTIAL

Herbal tea blending can be a fun activity with a group of children. Visit a health food store to choose an array of herbs and spices. With each flavor in a separate bowl, allow the children to scoop their choices into an infuser mug or small teapot. With an adult supervising the hot water and the infusion time, prepare and then enjoy the teas.

When blends are created especially for children, they are most often caffeine-free herbal blends. Using sweet spices, sometimes including whole flowers like rosebuds, and bits of fruit like dried blueberries, the results can be a colorful dry blend and delicious brew that needs no additional sweetener to tame a craving for dessert. Colorful packaging and cute themes designed to attract the interest of young tea drinkers make it even easier to substitute an herbal blend for a canned soda. The *function* of brewing tea with children is not only sharing a healthful beverage, but also the pleasure of teatime.

Health Risks with Herbs

Simply being herbal does not make an herbal tea without some risk. The same precautions should be taken as with all agricultural products, buying good quality from a reputable retailer or selecting packaged herbal blends from a trusted company. Hundreds of books and resources are available to address potential side effects and to suggest preparations for useful blends.

One of the issues with using botanicals as functional teas is a potential conflict with prescription medication. It is always important to consult with a physician or pharmacist to determine if there are any known issues. Experienced herbalists may also be able to advise on the contraindications for some of the more powerful botanicals, including tea.

Spa Teas

Functional teas are sometimes called *spa teas*, usually focusing on their relaxing, toning, and detoxifying properties. These blends focus in particular on their beneficial properties and not on the flavor of the brewed tea. In some cases, the herbs are not flavorful and can also produce strong physical reactions. Detoxification programs (nonmedical) usually suggest cleansing the digestive tract, lungs, and blood by removing heavy metals from the body. A few of the common herbs brewed as teas are alfalfa leaf, anise seed, barley, cilantro, dandelion root, eucalyptus, fennel seed, fenugreek, ginger, milk thistle, peppermint, stinging nettle, and turmeric. Preparation of every herb differs. In some cases the leaves are used, while in others a tea is brewed by boiling only the root. The part of each plant that can be used and how it should be prepared varies. Informed use of herbs is important. Testing for possible allergic reactions before beginning any herbal health regime is vital.

Tea Spas

The combination of drinking tea at spas combined with physical spa treatments is gaining popularity. Some of the new businesses are designed as relaxing and meditative tearooms that also offer modalities like massage, reflexology, acupuncture, and meditation classes. The reverse is also true, that spas are adding a room to simply enjoy a tea experience as part of a day of luxury and rejuvenation. Some spas are now private labeling their own tea blends.

Bath Teas

Bath teas are botanical blends for external use. Available in prepackaged extra-large tea bags, the herbs are to be added to a hot bath. By crushing and cutting the products, they infuse more quickly in bath water. Bath teas are often recommended for relaxation or to treat some skin problems. An additional benefit can be the aromatherapy from the infusion of the herbs in the hot bath water. Blenders often add a flower or leaf for the beauty and relaxation of the fragrance alone. Green and white teas are also popular ingredients for bath tea and for skin care products.

For a do-it-yourself project, you can use disposable (empty) tea bags or a reusable bag made of gauze or loose-weave muslin, filled with one of the following combinations:

- To help soothe a skin rash, blend white tea with pulverized oats, mallow roots, and calendula flower petals.
- Sore muscles can be eased with bath tea blends of rosemary, thyme, juniper berries, eucalyptus, and sea salts.
- Relaxing, aromatic herbs are lemon balm, lavender, chamomile, and mint.

ESSENTIAL

To release more active ingredients from a bath tea blend, place the tea bag in a heatproof bowl and set it in the bottom of the bathtub. Pour three to four cups of boiling water over the tea bag. Allow it to infuse for ten minutes, making a concentrated solution. Add a stopper to the tub or close the drain. Empty the contents of the bowl (infusion and tea bag) into the tub and add water for the bath. Most bath herbs will continue to add essential oils to the water and aromatics in the water vapor.

Tisanes—Herbal Teas

Another word commonly used for herbal teas—those containing no *Camellia sinensis* leaf—is the European word *tisane*. Tisane literally means an infusion of dried herbs consumed as a beverage or for its medicinal effects. It was first used in the fourteenth century C.E., and is derived from the Greek word for a drink made from crushed barley.

Tea shops, both virtual as well as brick-and-mortar, need ways to categorize their large inventory of teas. This helps customers search quickly for a flavor they want. Tisane is used interchangeably with the term herbal tea. This usually means that the ingredients are 100 percent herbal and contain no caffeine. But this is not always the case. It can also mean that a black, green, oolong, white, or pu'erh tea has been blended with a significant amount of herbal products.

Ayurvedic Teas

Ayurveda is a system of medicine developed in India, with origins recorded in texts as early as the sixth century B.C.E. Many of the practices are popular today, and it is becoming more common to see tea companies blend products with Ayurvedic herbs, recommending applications and benefits from this system.

Some of the Ayurvedic teas and a few of the traditional herbs used to blend them are:

- **Kapha:** for elements of water and earth, with lemon balm, ginger, cinnamon, cardamom, and pepper. It is usually sweet.
- **Pitta:** blended to address the element of fire with hibiscus, rose petals, chamomile, and peppermint.
- **Shanti:** fights stress and encourages peace of mind; might include tulsi (Holy Basil), fennel, orange peel, and spearmint.
- **Ujaala:** restores balance and harmony, with blends of ingredients like black tea, coriander, cloves, marigold, and calendula.
- **Vata:** a calming tea blended on principles of air and movement, with herbs like lemongrass, orange peel, licorice root, and chicory root.

Herbalism

Medical science began as herbalism. Even cave-dwelling ancients gathered herbs and prepared healing potions to treat illness. Evidence gathered from excavated sites includes remains of plants that are known today for their medicinal qualities. Some of the herbs recorded in documents from ancient China, Egypt, Greece, and Rome are exactly the same as herbal remedies employed today: honey, thyme, juniper, cumin, garlic, mint, poppy, saffron, aloe, elderberry, fennel, and many more. Noted healers throughout the ages who recorded their work helped establish schools of medicine with herbs and nutrition as the core teaching for maintaining health and treating disease.

ESSENTIAL

> Modern pharmaceuticals are still very closely linked with traditions of herbal medicine. There is always hope that, through the continued study of plant lore and the history of their healing qualities, there might be an undiscovered remedy or treatment for one of the diseases that still plague mankind.

Far from disappearing, the practice of herbalism is still practiced around the world. It is not only taught in medicinal schools of thought like Ayurveda and traditional Chinese medicine; it is also supported by herbal guilds around the world. Practitioners proudly preserve and share the collected wisdom. It is from this pool of experience that pharmacologists sometimes discover new opportunities for prescription medications.

North American Herbal Tea History

When the pilgrims first arrived in North America, they brought seeds and rooted specimens of familiar plants for medicinal uses as well as for food sources. Some thrived, but many did not. The transplanted Europeans turned to Native Americans for advice on how to use indigenous plant species to substitute for species they lost. Additionally, the pilgrims discovered new herbs and vegetables, incorporating them into their medical lore and menus. Later, when the colonists revolted against the high taxation of imported tea (the true tea, *C. sinensis*) and boycotted shipments, they were very appreciative of the shrubs that helped replace the brew that filled their afternoon teapots. One of these was *Ceanothus americanus*, a native North American shrub with yellow leaves and a minty scent that even earned the name New Jersey Tea.

Common Herbs Brewed as Tea

The following is a list of the herbs frequently selected for functional tea blends, with limited examples of the benefits they offer. In most cases, these herbs and flowers are known for many additional health applications.

- Anise seeds: digestive problems and coughs
- Chamomile flowers: headaches, relaxation, digestion
- Echinacea: infections like colds and flu
- Fennel: reduce swelling
- Feverfew: headaches, cold symptoms
- Lavender: eases sore throats and laryngitis
- Ginger: motion sickness, anti-nausea, and heart health
- Ginseng: fights stress
- Rosehips: calms coughs
- Rosemary: eases bronchial infections
- Sage: improves concentration
- Sarsaparilla: reduces fever
- St. John's Wort: fights lung congestion
- Yarrow: PMS symptoms

Of course, this barely scratches the surface of the vast body of work that has been shared for hundreds, and in some cases thousands, of years. New resources for herbalism and the use of herbal teas continue to share their knowledge of the subject. It is critically important to seek out the expertise of qualified professionals when considering any herbal treatment for health reasons. There are many books on the subject and organizations that offer workshops and training. You may be inspired to concoct your own healthful teas.

ESSENTIAL

Whether you're growing your own fresh herbs and flowers or browsing the bulk aisle in a local health food store, you will want to start with what you know and trust. Many herbalist books provide recipes for proven blends and instructions about how to prepare freshly harvested botanicals.

Brewing Herbal Teas

There is remarkable beauty and flavor in brewing herbal teas. Enjoying a delicious, flavorful tea rich in sweet fruit and spice can satisfy the function of relaxing and enjoying pleasure. Blends that have been ground for tea bags can quickly infuse with lovely colors of flowers like the brilliant red of hibiscus, or the smell of sweet spice like cinnamon. In a whole-leaf blend you may be able to spot tiny rosebuds or brilliant blue cornflower petals, small bits of apple, orange peel, or blueberries.

Herbs, flowers, leaves, and roots each require different preparations. Some brew (infuse) as quickly as tea leaves, while others may require longer infusions—even grinding or boiling (decoction) to draw out the flavors and chemical compounds and the best results. In general, infusion is the best method to draw the delicate oils from flowers and leaves. Using a rounded teaspoon of dry herbs or flowers per cup of hot water is a general rule-of-thumb. When using fresh herbs that have not withered and shrunk, you might need two to three times as much per cup of water. Whole herbs may need to steep up to 10 minutes to make a satisfying tea. If you are blending whole herbal products that infuse at very different rates, one becoming bitter while another is barely strong enough, you should either steep separately and then blend the concoctions or vary the percentage of dry material to achieve the desired balance.

Companies who package pre-blended tea have accounted for differences in the rate at which herbs infuse, providing a blend that will brew quickly and consistently. Most tea companies also provide suggestions about the best water temperature and length of time their tea should be steeped.

CHAPTER 12

Other "Teas"

With its new place in the public spotlight, *Camellia sinensis* has inspired adaptations of tea-like beverages and the renewal of old tea traditions. Innovation in the way tea is processed and brewed has allowed for new concoctions like bubble tea and a few renewed traditions like flowering tea. It is no doubt that as tea drinking continues to grow in popularity, creative minds will discover and develop even more. Some innovations may be found hidden in the past, while others might come as sudden bursts of inspiration. Tea lovers tend to be especially receptive to the cultural traditions and ways in which sharing it is meaningful.

Kombucha

A strongly brewed and sweetened black tea usually forms the base for this home-brewed fermented tonic called kombucha, in which bacteria grows and generates a pancake-like growth on the surface that is sometimes called a "mushroom" due to its shape. It is often called a cure-all tea with many different benefits. However, the lore remains mostly anecdotal without significant substantiating research. Medical science still issues many cautions, not only about its efficacy but also about the potential for contamination and subsequent harmful effects.

Kombucha is now available as a commercial ready-to-drink beverage. Using many different flavors of tea, such as chai and oolong, can make the experience more interesting. Several companies have recently introduced kombucha products that can be found in the healthy beverage areas in stores, and it is becoming a more familiar kind of "tea."

The History of Kombucha

As with many folk remedies shared cross-culturally, there are differing stories about kombucha's origins. Some believe so strongly in the healing properties of kombucha that it was called "the remedy for immortality" or the "tea of immortality" in China in the third century B.C.E., and later described as "the magic mushroom." In the early 1900s it spread to Russia and the rest of Europe. During World War II, sugar rationing made brewing kombucha more difficult, and its popularity dwindled. A Swiss company who promoted the health claims revived it in the 1960s.

Brewing Kombucha

Making a home brew usually requires a starter fungus, called a mushroom or a SCOBY (symbiotic culture of bacteria and yeast). This looks like a wet white disc, about a ½-inch thick and 6–8 inches in diameter. It is added to a freshly brewed (and cooled) half-gallon of sweetened tea along with a cup of the brew from the previous batch (a starter solution). The batch is then covered with a screen or woven fabric, then set in a warm place for one to two weeks to ferment. During this time, the SCOBY (also called the mother) will mature and reproduce another layer (the baby). Almost any tea flavor and a wide variety of sweeteners will work (artificial sweeteners must not be used, however). The tea can be brewed lightly for a gentler kombucha, and the amount of sugar or sweetener can be reduced for a tangy taste.

ALERT

Very little scientific information on the health benefits is available, but anecdotal reports of both horribly negative reactions as well as fantastic cures abound. Those who use kombucha believe that drinking it daily boosts the immune system, increases energy, eases joint pain, balances cholesterol levels, reduces blood pressure, and helps fight cancer. Another popular claim is that it also contains a number of beneficial B vitamins.

Cautions

Aside from doubts about using kombucha for health benefits, there is genuine concern about contamination and the growth of harmful bacteria as a result. Good practices are necessary, and there is a great deal of information available about cleaning the utensils used for fermentation and how to determine if the SCOBY is viable. Ventilation is required for outgassing during fermentation, but the covering must also be able to screen out insects like fruit flies. Finally, there is the potential for mold growth. If you intend to try making kombucha, please research the topic well before attempting it in order to minimize potentially health-threatening situations.

Anyone trying kombucha for the first time should check for allergic reactions. Begin by drinking only a small amount, no more than a tablespoon, and observe your reactions closely and objectively. Gradually increase the amount taken and monitor gastrointestinal reactions. An average daily use is 2–4 ounces three times per day, at mealtimes. Some recommendations are to take it either ten minutes prior to a meal or shortly after eating.

Flowering Tea

Sometimes called "blossoming tea" or "performance tea," this is a very entertaining and artistic form of tea. They are actually combinations of fresh green tea leaf buds and other flowers that have been hand-tied and compressed into a small bundle designed to open when infused in hot water. Dozens of designs have been created in the last few years, each with different flowers hidden in the center of a tightly wrapped ball of tea leaves, and each one opens to reveal a lovely flower. The long green or white tea buds wrap around osmanthus, globe amaranth, chrysanthemum, jasmine, or lily. Flowering teas are all made by hand. These little works of art are most often used for special occasions or as decorations, but the tea brewed from them can also be enjoyed.

Infusing Flowering Tea

Flowering tea should be infused in a glass container that can tolerate hot water, usually a large cylindrical vase about 4 inches in diameter, a large glass (such as a brandy snifter), or in a glass teapot. The flowering tea bulb is placed into the bottom of the container and hot water (under 200°F) is added slowly and gently.

Almost immediately, the tea leaves will begin to draw away from the round bulb. They will unfold slowly, one by one, to reveal the flower within. Within a few minutes, the entire performance will be complete. The water will be infused with the flavors and colors of the leaves and of the flower. Once the flower is open, the tea should be decanted before it becomes too strong to drink, or before the water becomes too dark to clearly enjoy the beauty of the flower. It can be infused several times as a beverage, and will last at least a week as a decoration.

ESSENTIAL

Flowering teas are often sold in gift sets with the glass container, several different tea flowers, and complete instructions for infusing and enjoying the performance of these unusual teas.

History of Flowering Tea

What was originally a folk art practiced in tea-growing communities was revived in the 1990s in Fujian Province, China. Innovations like this not only provided interesting new products to delight new tea drinkers, but also revitalized a cultural tradition and provided many new jobs for women. Tong Yun, who grew up on her family's tea farm and eventually took over the management of their business, generated dozens of new designs, and restored the craft into prominence in the Chinese tea business community.

Ready-to-Drink Bottled Teas

The convenience of bottled teas attracts individuals who want to reduce their consumption of carbonated sodas and drink more tea, but don't want to take the time to brew it themselves. Beverage companies of all sizes have responded with hundreds of delicious flavors. In most cases, basic green, black, and white teas are blended with additional flavors and then often enhanced with the addition of herbal supplements. Some popular choices are mixed with fruit juices. Some of the most popular flavors are tea with lemonade, peach-flavored tea, and raspberry-flavored tea.

FACT

A 2011 tea industry report by market strategists, Mintel Group, Ltd., found that bottled tea as well as refrigerated ready-to-drink (RTD) teas had increased overall tea sales by more than 30 percent in five years, saying, "The market continues to thrive on the pro-health perception of tea coupled with the fact that manufacturers have been savvy in bringing out consumer-preferred teas in innovative flavors and the convenient RTD format."

One of the major differences between the various RTD choices is whether or not they are made with brewed tea or infused with tea extracts and synthesized flavors and additives. RTDs are usually intended to be consumed as a cold beverage or served over ice, and are crafted by professional tea blenders for desirable flavors rather than for the energy boost.

Even though some of the new tea energy drinks are tasty, they are most often formulated for the extra energy they provide. Labeling and promotional material may even suggest the number of hours of additional alertness the beverage will provide. It would be rare to find an actual brewed tea as the base for an energy drink. More likely, a tea extract is only one of many ingredients in a blend of various juices and supplements.

Bubble Tea—Boba Tea—Pearl Tea

What began as a spontaneous, creative moment became a new tea craze that quickly spread around the world. In Taichung, Taiwan, in 1988, product development manager Lin Hsiu Hui was attending a staff meeting of the Chun Shui Tang Teahouse. While enjoying a popular dessert, a sweet tapioca pudding named *fen yuan*, she impulsively poured some of it into her glass of iced tea. The innovation instantly became popular at their teahouse. The word quickly spread, and variations on the original recipe were served in many other Taiwanese teahouses. The recipe and variations then spread to Japan, South Korea, China, and to many western countries.

One of the first adaptations to Ms. Hui's original black tea recipe was using the larger variety of black tapioca balls. But other tea flavors and many differently flavored sweet syrups proved to be equally popular with customers. There are now hundreds of different recipes, many of them no longer using real tea, some even substituting coffee. The drink is so popular today that there are several brand-name chains with multiple stores on different continents serving only bubble tea. Gradually, traditional tearooms are also beginning to offer variations of bubble tea as options to the traditional brewed tea.

The key to making bubble tea is proper preparation of the large, dried boba tapioca pearls in advance. They must be cooked for about fifteen minutes and sweetened with a syrup, then allowed to cool. Spoon the desired amount of cooked and sweetened tapioca into a glass, then add a favorite tea (strongly brewed), and top it off with milk and/or fruit juice. One variation is to make a tea and fruit smoothie in a blender with crushed ice to make it thicker and colder before stirring in the prepared tapioca pearls, allowing them to be suspended in the drink rather than sinking to the bottom of the glass.

Tea Concentrates

The history of Russian tea and the use of the traditional samovar created what is probably the first tea concentrate. Still used today, the samovar is a multichambered tea server with a small chamber at the base for burning charcoal to keep the tea and water warm for an extended period of time. A strongly brewed black tea is kept warm and usually becomes concentrated (a desirable result) as it sits over the heat. When served, a spigot at the bottom dispenses the intense tea, which is then mixed with the heated water, milk, and sugar to taste. Traditionally, the preferred taste was very strong, using some of the smoked teas, like Lapsang Souchong and Keemun.

ESSENTIAL

The general rule for the strongly brewed black tea concentrate assumes that it be four to five times stronger than the average tea served. This allows for variation in strength and for additions of milk, sugar (or jam, a Russian tradition), and water.

Commercial Concentrates

Tea concentrates are now produced commercially and packaged for both individual use and for restaurants. This is very helpful for serving large groups quickly, requiring less labor and equipment. This is also a popular innovation with caterers and event planners hosting large tea parties. While there are many different flavors, one of the most popular concentrates is masala chai and many other different chai blends. With the addition of boiling water, the final cup is instantly ready to serve.

Homemade Concentrate Recipe

A do-it-yourself concentrate recipe uses one cup of black loose-leaf tea or eight tea bags to a quart of boiling water. Use heatproof glass containers or stainless steel, not aluminum. The steeping container should be free of oils and aromas from previous usage. Steep for at least ten minutes, and store in a glass container until it is time to serve. One quart of this concentrate should serve about fifty cups of hot tea, using one tablespoon of concentrate for each. Black teas and herbal teas are usually preferred for concentrates, as green teas can become bitter with hot water and long steeping times, and can be more temperamental to serve. In order to concentrate green tea, use even more tea, lower-temperature water, and steep for a shorter amount of time. The concentrate will not be as strong as the black tea, and so it will be important to taste-test the ratio of concentrate to water in order to serve the best tasting cup to guests.

ESSENTIAL

To more easily serve warm tea to a large adult crowd, begin by having everything pre-warmed. Store the teapots, teacups, and saucers in a slightly warm oven or on top of an electric blanket before filling. Pre-heat the concentrate before measuring it into the warm teapots, then fill the teapots with heated water and serve immediately. Covering the teapots left on the table with cozies (custom fitted teapot blankets) will help keep the pot warm so that guests can serve themselves.

Tea Extracts

Tea extracts, especially green tea extracts, are available as a supplement in most health food stores and from supplement companies. Specific concentrations of epigallocatechin gallate (EGCG) and other active ingredients are (or should be) accurately listed on the label, and most products will also include caffeine information. Powdered extracts are packaged in capsule form but liquid extracts are also available.

ALERT

While it isn't possible to replicate the results of medical studies using tea by drinking it in brewed form, it could be possible using tea extracts. For anyone with health concerns, however, the use of concentrated extracts should be discussed with a physician. There are potential side effects associated with using extracts, especially in high doses.

Being able to precisely control the amount of tea you consume each day may be appealing to some. Not having to actually *drink* tea in order to receive the benefits may have certain applications to others. However, in our fast-paced, take-a-pill society, one of the greatest health benefits of drinking tea is the potential for stress reduction, sensory stimulation, and the social interaction it can offer. Consuming tea in extract form eliminates this benefit, and it is a significant loss.

QUESTION

How are extracts made?
There is a three-step process often used to make tea extracts. The leaves are first soaked in an alcohol solution to infuse the active ingredients. This is then reduced and concentrated even further before it is finally dehydrated into powdered form.

Freeze-Dried Tea Powder

Instant teas, or freeze-dried powder teas, are usually made from a concentrated extract that has been further dried under heat and pressure before spray drying or vacuum drying. There are some concerns that this process increases the concentration of fluoride and reduces the amount of antioxidants. There is very little scientific study comparing the health differences between brewed tea, tea extracts, and freeze-dried teas.

Tea-Infused Foods

Processed tea concentrates and powders in addition to regularly brewed teas have found many new applications in foods, both in commercial products and in foods prepared by home cooks and restaurant chefs. Some popular products on the market today include:

- Tea mints—a powerful punch of tea powders and extracts are added to oils and other food extracts, then molded into attractive shapes.
- Tea chewing gum—made with tea powders, these are sometimes advertised to provide an equivalent energy boost to drinking a cup of brewed tea.
- Tea chocolates—chocolate candy is sometimes made with powdered tea or blended with tea concentrates. Filled chocolates may also contain matcha powdered tea, or sweet fillings that include tea extracts.
- Tea candy—hard candies flavored to resemble favorite teas are usually made with tea extracts.
- Tea jams—made with a strongly brewed tea or tea concentrate that is substituted for the water in which fruit is cooked with sugar. Whole leaves may also be added with the fruit.
- Tea rubs—pulverized tea is mixed with other spices to form a dry powder blend that can help flavor meats, fish, or grilled vegetables.

Rooibos and Yerba Maté

Two very different herbal teas from two different continents are so frequently referred to as teas, and therefore confused with real tea, that they should be mentioned. And because they each have such unique traditions, they deserve special consideration; hence their inclusion here. Each of these two herbs provides health benefits comparable to *Camellia sinensis*, and are prepared and served in similar ways.

Rooibos

Tea shop menus and shelves of tea brands in grocery markets may include something called red tea that is not actually made from *Camellia sinensis.* Some of the confusion comes from increasing awareness that the traditional Chinese reference to fully oxidized tea (categorized as black tea) is "red tea." As western tea retailers begin to use the Chinese description for the category, it can be confusing, even for long-time tea lovers.

Rooibos comes from the tiny, needle-like leaf of a South African native shrub called Red Bush, a member of the legume family. It is now a well-known and easily available herbal tea. It has a natural sweetness and brews a soft red liquor. Not particularly sensitive to the temperature of the water or the length of steeping, it is an easy beverage to brew and serve. It can be found unblended, but is more often combined with other herbs and essential oils for additional flavoring. Some popular flavor combinations are rooibos with vanilla, orange, or chai spices.

History of Rooibos

In 1772, Carl Thunberg discovered that rooibos was one of the plants used as a medicinal herb in the Cederberg region of South Africa. Dutch settlers near Capetown began processing it and using it as a substitute for expensive, imported teas. In the early 1900s, a Russian settler developed a method for processing the tiny leaves similar to a Chinese black tea, allowing them to completely oxidize to develop a natural sweetness and more intense flavor. Major cultivation began in the 1930s, after the longstanding difficulty in gathering the tiny seeds was finally overcome.

FACT

South African farmers who first collected rooibos seeds could not force germination without damaging the seeds while attempting to scarify them, a process by which the seeds are abraded to aid germination. Dr. Peter le Fras Nortier worked with local natives and met a woman who supplied him with seeds she had "stolen" from ant mounds. The ants had cracked the shell of the seeds without damaging them. Soon thereafter, these seeds became the most expensive vegetable seeds in the world.

Brewing Rooibos

Rooibos herbal tea is very tolerant of different temperatures and times for infusion. It is usually recommended that the tea be steeped between three and five minutes. The one frustration that some tea people express when brewing loose-leaf rooibos is that the fine needles catch in some wire mesh infusion baskets and can be a little more difficult to clean. Rooibos can be served both hot and cold.

Health Benefits of Rooibos

Rooibos is high in antioxidants, so it offers many of the same health benefits as the *Camellia sinensis* when consumed, including anti-inflammatory properties, improved circulation, and digestive aids. It is naturally caffeine-free and is a source of magnesium, zinc, and iron. In South Africa, it is sometimes suggested to the elderly as a digestive aid, and given in diluted forms to babies with colic.

FACT

Rooibos gained great popularity after it was featured in the PBS series *No. 1 Ladies Detective Agency*, based on the bestselling book series of the same name by Alexander McCall Smith. Set in Botswana, Africa, the protagonist of the story, Precious Ramotswe, frequently serves clients and guests a cup of "bush tea." This is one of the many names for rooibos.

Yerba Maté

Yerba maté (*Ilex paraguariensis*) is an evergreen shrub in the same botanical family as holly. It grows in several locations in South America, such as Argentina, Brazil, Paraguay, and Uruguay, but was first cultivated by a slightly nomadic Guarani people who lived in southern Brazil. Yerba maté does contain caffeine, but the amount can vary greatly. The flavor of the prepared yerba maté can also vary with the terroir where it was grown and the season in which it was harvested.

Brewing Yerba Maté

The maté is brewed inside a gourd called a *guampa* or a *maté*. Dried leaves and twigs are placed inside the gourd and then infused with warm water (not boiling). The gourd is passed around a circle of family or friends and drunk through a metal straw called a *bombilla* or *bomba*. When the brewed "tea" is consumed, more warm water is added and the gourd passed around again, until all of the flavor has been drawn out. If lightly brewed, the flavors are usually vegetal, like a green tea. If boiling water is used or if the leaves are steeped too long, the infusion may become bitter.

There are many traditions for sharing yerba maté in a group with the guampa and bombilla. But it is now available in tea bags and ready-to-drink forms, sometimes flavored with sweet spices and dried fruit. It is often served with milk or juice, and may be served with meals and afternoon snacks.

Health Benefits of Yerba Maté

The natural caffeine is a stimulant and is often used to increase alertness and focus, similar to coffee and tea. But yerba maté is also high in antioxidants, offering some of the same benefits as tea for weight control, increased energy, and digestion.

CHAPTER 13

Buying the Healthiest Tea

The healthiest cup of tea is, almost always, the freshest tea that has been well packaged and properly stored. A healthy tea can change the way you feel, open your senses, and infuse a feeling of contentment. Sometimes the most familiar and readily available brands, the flavors that have been with you since you were a child, provide comfort and solace. However, there can also be a bit of adventure to buying tea in a specialty store, where a world of choices is available. On this adventure, some of the healthiest teas can be discovered with the help of a knowledgeable guide.

What Is Healthy Tea?

Choosing a tea can be a very personal decision. Many people find a particular comfort in the familiar flavors from childhood—the brand that was an everyday staple, or the blend that was a special holiday treat. Tea lovers frequently describe an experience with a particular tea that, even after years of tasting varieties from around the world, will suddenly be the most remarkable and memorable they've ever tasted. The tea sage Lu Yu wrote, "Goodness is a decision for the mouth to make."

Studying the scientific research on tea demonstrates that there are similar health benefits in almost every tea. Therefore, it's difficult to choose one for a single medical purpose. It is much simpler and probably more effective to develop a habit that improves overall health. Realizing that tea is one of the superfoods, with many overlapping benefits to all teas, the choices become easier and you can be guided by your personal sense of what is "good" to choose and what is also "healthy." Some of the criteria for selecting healthy teas may include some of the following:

- The flavor of the tea is one that perks up your senses and appeals to you. Forcing yourself to drink an unpleasant cup of tea because of its health properties is like choking down a spoonful of medicine. Find a single tea, or develop an assortment of teas, that appeals to you and will lure you to the cupboard more often, to establish that healthful habit of tea drinking.
- There is a good tea for every time of day. There are teas to fit every mood and occasion. Discover morning eye-openers, a collection of flavors for afternoon break, and companions for an evening meditation.
- Identify tea drinking with positive moods. In the midst of a crisis, the soothing sip of a good "friend" tea can sometimes bring the calm needed. During a conflict, discussing the problem over tea can help relax the tension.
- Good teas vary in the amount of caffeine they brew. Appreciating how caffeine invigorates also informs you at what time of day it can be consumed without compromising the quality of sleep.

- There are good teas for every food. In the same way that wines can be paired with food, teas also blend well with the dining experience. Good teas can enhance the experience of a meal.
- Good teas are comfortably affordable. There is a wide price variation in excellent teas. Staying within a budget does not have to limit the tea experience or the quality that establishes a healthy daily regimen. Certainly there are jaw-droppingly expensive teas, but these are not necessarily healthier than delicious choices that brew for under a dollar a cup.
- The best teas take you on a journey. Sometimes the journey is down memory lane. Others take you to a land and culture you've never investigated before. Tea and meditation can become a personal, spiritual retreat. Tea with family and friends can enhance relationships.

QUESTION

What is a bad tea?
One of the clearest examples of a bad tea is one with an unpleasant aftertaste. There can be different reasons for this, but it often indicates a problem with the production, or the use of lower-quality flavoring oils. It is also possible that a tea not handled properly can be contaminated by external odors, or can absorb moisture and develop mold. Tea that has been stored on open shelves in glass containers can fade in both color and taste, degraded by UV rays. These are issues that can quickly and easily be detected.

Tea Bags versus Loose-Leaf Tea

The differences between the two methods of packaging tea sometimes seem to suggest a hierarchy between novice and advanced tea drinkers, which is unfortunate. Almost everyone has an occasion where a tea bag is the best choice. And most of the large brands are now packaging better-quality teas in convenient sachets. Some purveyors offer exactly the same tea with both options.

On the other hand, watching a whole-leaf tea survive "the agony of the leaf" as it rehydrates and is restored to its original form is a sight to behold—even to one who knows very little about the rest of tea lore. Most importantly, just being loose-leaf does not indicate a high-quality tea, and cut tea in bags is not inherently of poor quality or less healthy.

Bagged Tea—Sachets

Tea bags, also known as sachets, are made of very fine filter paper, nylon, or food-grade plastic. The tea used to fill them must be cut into small bits in order to pass through the mechanized process without clumping. This finely cut tea is a combination of "fannings" and "dust." Being cut and powdered also makes the tea infuse more quickly. The tea selected for this packaging is usually not the highest quality, as compared to hand-plucked artisan teas, but can still be an excellent tea. The actual tea chosen, as well as the handling of the tea during processing and the secure wrapping of the individual bag to protect the tea from degradation by air, light, heat, moisture, and aromas, all contribute and help determine exactly how healthy it will be.

ESSENTIAL

It is often said that the wrapping for a tea bag costs more than the tea. This is probably true with a great many teas, and is reflected in the cost. The cost of brand name tea bags can vary from less than a nickel (USD) per cup to about a dollar (USD). And when purchasing tea in tea bags, the wrapper is critically important to preserving the quality of the tea. Considering how quickly the tea can deteriorate, a simple paper wrapper does not offer much protection. The optimum wrapper is foil that blocks light, moisture, and vapors. Food-grade cellophane is also an effective wrapper if the tea bags are not stored in strong light.

Brand Name Tea

Because of the expense of manufacturing tea bags, they are usually only sold by larger companies with a recognized brand name like Bigelow,

Celestial Seasonings, Choice, Good Earth, Harney & Sons, Lipton, Mighty Leaf, Numi, Peet's, PG Tips, Red Rose, Republic of Tea, Stash, Tazo, Tetley, Twinings, Yogi Tea, and Yorkshire Gold, to name a few. These companies produce flavors that are easily identifiable and remain consistent year after year, due to a staff of professional tea blenders. There may be more than thirty teas blended to maintain the integrity and consistency of an individual flavor profile. Most of the teas listed here taste the same now as they have for many years—a remarkable feat.

QUESTION

Are the silken tea bags better?
The fabric is not real silk; the adjective "silken" evokes the sense of higher quality. There are different-quality products used to make the new styled, see-through bags. Some are nylon or combinations of plastic. Others are biodegradable products. None have yet been proven to be either healthier than paper or hazardous; however, opinions vary greatly about their safety. There are people who feel that they are a finer mesh, so there is less residue in the tea after brewing them than there is with paper tea bags. Other tea drinkers have concerns about infusing any plastic in hot water.

Loose-Leaf Tea

It may be true that whole, loose-leaf teas are healthier than finely cut teabag blends; however, buying and brewing them may seem more difficult at first. Like any new hobby or skill, there is a learning curve. But the essential taste test remains the same: *What tastes good?* After that, knowing the essentials about the basic tea categories and having a few tips up your sleeve can be helpful and reassuring.

- Locate a retailer that demonstrates knowledge of and respect for the tea—whether it's a brick-and-mortar store or an online e-commerce vendor. If they present the tea well, can speak with confidence and fluency, show respect for individual tastes, and package the tea you choose with care, they are more likely to have selected quality products and keep them in optimum conditions.

- Begin with teas that are familiar to you from having enjoyed them in tea bag form. For example, if you've only tasted black tea in tea bags, don't start with a loose-leaf green tea. Notice the difference between the quick-brewing tea bag and the slower-brewing loose-leaf. Are there differences in taste? With this knowledge, you may then consider which you prefer.

- Purchase the smallest amount. Two-ounce packets are usually the smallest weights sold by retailers. Two ounces equals 56 grams, so, assuming 2–3 grams per cup, this small packet would brew eighteen to twenty-eight cups. This is enough to share with friends at a tea-tasting party.

- Note that whole leaves exhibit very different physical characteristics and can make the package seem more or less full. When comparing tea by weight, a package of more open and fluffy leaves will be larger than one with rolled leaves. One example is the difference between tightly rolled Gunpowder green tea and fluffy, open-leaved Bai Mu Dan white tea. Buying by weight will seldom give you the same-sized packages.

- If recommendations for brewing are not included with the tea purchase, ask the retailer. Most Internet sellers give brewing suggestions along with the descriptions of the tea on the sales page.

- Take a moment to study the tea at each stage: the dry leaf, wet leaf, and liquor. Appreciate the sensory experience of the tea at each stage. With so many choices, consider if this is a tea you would buy again, or if you want to try a different tea.

- Keep a journal with information regarding the teas you try and the retailers you grow to trust.

Where to Buy Good Tea

Tea seems to be popping up everywhere. There are more specialty tea shops, more brands on grocery store shelves, more online tea businesses, and selections in gift shops and kitchen stores. There are many reasons to buy different teas at various kinds of stores: the convenience of a quick package while grocery shopping, finding something unusual at a tea shop, even ordering directly from a grower online. However, for someone hoping to improve overall health by developing a daily tea program, finding the best tea may require a little legwork.

ESSENTIAL

How the tea is packaged, for both tea bags and loose-leaf teas, tells you a great deal about the professionalism and experience of the retailer. Inadequately wrapped tea or improperly displayed teas reveal the amount of respect the seller has for the products and the clientele. Selecting a healthy tea begins with locating one that is fresh and well presented. This is far more critical than the issue of bagged versus loose-leaf tea, or the cost of the tea.

Grocery Stores

The beverage aisles in general food markets are increasing the space for tea brands, even crowding out coffee in some grocery stores. Where there were once just one or two brand name teas, each with very limited selection other than basic black, there may now be a dozen brands, each with a diverse line of flavors. Now you can also find green, oolong, white, and herbal or functional teas in convenient tea bags. (Pu'erh is not as common in this form.) Customers can find their lifelong favorites along with tempting new treats in colorful boxes. Reading the boxes and checking ingredients on the labels can be a first step to learning more about the wide world of tea.

Health Food Stores

Health food stores tend to stock more brands of functional teas, purchased for particular health reasons rather than for the flavor. Of course, the flavors in many of the herbal and functional teas are delicious as well as beneficial. Increasingly, health food stores are adding a line of serve-yourself bulk tea to their pre-packaged brands, and are hiring personnel who have studied tea and herbalism and can advise on basic tea information.

Specialty Tea Businesses

There are more than two thousand specialty tea retailers in the United States alone. Some of these represent the traditional restaurant-style tearooms serving variations on a British-style, Victorian-style, country-style, or Asian-style tea. These usually offer a large selection of tea, with options in each major category, along with a traditional menu. Most also have a retail shop for the customer to purchase tea and tea accessories to replicate what and how they've been served.

Tea shops without food service are generally able to stock a larger and more specialized selection, concentrating fully on the tea and how it is to be brewed. They frequently offer samples of teas, sometimes even offering to brew a special cup to allow you to test a new flavor before buying. A knowledgeable staff member will be able to explain the tea's origins if it is an unblended tea or discuss the characteristics of a blended tea. Many tea shops also offer classes and tastings that provide an excellent way to broaden knowledge and experience. Meet-ups and special events bring tea lovers together to share the adventure.

Virtual Tea Shops

Because the tea industry is growing rapidly and online tea sales can be a fairly easy and inexpensive start-up, this has become a very attractive and popular home-based business. Some merchants are very well informed, have traveled extensively to meet growers, buy in large international markets, and can offer quality products and personalized service to their customers. In fact, starting an online store might be a first step for someone preparing to open a physical tea shop. Some very knowledgeable tea entrepreneurs begin this way and grow into their larger dream tea business gradually, developing a loyal customer base with e-commerce, online events, and all of the new tools of communication.

Some online tea retailers can also provide educational programs with newsletters, blogs, and webinars. They usually take great care in describing their tea products and recommending a preferred brewing method. One rather common practice for online merchants is to include a sample of a similar tea with the shipment. This is a small gift to help customers expand their awareness of more teas, and to encourage them to return for another shopping trip.

ALERT

It is easy to take a weekend seminar, or read a few books, then launch an e-commerce website. Unfortunately, there are some of these entrepreneurs who know how to build a beautiful website but have very little invested in their own tea education. They are, therefore, not able to give adequate support to their customers, may not know how to properly store and package tea, and may not know how to select a quality inventory.

Tea Math: The Cost of a Cup

When tea was first sold in both Europe and the colonies it was so expensive that the ladies of the house kept it locked away and wouldn't allow servants to prepare their tea. At a 2013 lecture at the University of California, Davis, Hong Kong tea master Ip Wingchi served ten different teas and told his listeners that a tea from any category (like oolong) can be purchased within a price range of $10–$10,000 per pound. These ranges are extremes. It would be nearly impossible to find an oolong tea for $10 per pound and, believe it or not, $10,000 is not the most paid for a pound of oolong tea. Rare teas at auction sell to collectors for much more.

ESSENTIAL

James Norwood Pratt, author of *The New Tea Lover's Treasury* and *The Tea Dictionary*, frequently speaks of fine teas as an affordable luxury. Some very fine tea can be brewed for less than a dollar a cup and served in such a way that you experience a pause in the typical hubbub of the day. Tea can be a way for you to enjoy a moment of elegance.

Calculating the Price of a Cup

In the regular world, if a pound of tea costs $100 but makes 200 cups of tea, then the cost of a single infusion is fifty cents. If there are multiple infusions, the value is increased. Considering that there are 453 grams per pound and most people use between two and three grams to brew a single cup, comparing the value of tea becomes a simple math problem. We can compare the list prices of some of the most familiar brand-name teas, taking into account similar tea blends and packaging, to calculate their approximate prices per tea bag.

Brand Name and Tea Flavor	Manufacturer's Suggested Retail Price	Cost per Cup in Dollars
Red Rose Original - 100 tea bags + figurine	$3.75	0.04
Lipton Black Tea - 100 tea bags	$5.00	0.05
PG Tips - 240 tea bags	$25.00	0.10
Twinings English Breakfast - 100 tea bags	$9.99	0.10
Taylors of Harrogate, Yorkshire Gold - 80 tea bags	$15.10	0.19
Bigelow Constant Comment - 120 tea bags	$17.75	0.15
Celestial Seasonings India Spice Chai Tea - 120 tea bags	$17.94	0.15
Kirkland Signature Japanese Green Tea (Ito En) - 100 tea bags	$16.27	0.16
Stash Double Bergamot Earl Grey Black - 90 tea bags	$14.95	0.17
Tazo Awake English Breakfast Filterbag Tea - 24 tea bags	$4.95	0.21
Good Earth Chai Tea - 108 tea bags	$23.94	0.22
Republic of Tea British Breakfast - 50 tea bags	$11.00	0.22
Traditional Medicinals Echinacea Plus (Organic) - 96 tea bags	$26.94	0.28
Choice Classic Black - 96 tea bags	$27.54	0.29
Yogi Chai Black (Organic) - 96 tea bags	$28.14	0.29
Harney & Sons Earl Grey Imperial - 30 tea bags	$10.95	0.36
Mighty Leaf Organic Breakfast - 100 tea bags	$54.00	0.54
Tea Forte Earl Grey (Event Box) - 49 pyramid infusers	$48.00	0.98

ESSENTIAL

Tea bags are standardized in the sense that the net weight in the bag is calculated to brew what the manufacturer considers a good 8-ounce cup of tea with a two-to-three-minute infusion. This is, of course, an average.

Large Brands

In the early 1800s, tea was still sold only in bulk, which made it more difficult to control the quality and to keep the tea (which was very expensive) from being adulterated by blending it with non-tea substances to stretch it. One of the first merchants to package tins of tea was Frederick John Horniman, a nineteenth-century British merchant, who by doing this guaranteed the quality of his brand. Other companies realized the value of packaging tea, and soon there were four major brands selling it: Lyons, Brooke Bond, Ty-phoo, and the Co-op Wholesale Society of Manchester. Perhaps the most famous of all tea brand names is Lipton, created by the Scottish-born grocer Thomas Lipton, who became a tea entrepreneur in the 1890s.

The major tea brands continue to provide remarkable consistency of flavor and quality. They design products with flavor profiles—like recipes—that taste the same no matter how much a given year's harvest may have changed. This requires experienced tea tasters to blend tea from many different sources. Some of the most famous blends require tea from as many as thirty different regions to maintain the exact flavor.

FACT

In his early marketing, Thomas Lipton advertised with the phrase "Direct from the tea garden to the teapot." He was, of course, speaking of his own plantations in Ceylon (now Sri Lanka). But there are growers in Sri Lanka, Darjeeling, and some other countries of origin who sell their tea directly to customers around the world. If health and freshness are important factors in selecting your tea, these may be options you wish to consider.

Small Tea Retailers

There are several advantages to shopping for loose-leaf tea from small, independent tea merchants. One is being able to select teas based on the beauty and aroma of the dry leaf, or after tasting a brewed sample. Small retailers can give personalized service. They become familiar with your tastes and can recommend teas that will be the most satisfying. Small tearooms tend to order less volume and maintain a smaller stock of each kind of tea, so the turnover can be much faster and the tea is then fresher. They can focus on the kinds of teas that their customers prefer and increase their own inventory based on this demand. Small retailers are usually very much invested in providing education for their customers through classes, workshops, and other special events.

What's Right for You?

Tea lovers seldom have a single favorite tea brand or flavor of tea. Most enjoy different categories (black, green, white, oolong, pu'erh, herbal) at different times of day. A personal tea cupboard usually reflects many different moods and ways of enjoying tea. And many tea lovers are like foodies, always seeking to broaden their experiences. People's tastes change with the season; something spicy for winter, or light and citrusy for summer. Curiosity lures us to try new things like the fresh harvest from the first flush in Darjeeling, or the complexity of a hand-rolled oolong. And it's always nice to be able to reach for a trusted functional tea to soothe an upset stomach or inspire sleep.

For everyone, the right tea for any given moment will be found by gathering a selection that satisfy many different moods and tastes. At the risk of crowding a cupboard with a few too many boxes and canisters, one of the healthiest aspects to all kinds of teas is adventure and exploration in the comfort of home. There is an expression that tea people *travel the world in their teacups*. The best teas are like guideposts to the next delight on that path.

The North American Tea Championship (*www.teachampionship.com*) conducts annual competitions in all major categories of tea. Participation by the tea businesses is purely optional, so not all brands submit their products. Professional tasters analyze and grade the samples. The results are published in the "World Tea Buyer's Guide," available online at *www.teachampionship.com/images/pdf/BuyersGuide-Final-Online.pdf*. The publication includes interesting descriptions of each category with some of the criteria for analysis, as well as lists of entries that received first, second, and third place recognition.

Tea Education

Every new tea experience furthers your own tea education, discovering what tastes good and what does not. Most serious tea lovers consider themselves to be lifelong students of tea, continuously adding to their body of knowledge, knowing that there is the potential to span more than any one person's lifetime. A hobbyist can also delight in learning something new every day with every new tea. A professional can devote study to a particular aspect of tea and never reach the end of what there is to know. There are many ways newcomers can turn to tea professionals to advance their interests. A mark of wisdom on the part of any tea professional is that they consider themselves perpetual students, and they delight in what every experience offers. The study of tea can be as humbling as it is fascinating. Here are some opportunities and events through which you can learn more about tea.

Tea Books

Tea history, tea cultures around the world, tea brewing and serving are all covered in dozens of classics by respected authors. While they are not titles that appear on famous bestseller lists, and libraries and bookstores may not have much invested in this very small niche, tea literature is an important aspect to delving into the world of tea. There are certainly differences of opinion between the writers, varied spellings in the foreign languages that can drive one crazy, and even conflicting recommendations about best brewing practices. But all are colorful intros into this new world.

Importantly, a bit of study before venturing to a class or buying a first artisan tea can be an excellent investment.

Tea Tasting

One popular event in the tea community is a hosted tasting, where a group of four to six teas is served and discussed. The host or teacher usually presents information about the country of origin and the way in which the tea being served was produced, as well as brewing and serving suggestions. Many tea shops and tearooms offer these to regular customers, especially when introducing new items to their menu or when a new season of teas arrives.

Tea Classes

In addition to tea shops, basic introductory classes are also sometimes held for continuing education programs at colleges, libraries, adult education communities, and recreation centers. A beginner class will touch on the types of tea, probably serving samples of each, with guidelines for brewing. Some classes focus on a particular country of origin or a specific period of history, a category of tea or a broad overview, touching on the high points of the 5,000-year history.

Tea Festivals

There are a growing number of consumer-oriented tea festivals around the world. A festival can be one or two days long, and there are usually classes, tastings, and several vendors with specialty tea items. Some events are exclusively tea-focused, while others combine both tea and coffee.

Tea Tourism

Tours to tea farms, factories, and markets of the countries of origin such as China, India, Japan, Taiwan, Argentina, and Korea are a fascinating way to experience a new culture and venture off the traditional tourist path. The hands-on experience, picking fresh leaves and then following them through the entire process, is a quality education that no book or workshop can provide.

Tea Sommelier—Canada

The Tea Association of Canada offers a Tea Sommelier course, currently available for certification at many colleges. The curriculum is designed to prepare the graduate to work in food service, designing tea menus and recommending food pairings as a wine sommelier would.

Specialty Tea Institute—Tea Association of the United States

STI forms the educational extension of the Tea Association of the United States. It offers introductory level study for tea enthusiasts as well as continuing education for tea professionals who want to work in the industry. There are currently four levels of certification, with the completion of Level Three being the qualification as a Certified Tea Specialist. Live classes are held at various locations around the United States.

QUESTION

What is a tea master?
The designation of tea master holds no absolute determination. It is respectfully used in reference to a person who is extremely knowledgeable about tea, and who has spent most of his professional life working in production and/or education. A tea master is also the person managing the harvest and production of fine artisan teas at a factory or estate. Unfortunately, the title has been degraded in some western countries, where there is very little understanding of true mastery, and where some are referred to as "masters" for marketing purposes.

World Tea Academy—Online Study

The educational division of World Tea Expo, a trade show for tea professionals with an extensive on-site curriculum, recently launched an online program designed to assist tea business owners with staff training. Online classes and video demonstrations are scheduled so that classes of limited sizes meet online and train with the professional staff. Course work includes forums and group discussions. The course of study begins at a basic, introductory level, then continues on to advanced professional training.

Tea as an Integrated College Program

In 2013, the University of California at Davis launched an interdisciplinary study of tea with coursework spanning several departments: Art, Art History, Humanities, East Asian Studies, Philosophy, Agriculture, and the UC Davis Confucius Institute. The program offers students a broad education in the world of tea at a graduate level.

CHAPTER 14

Brewing Healthy Tea

One argument from coffee drinkers who resist the seduction of whole-leaf tea is that the brewing is complicated and time-consuming. But compared with grinding beans, installing filters, and actually brewing the ground coffee, there may be very little difference in the basic steps of either daily brew. Ceremonial tea service certainly has every other beverage beaten, hands-down, for its complex preparation. But then, this exceptional opportunity to experience the elegance of tea practices is one of the most intriguing things about tea.

Brewing Basics

Brewing a cup of tea is actually simple and economical. It simply requires the cup and some water. Brewing a *healthy* cup of tea is only slightly more complicated. You need a rather fresh tea that has been stored well, a cup, and good-quality water. Of these three things, the water is the most critical component. Certainly, there are enormous differences in the amount of anti-oxidants, polyphenols, tannins, and thearubigins in the tea; but the simple fact that a cup of brewed tea is 99 percent water makes it far and away the most important contributor to the health of what you drink, as well as the flavor you will enjoy.

FACT

Long before the classic teapot, tea was brewed in a simple bowl, similar to a rice bowl. In ancient China, the bowl gradually evolved and became specialized for tea. The first addition was a lid to keep the tea warm that could also be used as a strainer, keeping the leaves from slipping into the mouth. Eventually, a third piece, a saucer, was added to secure the cup and to help prevent burning the fingers while holding the cup.

The techniques with which tea is brewed and the equipment—an elegant tea set, formal ceremonial tools, or a simple mug—creates ambience and may enhance the pleasure of the moment, but has very little to do with the nutritional value of the actual tea. However, in the long run, being able to create a bit of beauty and sharing pleasurable moments with friends and family can be very healing. Learning some of the tried and true techniques to healthy tea brewing will certainly expand the possibilities of what tea drinking can become.

Tea Balls and Tea Bags

Two early inventions changed tea drinking for westerners. One was the infuser called the tea ball or tea egg. The second was the disposable tea bag accidentally invented by Thomas Sullivan, an American tea importer. Both innovations kept tea leaves confined so that they could be neatly controlled.

Tea Balls

Silversmiths in the late 1800s enjoyed a great demand for fanciful, perforated balls with lids that could be filled with tea leaves, then suspended by a thin chain into a teapot or directly into a teacup. The beauty of these pieces makes them of interest to collectors today, though they are not as frequently used. One of the associated problems is that tea leaves expand as they rehydrate and crowd the tea balls, so that the tea does not infuse as well. A second issue is that the leaves are a little more difficult to clean out of the ball.

The Tea Bag

The tea bag came a bit later when American tea entrepreneur Thomas Sullivan sent samples of his teas sewed into small cloth bags as substitutes for more expensive metal tins. His customers did not understand Sullivan's intention and brewed the tea sample without opening the bag. They were delighted with the convenience of this new innovation and immediately ordered more of their tea in the handy little bags. Sullivan quickly found a way to produce more bags and is remembered today as the inventor of the tea bag. Tea bag designs continue to evolve, and it is the most popular way to brew tea today. And while most bagged tea is manufactured to brew a full-bodied cup without bitterness at almost any temperature, there are usually suggestions printed on the package.

ESSENTIAL

One controversial tea bag practice is "dunking." Agitating the tea bag up and down in hot water helps move the water through the leaf inside the bag, forcing it through the cut bits of leaf, fannings, and dust so that more flavor is drawn out and the tea leaves are less likely to clump together. However, it is unattractive, can be messy, and is considered to be very poor etiquette.

Cost of Convenience

The problem with both tea balls and tea bags is that, as the tea absorbs water, it expands and fills the bag or the ball, preventing water from flowing evenly through the leaves to extract the full flavor. To alleviate this problem, tea leaves are now cut into tiny pieces and blended with fine particles of tea called fannings and dust. There are not definitive studies on whether or not the chemical compounds in the leaf are reduced, but it is generally thought to be so. Even though tea bag designs have improved and most kinds of tea are sold this way, fine-quality teas are not likely to be used in their manufacture.

Beyond the Basics

Tea can be exorbitantly expensive and so complex that it prompts a lifetime of study. Some techniques for brewing fine tea involve several steps. In addition to the amount of tea, temperature of the water, and choice of cup, other "rules" for preparation (really just suggestions) can include the way in which the tea is placed in the brewing vessel, how the teapot is prepared, the way the water is poured over the tea, placement of the brewing tools, hand positions during the process, and many more. Attention to these details is not always restricted to ceremonies. For some tea lovers, it is a matter of style. Tea aficionados develop some of these disciplines in their personal style in order to precisely control and maximize the experience. One example would be brewing the leaves in a pre-warmed teapot versus a cold teapot in order to hold the water at a more even temperature. Also, swirling the water stirs the leaves in the pot so that the leaf surfaces are equally moistened. Hand position on the teapot or *gaiwan* (the Chinese lidded tea bowl) can be both a gesture of elegance and an efficient way to ensure that the tea is not spilled.

Water: 99 Percent of a Good Cup of Tea

Lu Yu, author of *The Classic of Tea*, considered water to be the mother of tea. Many tea masters teach about the marriage of leaf and water. There is probably not a single tea author or tea educator who fails to mention the importance of selecting quality water for brewing tea. Many quote Lu Yu's original teaching, that fresh spring water is the best. Most people don't have a source of fresh spring water, but you do have different sources from which to choose. Selecting favorite water is just like selecting a favorite tea. Whether it's filtered tap water or bottled water, there is no "best" choice except to satisfy individual tastes.

Donna Fellman and Lhasha Tizer tell one of the most unique stories about brewing tea with special water in their book, *Tea Here Now*. They describe a Vietnamese tradition in which lotus flowers are filled with tea leaves just before they close at sunset. The next morning, just before dawn, dew will be collected from the lotus leaves and used to brew the lotus-scented tea as soon as the flowers open.

FACT

The differences in water can be demonstrated by conducting a water tasting. Select several different water sources such as fresh tap water, two-day-old tap water, boiled tap water that has cooled, filtered tap water, and a few different brands of unflavored, bottled water. Pour the same amount in identical glasses. Compare the smell, appearance, and flavor. Have an assistant number the glasses and switch the order so that your tasting will be "blind." Then, using the same tea for each, brew a cup with each water and compare.

The Flavor of Water

Water that has a pleasing flavor and feel in the mouth is usually good for tea. Fresher water is also preferred because it has more oxygen in it, and for this reason many tea drinkers use filtered tap water. However, many municipal water districts add chemicals like fluoride and chlorine to their water supply in concentrations that some people can taste. The plumbing in older homes can add unpleasant flavors, even minerals and rust, to the water. Private wells draw minerals from the ground water. In most instances, a good filter can eliminate these issues, greatly improving the flavor of the water.

Bottled water offers an option to poor-quality tap water, but there are some cautions there as well. Some bottled water is highly mineralized while others can leave a slightly oily sensation in the mouth and may affect the flavor of tea. Other choices, like distilled water, can have a flat taste, which can also detract from a flavorful tea. Lastly, poor-quality plastic can also give bottled water an unpleasant taste.

Heating the Water

The most important "rule" about heating water is to heat it only once. Do not fill a kettle and then boil it multiple times. Heat only what is needed, and then refill with fresh water for additional infusions. In this way, the water will retain a fresh and bright flavor. Repeatedly boiling water does tend to reduce the amount of oxygen present in the water and "flatten" the flavor.

ESSENTIAL

When using whole-leaf tea, it is important for them to have room to float in the water so that the hot water touches each surface evenly. Getting to know how a tea will change as it is infused is helpful for choosing a vessel. Whole leaves should be able to float in the water with all surfaces exposed.

In his book, *The Classic of Tea*, tea sage Lu Yu described the various stages of boiling water: the first, tiny bubbles the size of shrimp eyes or crab eyes, then fish eyes, then the size of pearls, and ultimately the full rolling boil. Each stage has a unique sound. Almost without realizing it, people who consistently use a kettle recognize the rumble of their water gradually coming to a boil and reach for it just before hearing the whistle. Although this is not as accurate as a beverage thermometer, most tea drinkers instinctively gauge the temperature they want for their tea by the sound of the water approaching full boil. Gaining popularity, electric kettles make brewing tea even easier, even though they lack the romance of the old-fashioned whistling teakettle.

Tea Leaves

One of the delightful moments of using whole leaves over cut leaf is watching them unfurl and return to their original form. Some artisan teas that are bud-only, like Silver Needles, stand vertically when they are brewed. Activated by the hot water, they can look a bit like little dancers in the water. Other teas, like Jasmine Pearl, slowly unroll. Using a glass teapot allows the tea brewers and guests to watch, like peeking through a window, and enjoy the entire process.

Handling the Dry Leaf

It is important to use a clean teaspoon or scoop to transfer the leaves from the bag or from your caddy. Because they are extremely hygroscopic (which means that they love water) and readily absorb moisture, they also absorb aromas from the air as well as other surfaces with which they come in contact. Measuring the tea in the palm of your hand risks flavoring it with soap or perfume, or another kitchen aroma if you've been preparing food.

How Much Tea?

Most people measure their tea with a teaspoon or a tea scoop. But most often, recommendations offered by the retailers are written in grams. This is because there is such a large difference between the large, flat, and fluffy leaves like a White Peony as compared to a tightly rolled green Gunpowder tea. A teaspoonful of each of these kinds of leaves would be very different. There would not be enough of the fluffy leaf, and far too much of the tightly rolled one.

ESSENTIAL

Compare a brand name tea bag with the same loose-leaf tea. Using a small digital scale, set to measure grams, open a tea bag and weigh out the contents. Most tea bags contain 2–3 grams. Set this aside and weigh out an equal amount of the same kind of tea as whole leaf. Then compare the visual differences between the two. Then brew a cup of each and compare the aroma and flavor.

Fortunately, once you brew a new tea, the experience will guide the next cup: more or less tea, more or less brewing time. The more experienced you become with various whole-leaf teas, the more instinctive the brewing will become. The accuracy of weighing tea by the gram is essential to the professional tea taster, less so for the tea lover. Considerations like "how much tea" become part of the intimate relationship you develop with the leaf.

Multiple Infusions

There is an expression for brewing whole-leaf tea with the intention of creating multiple infusions that gradually rehydrate and restore the leaf: *the agony of the leaf.* With several brief infusions, the leaf gradually unfolds from its twisted or wrapped form and the flavors peel off in thin layers like those of an onion. The possible number of infusions may be as few as two or as many as seven, each one still offering an interesting cup. This is an important element of the gongfu tea service. But it is also a technique that some tea lovers use privately, brewing a batch of tea several times during a day, with a strong breakfast brew, moderate mid-day cup, and gentle evening tea.

Washing the Leaf

There is a step in brewing whole-leaf tea where the server "washes" the leaves with a quick rinse of warm water—about thirty seconds—and then discards that liquid. There are many interpretations for why this is done. One is that, being an agricultural product, the leaves are rinsed to remove any extraneous dust that may be present. Another reason is that during the time the tea has been shipped, repackaged, and then stored, some of the leaves were broken and the small bits are rinsed away. Another reason is that the surface of the leaf is thought not to offer the best flavor. A quick rinse opens the surface cells and reveals the sweeter flavors within. Try it and decide if this is a step you wish to incorporate into your own brewing practice.

Teapots

Teapots are made from many different materials, in a variety of sizes and shapes. Some of the smallest are designed for serving Chinese-style tea to a small group, and larger ones are generally used for serving Western-style tea to several people. Teapots of all sizes can be made from Yixing clay, fine porcelain, earthenware clay, silver, glass, stainless steel, and cast iron. Select a teapot based on the number of people to be served and your preferred method of brewing. In general, add only the amount of tea to the pot and only enough water so that, after steeping, there will be no water remaining on the leaves that might become bitter. Many teas, both loose leaves and tea bags, will brew a second flavorful pot. But you may have to allow a longer steeping time for the second infusion.

Teapots tend to develop a patina on the inside with frequent use. This discoloration troubles some, who prefer to wash it away to keep the inside of the teapot as spotless as the outside. Others take pride in the coloration or staining on the inside of the pot as it ages, and feel that it contributes a bit of flavor to each future use. With this in mind, some tea lovers reserve certain teapots for a particular kind of tea; for example, one for brewing green tea and another for brewing black tea.

Brewing Tips for Western- or British-Style Tea

The round-bellied teapot is usually associated with a "proper" British afternoon tea. Tea bags are often preferred to brew in teapots, because they can easily be removed as soon as the liquor reaches the desired strength, and cleanup is simplified. When putting whole-leaf tea directly into the pot, there are two methods for controlling the period of time that the leaves are steeped so they can be used for a second infusion: the one-pot method, and the two-pot method. With both methods the amount of tea is the same, usually one tea bag per person or one teaspoon (or adjusted amount for the tea) per person, plus one for the pot.

One-Pot Method

Tea is added to the teapot and just enough water is added for a first serving for all guests. The tea may be added as loose leaves, or can be contained in an infusion device such as a basket, tea ball, or tea bag. All the tea is served for the first infusion so that excess tea does not sit with the leaves, becoming bitter. Freshly boiled water for a second infusion is added when needed. Once again, only the amount of water that will be poured is added to the pot.

Two-Pot Method

A full pot of tea is brewed in one teapot, and then decanted into a second one for serving. The first teapot with the leaves can be set aside, and then brewed a second or third time. The advantage is that the full teapot can be kept on a votive candle warmer or electric warmer, and served over time without additional brewing.

Brewing Rules

It cannot be said often enough that a good cup of tea can only be determined by individual taste. There are guidelines, but there are no exact recipes or formulas to be followed that will satisfy all people or all tastes. Even the generalization that lighter teas are brewed with cooler water for less time can be limiting, and sometimes misleading. This brief overview of the tea categories should be considered a starting place, knowing that much of the richness of the tea experience is in experimentation.

Brewing Green Tea

Most green teas are sensitive to temperature and time, becoming bitter if infused with boiling water or if left in the water too long. Using water that is lower than the boiling point (180°F) works well for most green teas. Pour only the amount over the leaves that you will use immediately. Steep for one to two minutes for the first infusion, and possibly three to four minutes for a second.

Brewing Black Tea

Black teas can usually tolerate very hot water, almost to a full boil. In fact, many tea drinkers prefer the bold, bracing brew that comes from an aggressive infusion. But others like to peel away the layers of flavor of multiple infusions by beginning with a very light cup. Darjeeling teas are an example of black tea that may be better brewed with slightly cooler temperatures and less time.

By doing so, they are more likely to offer several good infusions. Most other black teas can also be steeped for longer times without astringency, for up to five minutes, though this reduces the number of times that the same leaves can be infused and still provide a pleasant cup.

Brewing Oolong Tea

Since oolong tea is more varied and complex as a category, there is not a standard practice for brewing. The range of low oxidation (green) to almost completely oxidized (black) leaves makes this impossible. Recommendations are to use techniques for brewing green and black teas relative to the type of oolong. For greener oolongs, use lower-temperature water, and for more fully oxidized leaf, use warmer water.

Brewing Pu'erh Tea

Like oolong tea, pu'erh is also a category with such enormous diversity that simple guidelines are of little value. The darkness of the brewed tea, the intensity of flavor, along with the mellowness provided by actual fermentation (rather than oxidation), mean that a short steeping will still be earthy and rich. On the other hand, some pu'erh teas can be steeped for more than ten minutes without bitterness. Brewing preferences will also vary between younger and more aged pu'erh. Because the flavor is so different from other teas, newcomers may want to visit a tearoom to sample or join an organized tasting before making their first purchase.

Brewing White Tea

Instructions for brewing white tea usually compare it with brewing green tea, recommending lower temperatures and a shorter steeping time. This results in pale liquor with a very subtle flavor. Using near boiling water and steeping for three minutes darkens the liquor and intensifies the flavor, releasing some of the definitive creaminess unique to white tea. The lack of astringency and bitterness allows this tea to be brewed many different ways.

One of the most important skills of a professional tea merchant is called "cupping." By infusing a tea under more stressful conditions, they detect nuances of flavor as well as possible imperfections in the tea. Using a larger amount of tea relative to the amount of water, then brewing it with boiling water for a longer period of time, the potential for bitterness, cloudiness, or other undesirable qualities quickly reveals itself.

Brewing Herbal Teas

When preparing bagged herbal teas and functional teas, it is highly recommended to follow the package directions. There are many herb blends where hot water and an extended steeping time are recommended to release the active ingredients. When using combinations of whole herbal products, it may be necessary to infuse some ingredients separately, such as boiling roots longer than steeping leaves, then combining the "teas" in the teapot or cup.

Brewing Flavored Tea

Tea leaves that have been flavored by adding food-grade oils have a tendency to lose flavor more rapidly than natural teas. For this reason, flavored teas do not usually produce very full-bodied second infusions, and may also have a shorter shelf life. Since black, green, and white teas are now available with added flavoring essences, the temperature at which it is brewed should be based on the basic category—boiling water for black tea but cooler temperatures for green and white.

Iced Tea

The story of iced tea first being served at the India Pavilion of the 1904 World's Fair in St. Louis is often interpreted as the origin of tea being poured over ice. Evidence to the contrary documents that iced tea was served in September of 1890 at a Civil War reenactment in Nevada, Missouri. Local newspapers reported that iced sweet tea had been served for the participants and described the cold tea as a luxury for hot southern summers.

Discussion on the difference between the two stories suggests that Richard Blechynden, the World's Fair tea merchant who was struggling to interest anyone in his tea, borrowed the suggestion to serve it cold and thereby popularized the innovative practice.

But even earlier, in the 1820s, cold tea punches were served in the South, blending tea with alcohol. A recipe in *The Kentucky Housewife*, a cookbook by Mrs. Lettice Bryanon published in 1839, combines a strong tea with a considerable amount of sugar, sweet cream, and claret that should be served cold.

FACT

> As a 2003 April Fool's Day spoof, Georgia State Representative John Noel and four fellow legislators sponsored a bill to the state House of Representatives to require that all restaurants serve sweet tea, and that "any person who violates this Code section shall be guilty of a misdemeanor of high and aggravated nature."

Brewing Iced Tea

Any tea can be brewed hot and then chilled and served over ice. But there are some teas that become cloudy when they are cold and look less appealing when served.

Some tips for brewing iced tea:

- Brew the tea at least twice as strong as you would for hot tea by using a higher ratio of tea to water to make it stronger. Do not steep it longer.
- Cool before pouring over ice, so that the tea does not become too diluted.
- Adding sweetener when the tea is still hot makes it dissolve more rapidly and evenly but assumes that everyone will want sweet tea.
- The best-dissolving sweetener for serving unsweetened iced tea to guests when it's already cold is a sugar syrup. This is thinner than honey or agave nectar and blends with the tea almost instantly.
- A pinch of baking soda (no more than ⅛ teaspoon per gallon) helps neutralize the tannins and reduces bitterness.

- Refrigerating tea can make it turn cloudy. Better to brew only what is needed for a day and then keep it at room temperature.
- Adding a sprig of mint or a lemon slice to the glass is both flavorful and decorative.

ESSENTIAL

One of the most attractive and festive ways to serve iced tea at a party is to loosely fill a tall glass with bite-sized pieces of frozen fruit that can be eaten, such as pineapple, seedless grapes, apple, strawberries, and blueberries, before adding the tea. Glasses can even be kept in the freezer prior to serving a party so that the glasses are frosty as the chilled tea is added. Even guests who prefer unsweetened tea usually enjoy the natural sweetness of fresh fruit.

Cold Brewing

Cold brewing is a technique that can be used with any kind of tea, and is the simplest and possibly the healthiest way to brew. Combine your choice of tea and water in a glass container, and refrigerate for eight or more hours before removing the tea. This method works especially well with green and light oolongs; flavors are smoother and sweeter. This does not risk the unhealthy bacteria that can grow in sun-brewed tea.

Taking cold brew a step further, new innovations of infusers suspend a vessel for ice over a small repository of tea, under which is the final pitcher to catch the brewed tea. As the ice melts, it soaks the tea, drop by drop. In very slow motion, the leaves are first saturated and then slowly give up their liquor. Each highly concentrated drop falls into the waiting pitcher. This is not a brew to be gulped, but to be savored with each sip. One tiny sip is an intense experience. This method is often used with Japanese teas like gyrokuro and sencha.

So Many Ways to Brew

Brewing innovations are being introduced to tea lovers every year. Many are designed for convenience. Others increase the elegance and delight in the tea experience. But they all seek to enhance the experience of the individual who wants to develop a personal taste for tea. The basics of brewing remain the same. Perhaps the one great secret to a fine cup is that there are no rules, only the invitation.

CHAPTER 15

Tea Brewing Tools

One of the most interesting things about the way we brew tea is that, even in these modern times, no matter how many time savers are invented, we never quite relinquish the old tried and true methods. There is a classic elegance and authenticity to the ancient methods and vessels. And, in some respects, brewing tea with them, taking the time to relax and enter into the moment, seems to brew the most healthful tea experience.

Almost Anything Will Do

Stepping into almost any tea shop can be surprising and slightly overwhelming to the uninitiated who are only familiar with western-style teapots and the well-known brands. The aroma of dozens of teas will fill the air. Walls are likely to be lined to the ceiling with canisters filled with dozens of flavors. And there are likely to be more "tea things" displayed than you ever imagined. Walls will probably be lined with shelves full of teapots, teacups, infusers, strainers, caddies, spoons, and other specialized paraphernalia. However, as extensive as the profusion of brewing equipment seems, even the simplest and most readily available things work just fine. A Mason jar or any heatproof glass tempered to withstand hot water can brew a very fine cup of tea. Other than being heatproof, the only additional necessity is that it be clean and free of aromas and oils. There is no need to purchase expensive accessories in order to enjoy beautiful and healthy teas. Almost everyone has the essentials in the kitchen cupboard. In fact, there are many people who prefer this simplicity, allowing the leaves to float in the water, unencumbered by restraints as they steep. The floating leaves are easier to pick out and snack on while they sip.

On the other hand, if you become more involved with tea don't be surprised if you begin to collect teaware and are tempted to practice many different ways to prepare and serve it. While the appeal of delicate teacups and interesting teapots does not change the flavor or the healthful qualities of the tea, the pleasure of serving guests with favorite teacups and fanciful pots can certainly enliven a quiet afternoon.

Which Way to Brew?

There is no single way to prepare any tea. There is no right or wrong. It's all about what tastes good to you and can be as simple or as complex as you wish. Preferences for brewing and serving become as unique to personal tastes as the selection of tea for the day. And in addition to tea being a healthy drink, the pleasure of preparing it can also contribute to our overall well-being and a personal ritual can even become an important part of the day. Having only one favorite tea or a single way to brew it is rare among frequent tea drinkers. In fact, different teas suggest completely different brewing methods and equipment. You may want to brew oolongs in a small glass teapot to watch the leaves open, or a pu'erh in a gaiwan to experience an association with ancient ancestors, or a flavored black tea in a six-cup ceramic teapot to serve a crowd. When rushed, however, a familiar tea bag flavor may be the one you reach for as you zoom out the door with your travel mug.

The Simplicity of Gaiwan Brewing

Most people assume that the tea bag is the easiest and most convenient way to make a cup of tea. But many who are familiar with gaiwans argue that it is just as easy and makes it possible to infuse the best possible flavor from the tea, and it is probably the most historic and still the most used piece of tea brewing equipment. In Mandarin Chinese, the word *gaiwan* literally means "lidded bowl."

It is a three-piece ceramic set with a bowl, saucer, and lid used for brewing an individual cup, but may also serve two to three people. The saucer design securely holds the bowl to keep it from tipping over, and also so that the individual drinking can grasp the cool saucer, tip the lid back, and sip from the lip of the bowl. The leaves float freely while steeping and can easily be infused several times. The lid is used to whirl the leaves in the water to make sure that the surface of every leaf is exposed to the water, but it is also used as a strainer, tipped slightly on the rim of the cup, holding the leaves back so that the tea can be sipped directly from the bowl. When serving others, the dry leaves can be displayed in the bowl before the water is added. After the tea is served, the wet leaves inside the bowl can be appreciated for color and aroma. In a well-crafted set, the lid can be tucked into the space between the base of the bowl and the saucer so that it will not have to be placed on the table.

As discussed in his *Classic of Tea*, Lu Yu explains that prior to the Ming Dynasty (C.E. 1368–1644), tea was prepared in simple bowls called *chawan* (*cha* meaning "tea" and *wan* meaning "bowl"). During the Ming Dynasty, the popularity of tea inspired the addition of the lid so the name changed to gaiwan, literally meaning "lidded bowl." Eventually, the third piece, the saucer, was added to protect fingers from the heat of the bowl, but also for hygiene, so the hand would not touch the bowl.

Heating Water

Since water comprises 99 percent of the contents in the cup, the benefits and flavors of the tea depend on the way the water is prepared. From a standard whistling kettle to some very elaborate commercial systems, being able to control the temperature of the water and having it at the ready are important considerations for brewing good tea.

A Simple Saucepan

Just as steeping the leaves can be very simple, there are also times when simple is best for heating the water. Using a saucepan on the stovetop allows for the preparer to observe the developing bubbles. The increasing size and activity of the bubbles in the water becomes the tea lover's thermometer. But they are also a vivid reminder that boiling water removes air and "flattens" the flavor that the water contributes to the tea. The adage "a watched pot is slow to boil" may have first been coined by an impatient tea lover! However, for those who want to increase their awareness of tea, making it a more focused, meditative practice, being able to watch the water reach its perfect temperature for the cup of tea may make the open saucepan a preferred choice.

Stovetop Kettle

The traditional western-style kettle with a spout, a handle, and even a whistle is usually made of a material that can sit above the flame or element on a stovetop. This style of kettle lives in the kitchen, is basically utilitarian, and almost never becomes part of a tea service. This style was inspired by Asian designs that were brought to the table. They are almost identical to a teapot, but used only to serve heated water. It is a spouted vessel that was traditionally heated over coals in a brazier. Today a ceramic water kettle might be used like a second teapot, but only for water. The water can be kept warm in the kettle, even over a votive candle heater, so that the tea in the teapot or the gaiwan can be infused again. Using a kettle in this way, the server does not have to leave the guests in order to brew more tea, and the service looks more elegant.

Electric Kettle

Electric water kettles sell at a range of prices that reflect their quality and options. There are some very simple options that start at around twenty dollars. More expensive brands and models offer additional features. The simplest kettle will usually heat water to the boiling point and automatically turn itself off, but will not maintain the water at the desired temperature. More advanced models can be set to shut off at specific temperatures, and some can maintain the water at an even temperature for constant serving. The convenience of having readily dispensable warm water is essential for busy tea shops. However, connoisseurs with a finely developed palate may prefer to heat small batches of water for each infusion.

ALERT

Even some rather expensive kettles may not be calibrated to an exact temperature. The settings may vary as much as ten degrees from the digital display. If water temperature is critical, it is always best to test it with a beverage thermometer.

Microwave

Many tea drinkers feel that microwaving water makes it taste flat, and some have concerns about using microwave ovens for personal health reasons. In general, however, there are two considerations when using a microwave to brew a good cup of tea. The first is that the water should be heated in the microwave prior to infusion. When the water is hot, then it should be poured over the tea to be brewed. The second is that odors lingering in the microwave from previous uses might flavor the water.

Assorted Tea Tools

Every year there are inventions to delight tea drinkers, from the newly curious to the old pros steeped in tradition. From tea bag users to loose-leaf aficionados, there is no end to creative gadgetry. Some are more decorative, and others are purely functional. The equipage can add to the tea experience in many ways, making it neater, faster, more whimsical, or more fun.

Tea Bag Squeezers

There are at least two different schools of thought about squeezing the last drops out of tea bags. One is that the tea bag should not be squeezed, so that the fine particles and dust that might make the tea cloudy are still trapped inside the bag. Contrast this with the other way of thinking, that it is important to glean every last drop from the tea. This second option is promoted through the instructions on some of the functional tea packaging, advising customers to maximize the beneficial ingredients. A totally different reason to squeeze the bag dry is for neatness, to avoid moving the dripping bag across a tablecloth or leaving a puddle in the saucer. Some tea bag squeezers look like tongs with flattened ends about the width of the tea bag. Others are made out of colorful, pliable plastic so that the bag can be slipped inside and pressed dry.

Tea Bag Holder

A tea bag holder is usually a small dish with a decorative or whimsical design, for the sole purpose of holding the used tea bag so that it does not drip on the table or look messy on the side of the saucer.

Strainers

Made of all sorts of materials from fine silver to hand-carved bamboo, strainers are designed to trap the leaves that escape through the spout when tea is brewed loose in a teapot without an infuser basket and then poured. Strainers are also used with the gaiwan, placed over a serving pitcher to catch stray leaves when the tea is decanted. Some strainers come as a two-piece set, where the perforated piece that sits across the rim of the cup can be rested in a matching cup or tray after its use, so that it does not drip or stain the tablecloth. Simple strainers can be just a mesh screen fitted into a ring with a handle to hold it securely over the cup or serving pitcher.

Wooden Tool Kits

A typical set of tea tools, sold in an attractive wooden container called a vase, holds five or six different pieces. It may include a funnel to neatly fill a teapot with dry leaf, a scoop used to dip into the tea caddy or bag, a needle to unblock a clogged spout, a digger to help pull spent leaf from inside the pot, a set of tongs to hold small teacups while bathing them with boiling water, and sometimes a matching strainer.

Pu'erh Tools

In addition to the standard set of tools, pu'erh tools include a wooden-bladed knife that can be used like a wedge to break the compressed cake into small pieces, a brush to sweep up the small bits and dust, and a tray over which the cake is broken apart. When these bits are collected in the tray or bowl, they are then swept with the brush into the brewing vessel, or back into the package or canister where the pu'erh is being stored.

Beverage Thermometer

This is an accessory that is a necessity for professional tea tasters, who must be precise with the water temperature, especially for "cupping," when they analyze the qualities of a tea. When comparing various teas for purchase, setting up precise comparisons is essential. Individual tea lovers who like to use these professional cupping techniques, or who like to brew their personal tea with precision, may also enjoy using a professional thermometer.

Digital Scale

A more accurate measure of tea leaves is by weight rather than by volume. A small digital scale is useful. As with water temperature, tea professionals needing to make exact comparisons of different teas must be able to control the variable of leaf quantity. A scale is also helpful for the home brewer to more accurately measure the tea instead of using a scoop or spoon.

Brewing the Tea

As important as the choice of water may be, the choice of vessel and attention to making the tea enhances all aspects of tea preparation. Well-brewed tea that tastes good inevitably offers more benefits to the whole body, including the experiences of relaxation and pleasure. Tea retailers and kitchen specialty shops usually offer a large assortment of accessories with which to brew tea. As simple as it might be to unite the leaves and the water in almost any clean vessel, there are many other options available.

Infusers

In the broadest sense of the term, an infuser is what contains the tea leaves while they are suspended in hot water, so a tea bag is also a simple infuser. Devices with mesh shaped to fit inside a teapot or mug are infusers. Perforated inserts of ceramic and stainless steel are also infusers. Tea-loving inventors continue to introduce new approaches to brewing a healthy cup of tea.

Tea Balls

Tea balls, also called "tea eggs," are small, perforated metal containers large enough to hold a teaspoon or two of dry tea. The container is suspended in the water by a chain so that it can be lifted out when the tea is strong enough. Some are as smooth and unadorned as an egg, but others are crafted with elaborate designs. The problem with most tea balls is that the leaves inside have inadequate space to expand. More finely cut leaves, like those for tea bags, will brew better than large, whole leaves.

Teaspoon Infusers

An adaptation of the tea ball is the perforated teaspoon. The curved bowl of the spoon is fitted with an operable lid so that the tea leaves can be held inside. The handle enables the tea drinker to use the device to infuse and stir at the same time. The same brewing problem as with the tea ball is associated with a teaspoon infuser, namely that the leaves are trapped in a space that does not allow for expansion. This is not an issue for a finely cut tea, similar to the tea that has already been cut for tea bags. But for teas like oolongs where the leaves will expand as they rehydrate, much of the flavor in the leaves will not be released.

Teapots with Infusers

Some infusers are custom-made to fit inside the teapot. They may be fashioned out of stainless steel mesh, or of the same ceramic material as the teapot, whether metal, glass, or clay. Good-quality teapot and infuser sets are designed so that the lid sits well on the rim of the teapot even after the infuser has been removed. One way to identify a lower-quality infuser teapot is if the lid does not fit snugly back into the rim of the teapot once the infuser has been removed.

Infuser Baskets

Stand-alone infusers similar to the infusers that are manufactured with the teapot also exist, most often made of stainless steel mesh. The shape may be cylindrical or conical, with a ring around the top that fits over the top of a mug or the lip of a teapot. The advantage to an infuser basket over a tea ball or tea bag is that the leaves float freely in the water during infusion. The best choice for an infuser basket is one that extends deeply down into the water of the teapot or mug. Some of the nicest infuser baskets come as a two- or three-piece set with the infuser's own snap-on lid and small tray. Dry leaves can be measured into it and taken with you to the office or out to dinner. After infusing, the basket sits neatly into the overturned lid, the lid serving as a saucer to contain any drips.

Infuser Mugs

Like the ceramic infusers made to fit inside teapots, there are comparable designs for mugs. These are three-piece sets that come with a mug, infuser, and lid. A very nice feature of these tea mugs is a lid designed so that it can be inverted to hold the infuser after the tea is brewed. Because the holes in the ceramic infuser tend to be a bit large, finely cut or broken bits of tea can slip through the holes. The infuser mugs work better for tea that is either whole leaf or in larger pieces.

Infuser Pitcher

Like an infuser teapot and infuser mug, the same concept is now available in tall glass and plastic pitchers. A mesh basket reaches at least halfway into the water, allowing the change of color in the brewing tea to be visible. The infuser basket can be removed as soon as the tea reaches the desired strength. These work well for attractively brewing and serving iced tea. but they are also very nice for brewing some of the more colorful tea blends that contain herbals, like hibiscus leaves, that add a vibrant red hue to the tea.

Infuser Baskets with Quick-Release Plungers

A newer innovation allows the infuser to sit on top of the cup or serving pitcher. A plastic basket holds the leaves and the amount of water appropriate to the container. Water is added to the cup and the lid closed. The leaves float freely in the water while brewing. When the tea is ready, a plunger can be depressed, releasing the tea into the cup or pot below. Another version of this technology is that the brewing container is not placed over the cup until the tea is ready, and the pressure from the lip of the cup releases the tea.

French Press

The French press is a rather narrow, straight-sided cylinder, usually made of glass or plastic. Tea leaves are placed into the bottom of the cylinder and then hot water is added. The lid into which the press is fitted is then placed over the opening while the tea brews. When it reaches the desired steeping strength, the plunger is pushed down. The attached tightly fitted screen or perforated plate presses the tea down into the bottom of the cylinder, effectively keeping the leaves separated from the water, stopping the infusion. The tea can be served directly from the carafe of the French press. Even though it was originally designed to brew coffee, it is very popular with loose-leaf tea drinkers. It is recommended that a press used for coffee should not be used for brewing tea.

Teapots

The image of the teapot is probably the most universal symbol for tea. Cultures around the globe have variations on the basic form and brewing techniques, but the basic anatomy of a teapot varies only slightly. Teapots are made with several materials, including various kinds of fired clay, silver, glass, stainless steel, cast iron, copper, and plastic. The parts of the teapot are:

- Belly—the brewing chamber of the tea.
- Spout—the mouth of the pot, which should be angled so that it does not drip.
- Handle—the way the teapot is grasped, oftentimes fitted with a thumb-hold to facilitate pouring. The handle should be designed so that the fingers can fit through it without touching the warm exterior of the belly of the pot.
- Lid—fits snugly into the belly so that it doesn't slip out when pouring. Somewhere in the lid, there should be a vent.
- Knob—sits on top of the lid and can be gripped to lift the lid out of the pot.
- Base—a foot that rests on the surface of the table.
- Strainer—set of holes in the side of the belly where the spout attaches, to prevent large pieces of leaf from clogging the spout. Not all teapots have a strainer fitted inside the pot.

ESSENTIAL

The teapot, as an object of art, is a combination of form and function. Ceramic artists for thousands of years have strived to create a perfect balance between the two. And, to the other extreme, sculptors with no concern for preparing tea often take their work to an expressive extreme without concern for functionality.

Yixing

Some of the most prized teaware for serious drinkers is made from a specific kind of clay found in the region of China near the city of Yixing in Jiangsu Province. The clay, also called purple sand clay, was first mined during the Song Dynasty (C.E. 960–1279). It was treasured for the unique colors, fine-grained smoothness, and the lack of potentially dangerous lead. Teapots made from Yixing clay are high-fired so that the clay vitrifies (becomes watertight). In this way, it does not require the application of a glaze. This leaves a matte surface that absorbs trace elements from the tea and builds a patina over time, coating the interior of the pot. For this reason, tea lovers usually reserve each teapot for a single kind of tea. One might be for pu'erh and another for oolong, the tea lover carefully developing the patina of the interior over many years of use with that particular tea.

True Yixing teapots are wonderful gifts for tea lovers. The abundance of colors and designs are attractive to teaware collectors. They can be very expensive; a good-quality pot for regular use is likely to start at around fifty dollars, but rare antique pieces can sell at auction for millions. The most expensive teapot in the world (as of 2010) was a Yixing teapot that sold at a Beijing auction for the equivalent of $2,000,000 USD. One of the living Yixing masters, Gu Jingzhou, made the pot in 1948. Prices for rare teaware by master ceramists are expected to continue to increase.

ALERT

Because they are so highly prized, there is the tendency for fraud with Yixing ware. They have also become attractive to imitators, who use lower-quality stained clay and lack the expert craftsmanship. It is important to study a bit about this lovely teaware and locate a knowledgeable and trustworthy retailer to start your collection.

It is recommended that most fine teaware **not** be washed with soap. This is particularly important for anything made of Yixing clay that has an unglazed, matte surface. Just as it absorbs the flavors and trace elements of the tea, it also retains the scent of soap and absorbs some of the oils. Washing with soap also disturbs the flavored patina that tea lovers purposefully allow to build up inside the pot. Yixing teaware should only be cleaned with boiling water. Similarly, the leaves should not sit in the teapot after they are spent. Use smooth, wooden tea tools to gently pull the large leaves out of the pot, then rinse the small bits out with water. Use boiling water for a final rinse, inside and out, including the lid. Leave the pot open and the lid overturned until they both dry completely before storing.

Fine Porcelains

Porcelain is a fine grade of clay that is generally white. Porcelain teaware is usually glazed to seal the surface from being discolored by the brewed tea. The most distinctive characteristic of porcelain is that it can be crafted with such thin walls that the piece is translucent. Fine porcelain is sometimes valued because of this translucency, almost as thin as glass. One of the popular glazes for porcelain is a light green celadon glaze.

Serving Tea

For countries with strong tea traditions, much about the culture is shared in the way it is prepared and served. It is an almost universal expression of hospitality and respect, sometimes welcoming a guest into a home but also setting a tone for an important business meeting. In some countries, formal tea service is an important part of the wedding ceremony and for others a casual tea time is an essential daily family gathering. Not only the tea that is served, but also the teaware used as well as the focus of attention and the artistic skill involved in creating the experience. Ancient traditions coupled with recent innovations inspire the way it is both brewed and served. There is often great meaning in the way tea is served, and many specialized tools have been created to enhance the art of tea.

Tea Caddy

When tea drinking first became popular in England and was an essential in every home of distinction, it was exorbitantly expensive. Special care was taken with storage in order to preserve the freshness and flavor of the tea, but also to discourage pilfering of something so valuable. There were two kinds of tea caddies: canisters and boxes.

Small, lidded boxes would be kept under lock and key by the lady of the house, sometimes in the lady's private chambers, and would then be presented at teatime. Originally made of wood, silver, or brass, they quickly became an important accessory in tea service. Larger boxes with several interior compartments were called tea chests. These were lined as best as possible to keep flavors from cross-contaminating each other. Some of the original tea caddies were ceramic, similar to ginger jars with tightly fitted lids. These are still used today as tea canisters, and are especially effective because they block light and seal out air and moisture.

Teacups

Teacups, like other teaware and tools, arrived in Europe with the early imports of tea. The original Chinese designs were small and simple without a handle, holding just enough for about three sips of tea (about one to two ounces). This is still a standard cup for Chinese tea, especially for the gongfu tea ceremony.

The cup size gradually increased and Europeans added the handle, probably inspired by the posset cups for hot milk and wine or ale, some of which were double-handled, one on each side. The single-handled cup served with a matching saucer became popular to secure the hot cup, somewhat similar to the saucer in a gaiwan set.

Other vessels especially for drinking tea are:

- Russian tea glasses, called *podstakannik*, are removeable straight-sided glass cylinders set into metal bases with handles.
- A *yunomi* is a Japanese teacup with a cylindrical shape without a handle. They are usually ceramic and beautifully decorated, often crafted by fine artists.
- Turkish tea is often served in glasses rather than ceramic cups or mugs, to show the difference between strong and weak tea.

FACT

Teaspoons evolved during England's Georgian period (c.e. 1714–1830). Smaller demitasse-sized spoons had previously been available, but were rare. The new larger size was more appropriate for measuring the scoop of dry tea per person into the pot, and for stirring milk and sugar into the cup.

Tea Strainers

Tea strainers (also included in the discussion on brewing tea) are relatively simple tools for serving loose-leaf teas when there is not an infuser in the teapot to catch the leaves. When a strainer is used as part of serving tea, it tends to be a bit more attractive than a simple mesh screen, adding to the interest and elegance of sharing teatime. Some are elegant silver pieces with handles that can rest on the rim of a teacup, while others are efficient stainless steel. One relatively inexpensive style, available in many tea shops, is a small gourd cut in half lengthwise and fitted with a bit of screen in the bottom of the larger section. Interesting and artistic tea strainers have also become collectible tea items.

FACT

One of the earliest strainers was found as part of a vessel discovered in Palestine dating back to 1300 b.c.e. A cluster of seven holes had been punctured in the side of a container made of earthenware clay, where a spout had been attached. The purpose for the strainer of that piece is unknown.

Ceremonial Equipment

Two of the most famous tea ceremonies are the Chinese gongfu tea ceremony, and the Japanese chanoyu, or the Way of Tea. Of course, there are many more traditions, but these two are examples of complex and elegant preparations based on rigorous historic traditions.

Gongfu

There are almost thirty different steps to the formal Chinese tea ceremony. It begins by respectfully welcoming guests, which may include lighting incense, providing food and entertainment, and carefully showing the guests every step of the brewing process, beginning with the dry tea. Particular focus is on the leaf. In addition to the gongfu teapot and small Chinese-style tasting cups, there is usually a large bowl in which the teapot can be "bathed" with hot water, or even a special gongfu table with perforations or slats so that the water drains into a chamber or tray hidden below.

Chanoyu

The formal Japanese tea ceremony is one of the most unusual, as compared to Western-style tea. Using a powdered tea, such as a finely ground matcha green tea, the event has very little to do with the plant or the leaf (unlike the Chinese gongfu ceremony). For chanoyu, even the welcoming walk through the garden and the lowered entrance to a teahouse used only for tea service, are integral parts of the complete experience. The ceremony may be conducted in venues other than a full teahouse, but there is an effort made to create the sense of elegance and meditation. A simplified tea service of matcha tea in the Japanese style can be prepared using the same tools, without the lengthy ceremony.

The main utensils for serving tea chanoyu-style are:

- Chawan—a shallow tea bowl in which the powdered tea is frothed and then served.
- Chasen—a bamboo whisk used to whip the tea.
- Chashaku—a long tool carved from bamboo or other wood, with a curved end that scoops a small amount of tea into the chawan.
- Natsume—a small container with a tightly fitting lid for the matcha.
- Chakin—a cloth used to wipe the tea bowl.

Automatic Systems

Bringing tea into the fast-paced modern world, recent innovations in automatic tea brewing are making their way into workplace break rooms as well as the kitchens of those who need their infusion to be ready in just a few seconds with very little mess.

Single-Cup, Automatic Brewing Systems

Systems that heat water and then force it through the dry beverage material (coffee, tea, cocoa) are becoming widely available in the marketplace. Some brands seal a pre-measured amount of the product into a disposable plastic cup. The system then punctures the sealed lid and injects hot water into it for steeping. When finished, the brewed beverage is dispensed into the cup waiting below. Some systems offer fill-yourself containers that are not disposable but can be washed out and used repeatedly.

Automatic Iced Tea Systems

There are systems for making iced tea that use both tea bags and loose tea. The automatic shutoff feature works well for large groups, especially when freshly brewed tea needs to be supplied throughout the day.

Tea to Go

Even though tea generates an aura of relaxation, meditation, and social and family gatherings, in this modern and fast-paced world, people still like to carry their tea with them. In Asia, double-walled thermos bottles are seen everywhere. Everyone carries their individual bottle filled with leaves, to which they can add water throughout the day. And of course there is the ultimate convenience of tea bags that can easily be carried with you and brewed almost anywhere. One handy invention is called a tea wallet, usually made of an attractive fabric, that will hold two or three tea bags and fit comfortably in a purse or pocket.

Double-Walled, Insulated Tea Bottles with a Filter Screen

Using a more casual style of tea brewing, the glass or food-safe plastic bottles that can be carried for all-day tea actually infuse the tea loose in the water, similar to drinking from a glass or gaiwan. One tip is to use less tea, so that it is always a milder flavor and not inclined to bitterness. There are the double-walled bottles that have only a screw-on lid, others that have an additional filter screen attached to the top of the bottle to strain the leaves when drinking, and still others with many different ways to separate the leaves and water.

Disposable Tea Filters and Bags

Various sizes of filter paper sacks are sold, so that you can make your own tea bags with either a favorite loose-leaf tea or your own tea blends. The largest is adequate for brewing tea for a crowd while the smallest is designed for single cups.

Caring for Tea Equipment

In general, teaware is not cleaned with soap or detergent, preventing any additional and unwanted flavors and oils from being added to the flavor of your next batch of tea. Some people use baking soda to scrub the stain from inside the pot and make it look shiny and new again. Boiling water is usually used to clean tea equipment immediately after use; then it is allowed to dry completely before the piece is stored. Leaving the lid open on a teapot will help the interior dry. Vigorous rubbing with a cloth towel also helps shine the surface.

Another variation on cleaning teaware without soap is to run it through a dishwasher on a regular or delicate cycle without adding detergent. The heat of the water and the heated drying are usually adequate to sanitize the teaware and tools.

CHAPTER 16

Tea Storage

Most tea has a shelf life, during which time it is the healthiest and most flavorful. Even though it doesn't deteriorate like fresh produce, the flavors and aromas diminish and the health benefits are reduced. Knowing how to shop for quality products and then how to store them is important. There are "aged" teas that increase in value over time, but this is a very limited category of high-end teas that require an even more controlled environment than other teas.

Shelf Life: Tea's Life Span

The life of a tea product begins as soon as it is harvested, processed, and prepared for shipment from the country of origin. Care must be taken that the leaves remain dry and cool, and that they are wrapped in airtight containers to retain freshness and to keep the leaves isolated so they will not be contaminated by unwanted aromas. Carefully controlling how the leaves are handled from the field to the final destination is essential. Consumers seldom know how much time has elapsed since the tea left the field, but they can still make some very informed decisions about buying quality teas and then properly storing them. This will most certainly brew the best possible cup.

ESSENTIAL

When Thomas Lipton bought tea plantations in Ceylon (now Sri Lanka), his advertising stressed the company's control from the plantation to the store. This gave customers a sense of confidence that his brand would be the freshest tea possible, and that his company would provide consistent quality. These issues continue to be concerns for tea lovers today.

Enemies of Tea

The enemies of tea are air, heat, light, moisture, and other foreign aromas. Buying a tea that has been packaged well and then selecting a good location in your home in which to store it are important parts of brewing a healthy cup. In some cases, the packaging for the tea is more than adequate to seal in flavor and freshness. Other teas with less protective packaging may need to be stored in an airtight, opaque container. By securing the freshness and the viability of the powerful antioxidants, like the catechin epigallocatechin gallate (EGCG), along with the other nutritional components, the tea is healthier. For anyone making tea part of a health regimen, freshness and storage are as important as they are for a connoisseur preserving the delicate flavor profile.

Blocking Air

When individual tea bags are stored in foil or other high-quality overwrap, they are also airtight. Retailers selling loose-leaf tea are usually careful to select packaging that also serves as good storage at home. One good option is a thick, food-grade pouch that can be resealed. An additional way to keep air from degrading loose-leaf tea is to vacuum seal the container. Some retailers go the extra mile and vacuum seal airtight, food-grade pouches of their teas. This is particularly valuable if the tea will be stored, without being opened, for a longer period of time.

Once the tea is opened at home, it is important to close the tea after using it, and to force the air out of the bag as much as possible before resealing it. Storing the package in a cupboard also reduces drafts. If the tea is removed from the original packaging, it is important to store it in an airtight container with a tightly fitting lid.

Blocking Moisture

Most good airtight containers are also good moisture barriers. However, if the tea bags or loose tea comes in a paper canister or simple paper wrapper, give them a secondary layer of protection if they are to be stored for some time. In dry climates, this is, of course, less of a problem. But in humid coastal locations, it is more important.

Blocking Aromas

If the container is airtight and moisture-proof, the tea is probably protected from imposing, unwanted scents. Even with good containers, however, it is wise to keep tea stored separately from other foods or highly aromatic substances, such as onions or spices.

Blocking Light

One of the biggest mistakes that tea lovers make is storing loose tea in an attractive, clear glass jar to display the beauty of the whole leaves. Ultraviolet (UV) light quickly bleaches the color from the leaves and breaks down their chemical components. There are opaque glass containers that will serve better to preserve the life of the tea, and even well-sealed opaque glass canisters should be stored carefully. Tea bags individually sealed in colorful foil packets can make attractive displays and, if kept cool in the clear glass jar—not in direct sunlight or near a heat source—can be an effective way to keep your tea readily available.

Keeping Cool

It is important to keep your tea cool. Some of the warmest places in the home are the cabinets above the kitchen stove and refrigerator. As convenient as these cabinets may be, they are less than ideal for your tea. Another location too warm for tea storage is near a window that receives direct sunlight. And, rather obviously, proximity to the normal heat sources for a home is also a poor choice for storing tea.

Tea Bags and Sachets

Tea bags are also called sachets, and are usually sealed in individual envelopes. The wrappers, also called overwrap, can also be very effective storage containers, adding to the shelf life of the tea. The most protective overwrap for tea bags is foil, which blocks all the enemies of tea except heat. The tea inside remains fresh and is less likely to absorb other aromas than with other kinds of wrappers. The least protective is paper, which offers very little protection. Clear plastic or cellophane overwrap is also less effective than foil. Tea bags that are not well wrapped should be stored separately, in airtight containers.

Storage Differences for Various Types of Tea

While proper storage extends the shelf life of all teas, there is usually thought to be some differences in storage techniques recommended for the various tea categories. Most aficionados find that green tea degrades more quickly, and that black tea remains vibrant the longest. Oolong and white teas fall somewhere in between. But there are definitely certain teas that require more careful handling.

Flavored Teas

The flavoring concentrates added to tea can be very fugitive, and dissipate quickly once the tea is opened. Another issue with flavored teas is that they tend to generously share their fragrances with other teas stored nearby. For these reasons, they should be well sealed and stored separately from other teas. If all your flavored teas are stored in one area without compartmentalizing them to isolate the pungent aromas, you may find that all your teas take on a bit of the essence of the most dominant flavored tea.

Matcha

Matcha is especially vulnerable to moisture, absorbing it quickly and then clumping. But it is also vulnerable to all the elements. For this reason, matcha should be carefully stored and the container only opened long enough to take out what is needed, then quickly sealed again as tightly as possible.

QUESTION

Does tea actually become stale?
The answer is both *yes* and *no*. Most tea, when stored properly, retains freshness for about two years. Some teas last longer, and others actually improve with age. Improperly stored tea can lose flavor, become contaminated by absorbing unwanted odors, or deteriorate if exposed to moisture. You might experience the difference as the brewed tea having a slightly flatter taste with less of the original briskness and dynamics.

Tea Absorbency

The same mechanisms that make tea easy to scent and flavor also make it subject to contamination. Tea quickly absorbs moisture from the environment, similar to the way that sugar and salt form clumps. This tendency is referred to as *hygroscopy*. Tea is one of many hygroscopic (very absorbent) substances. While it is one of tea's creative abilities, allowing it to be scented and flavored, it is also a vulnerability.

Scenting

The hygroscopic nature of tea means that any aromatic substance in proximity while the tea is in dry form will, most likely, be absorbed. This is why pan-fried teas, like the famous green tea Dragon Well, have a slight flavor of pine smoke, and why the more intensely smoked black tea Lapsang Souchong can be crafted by storing it in baskets above aromatic wood fires. In the same way, tea stored with fresh jasmine flowers draws the delicate aroma of the flowers into the tea leaves.

ESSENTIAL

Scenting your tea is one way to revitalize it. If you have a tea that was lost in the back of the cupboard and it brews a lackluster cup, try closing it in a jar with a bit of fresh citrus peel, like orange or lemon, for a few hours. Another pleasant scent, and a staple in most kitchens, is vanilla extract. Add drops of the extract to an empty jar, and then add the dry tea leaves or tea bags. Shake vigorously to make sure the scent is evenly dispersed.

Twenty-Five Tips to Keep Tea Fresh

- Buy loose-leaf tea in small amounts (between one and four ounces) that will be used quickly.
- If you do buy tea in larger quantities—even tea bags—for a better value, separate what will be used within a short time to put into a container that you can open and close daily, and store the bulk of it more securely.
- Do not store tea near the oven or in a cupboard over the stovetop.
- Do not store tea on top of the refrigerator or freezer, or in the cupboard above them.
- Do not store tea in poor-quality plastic bags that might have a chemical odor.
- Storage containers should be opaque, preferably of stainless steel or tin.
- If you store tea in glass canisters, then keep them inside a cupboard or an area away from light.
- Do not store flavored teas near other teas.

- Store especially smoky teas like Lapsang Souchong away from all other teas, and make sure they are in an airtight container.
- Close containers quickly after selecting your tea.
- Do not fluff or shake loose tea leaves. This will actually disperse air throughout the leaves and cause them to degrade faster.
- Gently scoop loose leaves from the surface. Leave the remaining tea packed down inside the container.
- Be careful not to scoop with a wet spoon or scoop that might leave water or aroma behind.
- If you have to choose between pretty and functional storage solutions, go for functional. A small amount of tea can be displayed to guests in a smaller, pretty container.
- Double up when possible. Leave tea in its original package, then put that package into an airtight canister.
- If you want to invest in a larger amount of a limited tea (such as a new harvest tea), request that your retailer package loose tea in smaller batches that will not be opened until needed.
- Be sure the storage container is dry and free of odor before adding tea.
- Open the containers for tea as little as possible.
- If your brand-name tea is packaged in paper with less secure over-wrap packaging for each bag, store it in a larger sealed storage container to keep the tea fresh and flavorful.
- Plastic can give off aromas that affect tea, and many plastic containers are not airtight.
- Don't reach into a canister of loose-leaf tea with your hands. Natural skin oils can have aromas, and even the soap last used can impart a subtle smell to the tea.
- Save good, food-grade zip-top bags that were previously packaging for tea. When reordering the same flavor, they can be used to decant a small amount for daily use so the main bag is not opened as frequently.
- Unless tea bags are individually sealed in a more secure foil over-wrap, they will "share" flavors. It is best to store each flavor separately, even if you intend to serve them in a small basket or bowl as a selection to guests.

- A food vacuum-seal device can be used to seal tea for longer storage. Take out what you will use and then reseal the rest. This is more important in humid climates.
- Spice jars hold enough loose-leaf for several infusions. Buying ones that have never been used is recommended for fine tea. However, repurposing recently emptied ones can be an interesting experiment in flavoring your own tea.

Recommended Containers

Consider whether or not you are storing tea for short-term versus long-term or infrequent use. This will help determine the size and type of container you require. Most tea drinkers have teas that they use almost daily, with others held back for a special moment. Some attractive caddies or canisters can be kept close at hand, with just a few tea bags or a few infusions of loose leaves inside. The larger amounts of tea can be preserved in airtight containers in the cupboard, only opened to restock the more convenient caddy. If your tea is already packaged in a substantial bag, it is usually best to store it inside a larger container rather than decant it. Then, if you want to show the dry leaf to your guest, scoop the amount needed into a small condiment dish (white is best) or a small tea caddy.

Stainless Steel Canisters

Many retailers use large, stainless steel canisters to both store and display their tea. One beautiful and very traditional tearoom display is to line a wall behind the counter with shelves of these shiny canisters. The lid can be lifted from the top and handed to a customer to sample the fragrance of the tea without contaminating the contents. Sometimes the entire canister is brought down for the customer and the lid is waved over the top to waft the aroma into the air. Canisters like these come in many sizes, even small enough for home use.

Double-Lidded Stainless Steel Canisters

The best canisters for tea storage, though a bit more expensive, are double-lidded stainless steel canisters. These have a tight-fitting inner lid that slips snugly into the lip of the canister, with a second covering lid that is not quite as tight but still adds a layer of insulation against the elements. These also come in many different sizes.

Tea Tins

Some tea companies package both tea bags and loose-leaf tea in decorative tins. These tins are attractive and colorful, usually bearing the company logo and brewing information. The tea inside may be sealed in an inner pouch. Home tea cupboards are usually stacked with a selection. These have become collectibles and, in some cases, antiques.

Zip-Top Pouches

Resealable zip-top pouches are one of the most affordable containers in which retailers can pack and ship tea, but they are also good storage at home. Food-grade bags come in various densities and materials. After the tea is inserted, the air can be pressed out and the zipper closed, then the top edges heat-sealed for security. Even after the bag is opened and some of the tea used, the consumer can force extra air out of the bag and re-zip the seal to keep the tea fresh longer. Some even more effective products are now laminated with a layer of aluminum that is airtight and moisture-proof, using high-quality, food-grade polyesters (such as polyethylene terephthalate, or PET) to form an almost impervious barrier.

Wooden Tea Chests

Beautiful display chests make lovely gift items, and are sometimes sold with a collection of teas filling the compartments. Many of them, however, are not airtight. This is not a concern for foil-wrapped tea bags that can be nestled snugly into separate compartments, or for loose teas that are stored in airtight canisters within the chest. However, if the tea itself is not separately sealed, it is unlikely to stay fresh in a simple wooden chest, especially if it is a loose-leaf tea.

A Tea Cupboard

What begins as a single box of tea bags on the kitchen shelf next to the coffee and cocoa packets can quickly multiply and demand even more space. Packages of beguiling tea flavors can quickly fill an entire shelf. Then there are the collections of teapots, teacups, and infusion baskets that can grow to fill an entire cupboard. And, of course, there are the ongoing concerns about light, heat, air, and moisture. Some tea enthusiasts opt for a stand-alone cupboard that is completely removed from the kitchen.

ALERT

Warning! The tea habit can be so enticing that very devoted tea lovers dedicate an entire room to their collections, and consider it a place of escape for a private sip or a meditation moment. Cupboards separating various teas, shelves displaying teapots, books that wax poetic, and art that complements the experience can, when brought together, make a very pleasant space.

Cold Storage versus Room Temperature

A great debate continues about whether or not to refrigerate tea to extend its shelf life. At this time, the decision is a personal one and should be tested with lesser-quality teas before using more expensive, high-end tea.

Do Refrigerate

Some tea lovers feel that refrigeration actually improves the taste of the tea and makes it last longer. Two guidelines are important. First, if tea is stored in refrigeration it should be always kept refrigerated, not warmed and then chilled again. Consistency is critical. Repeated changes in temperature degrade the tea even faster. Second, tea should not be stored in a refrigerator with other foods that have strong odors.

Don't Refrigerate

The argument against refrigeration is that condensation tends to form inside the container. Even very high-quality teas are not completely dry. There may still be a small percentage of moisture in the leaf. Also, as soon as the container is opened, the hygroscopic nature of tea will draw additional moisture from the air. This is what will trigger condensation, additional oxidation, and the deterioration of the tea.

Aging Tea

A ten-year-old box of tea bags, forgotten in the back of the kitchen cupboard, tucked in behind the rice and cereal boxes, is not the same as an aged tea. It's just old! It might not be moldy and could still brew an acceptable cup of tea, or it could be used for other purposes (see Chapter 18), but it is not even remotely what one might consider "good."

Intentionally aged teas, usually pu'erh and some oolong teas, on the other hand, have enjoyed watchful care by an experienced tea aficionado or tea master. The craft of finely aging tea requires not only an understanding of how the elements will change the flavor and nature of the tea, and the patience to control every detail, but also an informed vision of the potential for the leaf. Not every tea will age well. A tea lover who is interested in aging tea must first be able to recognize the potential in a newly harvested tea, and then be willing to monitor it throughout its development.

Containers for Aged Teas

When purchasing aged teas, it will probably be recommended that they *not* be stored in airtight containers. These teas are still developing their mature flavors and need some amount of air and moisture, but must still be protected from other environmental changes, accumulations of dust, or invasion by insects. Large ceramic urns of unglazed earthenware clay with loose-fitting lids are frequently used for aging tea. Pu'erh tea is often wrapped in thick, acid-free tissue paper and stored in a presentation box. While there are less expensive paper options, traditional Chinese presentation boxes are lidded, covered with silk brocade on the outside, and lined with either silk or satin inside.

CHAPTER 17

Healthy Tea Traditions

Our personal and cultural traditions are our anchors. They connect us to ancestors no longer present, as well as family and friends with whom we still gather around the table. One benefit of studying tea history and international traditions is recognizing similarities and how these traditions actually stitch the world together. The essence of tea in every culture is peace and hospitality. With this realization, a cup of tea provides benefits that science cannot measure.

The Healthy Habit of Teatime

One of the healthiest things about teatime is how it makes you feel and how it can transform stressful situations with a bit of calm. Many of the medical studies conducted on populations where drinking tea is traditional show that the daily habit produces the most significant results. Humans are creatures of habit, and consistent tea drinking may not only provide some antioxidant protection but also a meaningful tradition and rhythm to enhance a healthy lifestyle.

Something as simple as relaxing with a cup of tea is one way to deal with difficult moments, but doing so regularly enough that it becomes habitual is proving to be highly beneficial. Usually healthier than drinking alcohol or taking a pill to relax, even the preparation of the tea can be soothing. Just sipping it from a favorite cup or mug may bring calm and comfort. Brewing it in a family heirloom teapot, handed down through generations, reminds you that there are people who care for you. Sharing a teatime habit with family and friends is one way to enhance communication and strengthen the bonds of support and trust.

De-Stress with Tea

For her January 2014 issue of *O Magazine*'s "From Oprah's Kitchen" column, Oprah Winfrey talked about "Oprah's Foolproof Stress Cure." Of course, her "cure" is tea. She describes in detail how she learned to make tea while visiting a family in India, and then brought the tradition home to the people in her own daily life. She concludes her column by saying, "It feels like an honor to share a cup of tea with other people. It feels like an act of grace."

Chronic stress causes, or negatively contributes, to almost every illness or disease. Developing techniques to deal with normal daily stressors and also with more challenging situations is an important life skill. When you can manage the feeling of being stretched too thin, then you discover the depth of your inner strength and external stressors are less likely to take the same degree of physical toll on your body. An ancient Chinese proverb says "A true warrior, like tea, shows his strength in hot water." Eleanor Roosevelt adapted the adage by saying, "A woman is like a tea bag; you never know how strong she is until she's in hot water."

A Personal Tea Practice

In the same way that airline staff prepares passengers for takeoff by reminding adults to put on their own oxygen masks before taking care of their children, you need ways to deal with your own tension and discomfort before you can help others. You cannot as effectively do what you want for others until you manage your own fears and stress. Everyone needs to develop a meaningful, personal program to maintain good health and a positive attitude. Along with exercise, good nutrition, satisfying work, and positive relationships, you can benefit from being able to relax and reduce daily pressures—such as stopping for a tea break. There should be moments in the day when you can recharge your batteries and rekindle a flagging spirit.

A personal tea practice might be a way to begin the day by taking a few minutes to focus on more careful and ritualized tea preparations. It can gradually enliven the senses and gently bring you to that place of alert readiness, prepared for the rest of the day. The ritual might involve a special tea, teapot, or teacup that, as the daily practice continues, becomes a trigger for the feeling of calm needed at other times. A similar tea ritual might also be a pause in the middle of the day to catch your breath, or an evening ritual to prepare for more restful sleep.

Dealing with Family Crises

Putting the kettle on to brew a pot of tea during a family crisis can signal the time to gather around the table to collectively deal with a difficult issue. Tea tends to be a bit more soothing than coffee. Selecting one of the herbal tea blends known to promote relaxation can work as well for a group as for an individual. Encourage the calm alertness of tea as an alternative to the energy boost of coffee. Whether it's coming to grips with a major health problem, a financial emergency, or the death of a loved one, having someone brew the tea can have a calming effect.

Tea and Conversation

The gift of gab isn't easy for everyone, but gatherings for tea may be slightly easier venues in which shy people feel comfortable enough to talk. Tea is often mentioned as a way to generate comfortable conversation, but this is certainly a benefit of the traditions rather than the leaf chemistry. In *If Teacups Could Talk*, author Emilie Barnes writes:

> *"The very act of preparing and serving tea encourages conversation. The little spaces in time created by teatime rituals call out to be filled with conversation. Even the tea itself—warm and comforting—inspires a feeling of relaxation and trust that fosters shared confidences."*

There are times when serving tea can help loosen the lips and break through uncomfortable moments of silence, and situations when the ability to make small talk is a valuable talent. Teatime can be a good place to practice. Scheduling regular times to focus on conversation—such as teatimes—can keep everyone in fine form for convivial chitchat.

ESSENTIAL

Anyone brought up in the south central and southeastern United States can confirm the same inclination to initiate conversation over tea, even if it's iced. The tall glass with clinking ice cubes, a slice of lemon or sprig of mint, a generous amount of sugar, and sweat dripping down the sides also symbolizes a time to relax and discuss the pressing issues of the day.

There are certain phrases or approaches almost guaranteed to stifle productive conversations before they begin. One way to set up a necessary conversation to be less threatening or confrontational is to ask, "Would you like a cup of tea?" As the brew works its legendary magic, the necessary discussion is more likely to begin more comfortably.

A Tea Lifestyle

There is no single definition for the tea lifestyle. At best, you may be able to point to a moment when the act of preparing and drinking it took on a meaning deeper than you ever anticipated. Or you may be able to look back over several years and track the highlights on a path to gradual appreciation for the ways in which tea enriches your life. At some point, the idea of being a tea person rather than a coffee person becomes conscious, adding another unique flavor to your personal identity.

A tea lifestyle can be both solitary and social. The value of peaceful relaxation in a private space can be balanced by larger public gatherings with others who enjoy sharing the passion—meeting other tea people. Tearooms frequently schedule meet-and-greet opportunities at themed parties, classes, or tea tastings. Online social networks are now connecting people from countries around the world who would otherwise never have the opportunity to meet in person. They can share insights, experiences, brewing tips, and reviews of their favorite brews.

QUESTION

How are people able to share tea experiences online?
There are tea clubs whose members receive identical packets of tea and instructions for preparing it with the same equipage, water temperature, and steeping time. Then they submit reviews describing their impressions, and the event coordinator compares the member findings and shares all comments with the entire group. Members living on different continents can participate, almost as if they are in the same shop. Some retailers offer tea of the month clubs that promote some of the same kind of connectedness between people on different continents, and video sharing can provide an additional dimension.

Tea Travel

In the late 1800s, when women in the United States and England were not allowed to dine in regular restaurants unescorted, tearooms provided places where they could meet with friends, offer pleasing menus, and guarantee a standard of safety and cleanliness. Modern tearooms still attract travelers (both male and female) who are seeking the same qualities—especially when they travel. Tea lovers tend to make a point of visiting the tearooms and tea shops in cities they visit. Tea magazines, books, and websites feature some of the most interesting destinations, which can turn into the reason for traveling unto themselves.

Some tea lovers are known to travel to historic tearooms as the highlights of their travel. The Lao She Teahouse in Beijing, China, is one such tea destination serving both tea and entertainment, with a history of having welcomed many famous dignitaries. In London, England, tea lovers can visit historic locations such as the original Twining's Tea Shop, opened by Thomas Twining himself. Babington's Tea Room in Rome is considered one of the most famous, opened in 1893 by Isabel Cargill when tea was still sold in pharmacies. In the United States, the oldest tearoom is reputed to be The Bottom of the Cup, located in The French Quarter of New Orleans, LA. The name refers to the motivation for opening tearooms there: it was illegal for psychics to charge for tea leaf readings, so they sold tea by the cup and then read the leaves for free. In Victoria, British Columbia, Canada, The Empress Hotel's tearoom is a long-time destination for tea lovers.

Specialized tour organizers with extensive tea experience offer travel to countries of origin, visiting farms and factories as well as important points of interest. One of the most treasured experiences for tea lovers is to visit a plantation where they can pick and process their own tea under the auspices of the local tea master. Several plantations have built comfortable guest quarters within the tea fields. These are opportunities for peaceful, personal retreats as well as training for tea professionals.

A Well-Stocked Cupboard

One of the most obvious indicators of a tea lover is a cupboard filled with packages of favorite flavors and teaware displayed in places of honor. The habit may begin gradually—starting with just a few brands and a simple teapot. Oftentimes, it's the desire to share the new hobby with family and friends that fuels expansion of the tea selections. Discovering a new brand or drooling over a new flavor blend can entice a tea person to fill their cupboard with far more tea than they will be able to finish in a reasonable amount of time.

ESSENTIAL

A crowded tea cupboard or pantry can signal the perfect time for a tea tasting. With loose-leaf teas, consider organizing the event by categories. Especially if you're overstocked with last year's green teas and the new harvest is approaching, you might want to clear shelf space. Or you could introduce friends to favorites in each different category: green, black, oolong, white, pu'erh. Limit it to a selection of five or six different teas. Provide information about each one and open the discussion for comparisons. If your tea abundance is in wrapped tea bags of well-known brands, suggest that guests select favorites and share their personal tea memories.

Brewing Memories

Tea memories are frequently some of the fondest memories from childhood. They are the settings when adults took the time to make you feel special and important, when the storytelling began, and scenes from earlier times came to life again. Tea experiences can be, in some almost inexplicable way, some of the most important moments of your life.

Tea Cultures

Tea is the second most consumed beverage in the world because it is so deeply infused in cultural traditions. Exploring a greater knowledge of tea traditions adds to our understanding of people around the world. Tea universally symbolizes hospitality, and is one of the most important ways to welcome guests. In many different countries, a guest is immediately offered tea—the best tea. Tea traditions demonstrate respect. In some cultures, businessmen begin negotiations with tea, the quality of which conveys respect and desire for successful dealings. Formal tea services are also included in wedding ceremonies as a way for the young couple to show respect for their elders. And tea has historically been used to convey beauty and peace. Expanding your awareness of worldwide tea cultures also increases the pleasure and benefit of drinking and sharing it.

Tea Seasons

Spring harvest of teas grown in Asia, especially China, Taiwan, India, and Japan, generates excitement among tea lovers everywhere. As with fine wines, connoisseurs are anxious to sample the new teas and compare the flavor profiles with memorable harvests of the past. Unlike wine, the spring teas should be sampled as soon as possible after they leave the factory, and specialty shops are usually quick to announce the arrivals of their first shipments. Of course, the same is true for the release of later season teas. Those who have a preference for autumnal teas wait with the same anticipation for that season's harvest.

Family Teatime

The original "high tea" was actually a family teatime in England, while "low tea" or "afternoon tea" was the social event. Afternoon tea was served in a parlor or drawing room on a "low table," in contrast to a dining room table used for a larger meal. Originally, the word "high" referred to the height of the table, the one where the family gathered at the end of the day for a substantial meal along with tea and conversation. The essence of the original "high tea" is being revitalized when families set aside special teatimes, where phones and other electronics are turned off and simple fare doesn't distract from what's really important—uninterrupted conversation.

All too often, modern family life unavoidably interrupts family mealtimes. Teatime also has an advantage because it is not considered to be one of the required daily meals. It is not an obligation. Even simple daily teatime can feel like a party.

ESSENTIAL

Borrowing a phrase from British tea tradition, the one who pours the tea is called "mother." Everyone loves to be the one in charge of the teapot and it's great fun to take turns, asking a child, "Would you like to be mother?"

Parents looking for more ways to spend meaningful time with their children are discovering teatime. In addition to starting a simple family tradition, exploring the fun of tea encourages it as a replacement beverage for canned sodas, and naturally sweet, flavored teas can eliminate the need for added sugar. Healthy fruit dishes served at teatime can replace nutritionally empty sweets. Preparation for a family teatime can be a fun way to involve children in the kitchen and teach cooking basics—even sharing some of the secret family recipes (or making them up together).

Tea is multigenerational, a beverage and an event enjoyed by all ages. There are precious few activities where an entire family can gather for the sole purpose of talking, practicing the art of conversation. What may begin as a playtime activity with a plastic tea set gift from a grandmother can grow into a cherished part of everyday life. Tea can become a lifestyle.

Tea in Education

There is a great deal that can be learned about the rest of the world by exploring the way in which tea is a part of life. And there is a lot you can learn about yourself when you experience and share what tea means in your life. There is, at this point, very little written as educational curriculum that can be used by elementary and junior high school teachers, but it is being developed by tea-loving teachers who use tea creatively in their classrooms and by professional tea educators who see the worldwide culture of tea as a way to explore many different subjects.

TED TALKS about Tea Bowls

Tea professional and tearoom owner Kyle Stewart of The Cultured Cup in Dallas, Texas, launched a project to take tea experiences into public schools. He wrote classroom curriculum that involved taking tea and Japanese-style tea bowls into schools, so that young children could experience the beauty and sensory stimulation of green tea. His work was included in one of the TED TALKS for children where he begins with the question, "What could we learn from a Japanese tea bowl?"

Additionally, Stewart takes his program into classrooms and works with teachers to blend tea into other subjects. Several teachers have developed creative and meaningful ways to use tea in their classrooms.

Second Grade Reading and Teatime

One Michigan second-grade teacher, Miss Karen, started a tradition of monthly tea parties. She would designate a reading theme for the month, giving her class a book list exploring that theme (such as fairy tales, seasons, plants, or music). At the end of the month, she would schedule an afternoon tea party, inviting parents and grandparents to donate some simple treats and join the class for tea, during which time the students would present their book reports and serve tea. Linking the regular tea parties with reading accomplished several things for these seven- to eight-year-olds. Reading became more important and more fun. Families became more involved in the relationship between the child's home reading and the classroom. They focused more attention on what their own child was reading, and the interests of other children at the same level. Reading generated conversations at home, at the park, and on the playground. Trips to the library had more purpose. Children practiced public speaking. Shy children increased their self-confidence.

Increasing Attention Span

A Northern California fifth-grade teacher was given a class of twenty-five "problem" students. Rather than have students who tended to disrupt the classroom intermixed with regular classes, they were isolated in a single, rather chaotic, group. The teacher immediately identified her first goal, and concentrated her work with the class on increasing their individual and group attention span. She felt that nothing would be gained until the students were able to listen to her, and that would require having their complete attention. Not having the entire class quiet was a problem because a single, acting-out student would easily distract everyone.

She brought her passion for tea into the classroom and divided the room into five groups with a special teapot for each group and a personal cup and saucer for each student. They each had a turn to be mother, with the honor of serving the tea while the teacher read aloud. At first, the students were able to remain quiet for only five minutes. The time gradually increased to where the teacher was able to read an entire chapter, about a half hour at a time. The positive impact of this reading teatime contributed to better classroom behavior throughout the rest of the day as well.

Making Memories with Tea Parties

Memorable tea parties can be simple or elaborate, spontaneous or intricately orchestrated, and can be inspired by the grandest day of the year or nothing more than the desire to share a few hours.

Keeping It Simple

There are times when bringing out a certain tea set creates a party mood. Bringing out the nicest cups and saucers, arranging the cookies on a plate decorated with a freshly picked garden flower, cutting the crusts off of the sandwiches, adding sprinkles to the cupcakes, lighting candles, playing music—all can transform what would otherwise be an afternoon snack into something memorable. When Anna Maria Russell, Duchess of Bedford, began the tradition of afternoon tea in England in the mid 1800s, it was simply to bridge the gap between lunch and a late supper. Her simple tea and toast quickly became a ritual on a grand scale in the English court.

Tea for Two

Whether it's a romantic rendezvous with fine porcelain or an afternoon in the playroom with a plastic teapot, a tea party for two usually focuses more on the conversation than the accoutrements. Children thrive when they enjoy the personal attention. Of course, so do adults. Valentine's Day is a perfect opportunity for both elegance and romance, as much as playtime tea parties.

Themes

Themed tea parties are popular. Television series like *Downton Abbey* have recently inspired many gatherings among fans, imitating the manor style and taking inspiration from their menus. Literary themes and authors like Jane Austen inspire tea events, and book clubs are known to set aside special meetings as tea parties. Themes can celebrate the changing of seasons and holidays, and honor accomplishments like graduations, promotions, and retirement.

Birthday Tea Parties

Not just for little girls and little old ladies anymore, birthday celebrations with a tea party format can go well beyond the sparkling tiaras and flowered hats. One caterer specializes in cowboy tea parties at a dude ranch near Las Vegas. Another tearoom in New Mexico offers tea and cigar gatherings for their gentlemen customers.

Ceremonial Tea

The number of tea businesses and tea professionals is growing. There are now many tea shops offering events based on cultural ceremonies. Japanese teahouses serve chanoyu, and Chinese tearooms offer gongfu. Students of these traditions and others also perform the ceremonial tea services in private homes. One relatively new form of ceremony created by a Taiwan tea master is the Wu-Wo tea ceremony, which means "without self."

Participants in Wu-Wo events set aside the rigors of other formal training and serve tea in an organized way that lacks the hierarchy of a teacher, master, or guide. There are seven basic principles:

1. There is no director. All participants are considered equal and follow an established timing for the event.
2. Seating is random. There is no hierarchy. Positions in the circle are drawn like a lottery.
3. Each participant prepares and serves a tea of his/her choosing.
4. There is an established way in which participants serve their tea to others, all flowing in the same direction around the circle.
5. The ceremony is conducted in silence.
6. Participants strive to serve their tea with their greatest skill, having an intention to concentrate and improve their technique.
7. No one expresses prejudice or distinction of one tea or one form of presentation over another.

Wu-Wo is considered to be an international ceremony, and is now practiced around the world with a growing number of events and conventions being scheduled every year.

Going All Out Tea Parties

At the opposite end of the tea party spectrum, from the simple fare with nothing more than tea and toast, are tea parties that don't hold back on the preparations or the calories. Tea parties are known for transformation, creating the ambience where a woman can feel like a queen for a day and a young girl can feel like a fairy princess. Sometimes tea can inspire you by lifting you out of the daily grind and adding a little sparkle to your day.

The most elaborate and expensive tea parties are probably winter holiday events at large hotels in major cities. With traditional winter themes, these are dress-up parties for all ages with magnificent decorations and bountiful treats that become local family traditions. Due to the great popularity, it is not unusual for these annual tea parties to sell out almost immediately.

Creating an all-out tea party at home can easily become a beloved family tradition. It can be an opportunity to wear the best party clothes, feast on fine confections, bring out the best china, decorate, and celebrate in a way that all ages will remember fondly. A large affair like this is not an easy endeavor for one person to manage; a team effort can make it simpler.

Tea Fundraising

Tea parties are becoming a healthy new method of fundraising. Some arts organizations blend their performing arts talents with culinary creativity to produce extravagant afternoon tea parties. It is not uncommon for these to become annual sold-out events. School arts programs as well as service organizations are discovering tea brands that offer tea fundraising to compete with the sale of candy bars and magazine subscriptions. It is increasingly popular to "private label" tins of tea so the tea package information continues to distribute information about the goals of the fundraising organization.

CHAPTER 18

Other Uses for Tea

Don't throw that used tea bag away! Even if you've steeped the life out of the leaves and barely a tint remains in the cup, there may be a second life for that old tea. Additionally, there are other ways tea can make a healthy difference in your life. Add tea's super antioxidants to recipes. Let those tea tannins replace some toxic cleaning chemicals. And use tea's astringency as part of your daily beauty plan.

Cooking with Tea

Some tea historians believe that tea leaves were used for cooking many years before the legendary emperor Shen Nong theoretically brewed the first cup. Fresh leaves may have been plucked and chewed, or cooked with other vegetables and meats, for more than a thousand years prior to Shen Nong's discovery in 2737 B.C.E.

As current interest in tea expands and the health benefits continue to substantiate ancient wisdom, creative minds investigate new and imaginative ways to bring it to the table. Dishes cooked with the dry leaf, or with infused tea, and even using tea to create flavorful smoke, are joining other favorite dishes on the menu.

Marbleized Eggs

A traditional Chinese food, marbleized eggs are cooked with brewed tea. Simply boil eggs in a strong black tea concentrate, or add black tea leaves to the pot of water while boiling the eggs. It not only colors the shell, but also colors the outer layer of the white inside the eggshell. Once the egg is cooked, lightly crack the shell but do not remove the pieces. Soak the eggs in the strong tea solution for four to eight hours. (Refrigeration is recommended for extended soaking.) Remove the shell, and you should have a pattern dyed into the white of the egg along the lines of the cracks. Using different teas will vary the color of the patterns on the egg and make an interesting presentation.

Tea-Flavored Rice

Replace the necessary amount of water with brewed tea to cook rice. Many different flavors will work well for this, both true teas and herbal blends. Some tea leaves are also delicious and attractive when cooked in with the rice. Whole-bud teas like Dragon Well or Silver Needle add a soft color and delicate flavor, and the tender buds become soft enough to chew easily after cooking. The finely cut pieces in tea bags create a speckled effect in cooked rice.

Cooking Vegetables

Add a tea bag or a tablespoon of loose leaves to the boiling water when steaming vegetables. Tea leaves can also be added to a stir-fry or sauté. For baked vegetables like winter squash, using a tea and spice blend as a rub to coat the surface adds a crunchy crust.

Tea and Spice Rubs for Meats

The conveniently ground tea inside a tea bag provides a ready-to-use ingredient in spice rubs for fish, poultry, and meat. Blend whole leaves with salt and dry spices, then pat generously on the surface of the food before roasting or grilling. When grilled, the whole leaves add a crispy, spicy crunch to the surface.

Smoking Fish, Meats, and Vegetables

Tea-smoked meats and fish aren't a new innovation, so it's nice to remember another classic. Adding tea to a smoking packet, along with other ingredients, is especially nice for fish and lighter flavored meats and vegetables. Lapsang Souchong tea works especially well with meats.

Meat Tenderizer

Tannins in black tea are particularly good for tenderizing meat. Mix strong black tea with meat stock, favorite spices, and a bit of oil. Cover the meat with the solution and refrigerate for at least four hours, then cook as required.

Marinades

Teas are showing up in many different marinade recipes, especially green tea, black tea, and chai blends. Their contribution to the recipe is not only additional flavor, but also tenderizing the meat.

Add to Baked Goods

Again, the finely cut tea inside tea bags is one option to spice up a cookie recipe. Finely cut tea can also be blended into cake batter or pie crust. Earl Grey or chai tea, with the strong flavors of sweet spices, are good choices. Try adding two tablespoons of tea into a recipe for sugar cookies or shortbread. If desired, the tea can be ground more finely in a food processor to mix easily into the dough.

Jams, Jellies, and Preserves

Adding tea gives an unexpected note to preserved fruit. Brew a tea concentrate to replace the water in a recipe, or add dry tea into the bubbling fruit. Use the finely cut contents of tea bags or, if you know the leaves will become tender, some whole leaves can be added as a mystery ingredient.

Tea Syrups

Infuse a tea concentrate about four times as strong as you would normally drink. Mix with an equal amount of sugar. Bring the mixture to a boil and reduce to a low simmer, stirring constantly. The sugar should dissolve within two minutes. Simmer eight minutes longer, for a total of ten minutes. Tea syrups are delicious poured over poached fruit, custards, or ice cream.

Smoothies

Tea can be added to fruit or vegetable smoothies in three ways: as a concentrated brewed tea, as the finely ground contents of a tea bag, or as a spoonful of powdered green matcha tea.

Tea Punches

Tea punches were the precursors to the Southern iced tea tradition. By the late 1800s, tea punches were already appearing in recipe books and being mentioned in social news columns. Brewed tea concentrate was mixed with fruit juice and then cooled in a springhouse (since ice was rare). Tea punches were often served with alcohol at adult parties. A few recipes from this era still exist, and can be found by a simple Internet search.

Beauty Treatments

Tea products are not only filling more space on grocery store shelves in beverage aisles, but the extracts and concentrates are also being added to beauty products. Some of these you can make yourself at a fraction of the cost.

Green Tea Face Mask

The higher astringency in green tea (more than black tea) helps tone the skin. Brew a strong cup of green tea, using about twice as much tea as you would use to brew a cup, and steep longer than normal. Allow it to cool completely. Mix the tea with rice or oat flour to form a thick paste. Apply gently, carefully avoiding the area around the eyes, and leave for up to thirty minutes. Gently remove by washing gently with warm water and a washcloth, rubbing to exfoliate. Pat dry and then moisturize.

Matcha Face Mask

Matcha, also a green tea with the higher astringency, makes a thick mask just by adding water to the powdered tea. Although a bit more expensive than brewed tea, it makes a dramatically green-colored mask. It can also be blended with flours to reduce the amount of tea needed to cover the entire face and still have a strong mask. Mix two teaspoons of matcha powder with an equal amount of water and one teaspoon of rice or oat flour. Stir together to form a stiff paste, and then spread it on the face. Let it set for fifteen to thirty minutes. Wash gently with warm water, pat dry, and then moisturize with your favorite cream.

Tea Bag Exfoliant

Brew two tea bags, and then set them aside to cool while you drink the tea. After you've finished your tea and the bags have cooled, rub them over the problem areas, such as patches of dry skin around knees or elbows. The tea helps remove dry skin, decongest the pores, and absorb impurities. Moisturize with your preferred cream, oil, or hydrating serum immediately after the treatment.

Eye Compresses

You can relieve tired and puffy eyes with chilled tea bags. Caffeinated tea works best for this. Completely hydrate the tea bags in warm water, making it strong enough to give you a light cup of tea—about half as strong as you normally would. This leaves a lot of good tea in the bags. Chill and then apply to eyes for ten minutes. Another option instead of using the actual tea bag is to soak brewed (unsweetened) tea into a soft washcloth, chill it, and then gently place the cloth over eyes.

Skin Toner

The astringency in tea, especially green tea, acts as an effective skin toner. Use as you would with any other toner and then moisturize after applying.

QUESTION

What is the difference between tea extracts, tea oils, and tea tree oils used in health and beauty products?
Tea tree oil is an essential oil made from the leaves of the *Melaleuca alternifloria* (related to myrtle) and is native to Australia. Tea oil used for cooking and beauty products is pressed from the seeds of the *Camellia sinensis* tea plant or another varietal in the family, *Camellia oleifera*. Tea concentrates are usually concentrates of the liquor infused from the leaf.

Blemishes

Moist tea bags can be held in place over a blemish for ten minutes to reduce swelling and promote healing.

Bath Tea Bags

Fill a large fill-it-yourself tea bag (or tie a small gauze bag into a bundle) with two regular tea bags or four teaspoons of loose-leaf tea (green, white, or black) along with three tablespoons of flowers and herbs such as lavender flowers, rose petals, rosemary, mint, and chamomile. Four to eight drops of essential oils can be added to the blend. Then tie the bath tea bag closed to secure the tea and herbs. The bag can be added directly to the hot bath water, or can first be infused in a pan of boiling water, making a slightly stronger infusion that can then be added to the bath.

Hair Rinse

Rinsing hair with a regular brew of either green, black, or white tea after shampooing helps remove any excess shampoo and is good for the hair and scalp. It will leave the hair clean, shiny, and smelling great. Many prefer white tea as it has less potential to add color and many like to have the tea slightly warm for comfort.

Freshening Smelly Shoes

Tuck your favorite flavored or scented dry tea bags into sneakers to absorb foot odor and to infuse the shoe with your favorite tea fragrance.

Athlete's Foot Soak

A mild infusion of black tea in a foot tub can be very soothing and also help reduce the infection. Infuse four tea bags in a quart of boiling water so that most of the beneficial compounds in the tea will be drawn out. Allow the tea to cool slightly until it reaches a comfortable "soaking" temperature. Pour it into a basin large enough to hold both feet and soak for ten to fifteen minutes. Rinse and then pat dry.

Tea Soap

Many expensive, luxury soaps are now adding tea as an ingredient. You can make your own by following standard homemade soap instructions, substituting a strong infusion of tea for the amount of water. Adding some finely ground leaves is an option that will give your soap a speckled look and also adds a roughness that acts as an exfoliant.

Facial Scrub

Homemade facial scrubs using either salt or sugar as an exfoliant can benefit from adding a bit of finely ground green tea or matcha powdered tea. Consider purchasing a simple, less expensive commercial scrub, then adding your own tea extracts or concentrates.

Ease Sunburn Pain

Cool a strong infusion of green tea, use it to soak a sponge or soft cloth, and then gently pat onto sunburned skin. Infused tea can also be added to a spray bottle or atomizer to apply without touching painful burns.

Tea Gardening

Your plants can enjoy their own kind of tea party when you use spent tea leaves to fertilize, hydrate, and mulch. Before you toss the bags into the trash, consider the value they may still have for your plants.

Compost

Used tea leaves provide a rich addition to a compost pile. Most families don't produce enough leaves to make much of an impression on a compost pile, but tearooms accumulate huge amounts of leaves every day. Gardeners who maintain large compost piles may want to contact a local retailer, offering to volunteer as a tea leaf recycling service.

Houseplants

When you've brewed the flavor from your tea bags, they can be buried in the soil of a houseplant to help retain water in the soil.

Potting Soil

Used tea leaves can be blended into a batch of potting soil to add nutrients and to help maintain moisture in the soil.

Mulch Roses

Rose bushes are particularly fond of used tea leaves being spread on the soil around their bases. The tea can be worked into the surface of the ground, or just left on top to absorb moisture and keep the soil beneath moist for the plant.

Grow Your Own Tea

Camellia sinensis plants can decorate your yard, as well as provide you with the freshest cup of tea you've ever tasted. Plants can be ordered from specialty nurseries, and added to your garden. While most tea plants favor warm climates with high humidity, there are new varietals being developed for greater diversity. In 2013, a project supported by the U.S. Tea Growers League (*http://usgrowntea.wordpress.com*) was launched by Tealet (*www.tealet.com*) to have tea plants growing in every state. To harvest your tea, pluck the new spring growth (two leaves and a bud). Dry the tea as a white tea or process minimally as a green tea (see following), then brew your own homegrown tea. Check with nurseries that specialize in the varietals for making tea. One in North Carolina is The Camellia Forest (*www.camforest.com*), which offers a dozen varietals along with instructions for growing and a video demonstrating how to pick, pan-fry, and roast your tea. In 2013, the United States League of Tea Growers formed an organization to support those interested in growing tea. With membership levels for both commercial and home growers, the association's mission is to encourage knowledge about specialty tea, and bring tea growers together in cooperative collaboration. Their Facebook page can be found at *www.facebook.com/usltg*.

Processing Your Harvest as a White Tea

Pluck the fresh buds and the first two leaves. Spread them on a flat baking sheet to dry undisturbed. Sun dry as much as possible, but keep them in a place where they are not likely to absorb moisture or other aromas. Without using any devices, it can take up to two weeks to thoroughly dry the leaves so they can be stored, but they can be brewed at this stage of drying.

Some ways to accelerate the drying are to use an electric dehydrator, or to spread the leaves on baking sheets and dry them at about 200°F. There will be very diverse colors in white tea, from silvery tips, to streaks of green, to reddish-brown hues on larger leaves. Drying time for this will vary, depending on the previous sun drying. The tea is dry when the leaves feel brittle and break easily.

Processing Your Harvest as a Green Tea

After picking the fresh tea, buds, and top two leaves, allow them to wither in bright sunlight until they start to soften and wilt slightly (an hour or two), or immediately pan-fry over a very low heat to stop the oxidation. Work in small batches. Pan-fry on a low heat in a clean pan or wok. Turn the leaves so they heat evenly but do not brown or burn. Stop and allow the batch to cool, repeating the process several times. When the leaves are completely softened and the aroma is sweet, place them in a 200°F oven for ten to twenty minutes, or until nicely dry. Your green tea can be brewed and enjoyed immediately.

Art Projects

Tea and fine arts have been partnered for thousands of years and across many cultures. Fine paintings and great literature both give nods to tea. The American painter Mary Cassatt painted several canvases featuring afternoon tea. Writers like Lewis Carroll, A.A. Milne, and Beatrix Potter frequently used teatime in their classic storylines. In a more day-to-day world, tea is finding its way onto the home craft shelf along with other supplies.

Tea Bag Folding

A form of mini origami paper folding was traditionally done with tea bag wrappers. Today, there are books and templates for this craft using small pieces of paper similar to the size of an unfolded tea bag in addition to recycling your saved wrappers.

Aging Paper

Soaking white paper with an infusion of black tea quickly darkens it to an ivory or golden yellow. Roughing or burning the edges increases the illusion. Prop designers use this technique to turn regular paper into something that looks like parchment or old scrolls. An inexpensive way to make your own wrapping paper is by tea-dyeing tissue paper, newsprint, or other absorbent papers.

Fabric Dye

Like aging paper, tea will also stain white cotton fabric to look more like an ivory or antique white. Brew a strong batch of black tea and completely submerge the cloth, allowing it to sit for at least thirty minutes. Make sure that there is a large volume of liquid in a large pot or tub, so that the entire bit of fabric will be evenly soaked, and move it around in the tea bath during soaking.

Pillow Stuffing

Tea pillows were mentioned by Lu Yu's *The Classic of Tea*, used to promote restful sleep and well-being. Dry leaves are stuffed into a small pillow that can be placed behind the neck or inside the outer case of a regular pillow. Change the leaves frequently.

Teaware Art

An image of a favorite teapot or teacup can be the art on personalized note cards. It's easier than ever to snap a shot, print a card, and pen a "wish you were here" note. A more ambitious project would be to photograph a personal teaware collection and pair it with famous quotes, like this one from *The Portrait of a Lady* by Henry James:

> *"There are few hours in life more agreeable than the hour dedicated to the ceremony known as afternoon tea."*

Another favorite is from Ralph Waldo Emerson's *Letters and Social Aims*:

> *"Some people will tell you there is a great deal of poetry and fine sentiment in a chest of tea."*

Paintings of family heirloom teapots, like the one a beloved grandmother brought with her from "the old country," are also treasured gifts. When a single teapot or teacup cannot be shared with the remaining family, small paintings or framed photographs can become the keepsake that jogs the memory and touches the heart.

Around the House

Amazingly, tea can be a handy, inexpensive, and nontoxic helper around the house.

Black Tea Wood Cleaner

The tannins in a strong infusion of black tea will help remove dust and restore shine to wood furniture. Soak brewed tea into a cotton cloth, or simply use moistened tea bags to vigorously rub the wood surface.

Absorb Refrigerator Odors

Dry unwrapped tea bags or tea leaves left in an open container can keep a refrigerator smelling fresh and clean.

Deodorize Cupboards

Tea works the same way in musty smelling cupboards as it does in the refrigerator. Scatter a few unwrapped tea bags throughout the shelves in kitchen cabinets and clothes closets. Herbal scents like lavender, chamomile, and rose are light fragrances for lingerie drawers.

Glass Cleaner

An infusion of tea can be used as a glass cleaner. Spray it directly onto the glass and then wipe clean, or soak a towel in brewed tea and then use it to wipe over the glass surface. This is also excellent for car window glass.

Resources

Because tea is an international experience with unique products grown in many different countries and cultures celebrating interesting traditions, the Internet has been an incredible tool for change, growth, and connections. Just a few years ago there were barely any tea books with photographs of the fields and information about the history. Now there are videos and online groups—an entire social network of tea lovers.

Tea Websites

TeaMap

TeaMap is a helpful resource for traveling tea lovers who want to find a good cup of tea at their favorite destinations, even if that may be just around the corner. Directory listings are provided by the retailers but then organized by city, state, and country.
www.teamap.com

The Urasenke Foundation

An international association promoting the Japanese tea ceremony, chanoyu, with community gatherings and education.
www.urasenke.org

International Tea Cuppers Club

ITCC is a worldwide tea community of people who share a passion not only for the finest teas but also for contributing to the refinement and evolution of the tea industry. Members participate in innovative Cupping Events, Member Hosted Events, the Community Board, and the ITCC newsletter.
www.teacuppers.com

International Tea Sippers Society

ITSS was created to help tea lovers of all preferences—from those who enjoy a glass of iced tea with meals to the whole-leaf gourmets—to connect directly with tea businesses, and join a network of fellow tea lovers for tea-focused travel, tea education, and other special events.
www.teasipperssociety.com

Tealet

A monthly tea club that describes itself as, "a bridge between tea growers and tea drinkers," providing more information about every tea to the consumer and more profit for the grower.
www.tealet.com

The U.S. League of Tea Growers

Growers in the United States who have organized to share their expertise and resources as well as promote education about growing and processing tea.
www.usgrowntea.com

United States Tea Association

The U.S. Tea Association makes tea interesting and fun, providing lovely photographs and interesting articles about tea and the latest health research.
www.teausa.com

Tea Association of Canada

The Tea Association of Canada is organized to support the tea industry in their country but also provides a great deal of education about tea as well as their professional Tea Sommelier course.
www.tea.ca

United Kingdom Tea Council

Filled with tips for brewing and the latest facts on health, this site can keep you well entertained with a great deal of interesting content, with a European focus.
www.tea.co.uk

Indian Tea Association

This is an extensive site about the teas of India, the growers, growing conditions, manufacture, auctions, and other more general aspects, including product health and safety. You can feel as if you get to know the people who craft these lovely teas by spending a little time browsing here.
www.indiatea.org

The Sri Lanka Tea Board

Search for everything you want to know about tea from Sri Lanka and the people who grow, manufacture, and sell it. The website provides the latest information on their fine tea.
www.pureceylontea.com

Tea Board of Kenya

Learn more about the tea industry in this African country. Much of the information they provide is about their current research to develop new cultivars and the growth of the tea industry there.
www.teaboard.or.ke

Tea Bloggers

Join dozens of conversations with real tea people who share their passion for *all things tea*. Bloggers share everything from recipes to travel tips, from a serious academic perspective to jolly tea humor.

TeaChef

Adagio Teas hosts some of the highest ranked and most useful sites. In addition to the Tea Map so that tea lovers can sip their way around the world, they provide an E-Cookbook with tea as an ingredient in every recipe.
www.teachef.com

T-Ching

An association of more than ninety respected tea writers who have contributed more than three thousand articles to this extensive site. Along with almost daily new posts is an archive that includes tea history and education with something for tea lovers of all kinds.
www.tching.com

Tea Guy Speaks

Journalist William Lengeman posts frequent articles on a variety of interesting tea topics, including book reviews, how-to articles, fun videos, and interviews with tea professionals.
www.teaguyspeaks.com

Tea Pages

Katrina Avila Munichiello, the author of *A Tea Reader: Living Life One Cup At A Time* and Senior Editor of *Tea Magazine*, shares regular blogs about her experiences working in the industry and her life as a tea lover.
www.teapages.net

The Tea Maestro

MSN calls Bruce Richardson "A leading tea expert involved in tea's American renaissance for over twenty years." His blog shares his experiences as a tearoom owner, author, publisher, and historian.
www.theteamaestro.blogspot.com

The World of Tea

Tea author Tony Gebely focuses on tea cultivation, culture, education, and brewing a good cup of tea.
www.worldoftea.org

The Devotea

Blogger Robert Godden aptly describes this blog as, "Lord Devotea's Tea Sprouts: In which life's eternal questions are ignored in favour of a cup of tea."
www.thedevotea.teatra.de

Association of Tea Bloggers

This worldwide association features more than seventy tea bloggers in many different languages with a little something for everyone.
www.teabloggers.com

Tea Festivals

The listing here includes festivals featuring only tea and tea-related goods.

Tea Lovers Festival—Los Angeles, CA
www.tealoversfestival.com

Rocky Mountain Tea Festival—Boulder, CO
www.rockymtnteafestival.com

Northwest Tea Festival—Seattle, WA
www.nwteafestival.com

Los Angeles International Tea Festival—Los Angeles, CA
www.teafestivalla.com

San Francisco International Tea Festival—San Francisco, CA
www.sfinternationalteafestival.com

Ottawa Tea Festival—Ottawa, Canada
www.ottawateafestival.com

Toronto Tea Festival—Toronto, Canada
www.teafestivaltoronto.com

Vancouver Tea Festival—Vancouver, Canada
www.vancouverteafestival.ca

World O-Cha—Shizuoka, Japan
www.ocha-festival.jp/english

Xiamen Tea Festival—Xiamen, Fujian, China
www.teafair.com.cn/en

Hong Kong International Tea Festival
www.hktdc.com/fair

Tea Education Resources

Just a few years ago, anyone who wanted to know more about tea had to seek out mentors and create their own experiences. There are now many more options available, both for those interested in expanding their own tea knowledge as well as anyone interested in finding work within the tea industry.

Specialty Tea Institute

STI is the educational program sponsored by the U.S. Tea Association. Two introductory levels are for more general interest. A third level is considered the beginning of their professional education.
www.teausa.com/14527/sti-tea-education-courses

World Tea Expo—New Tea Business Boot Camp

This boot camp is an intense nuts-and-bolts weekend for those considering starting their own tea businesses. From the sweeping "tour" of the countries of origin to the basic startup, students learn from successful professionals in the industry.
www.worldteaexpo.com/index.php/education

World Tea Academy

WTA is an opportunity to develop your tea education from the comfort of home. Work with leading industry educators, starting with the basics, but continuing at your own pace to increase knowledge and expertise.
www.worldteaacademy.com

Canadian Sommelier

A tea sommelier training program with eight nodules is offered at several universities in conjunction with the Tea Association of Canada.
www.tea.ca/education/tea-sommelier-program

World Tea Tours

Professionally led tours to tea growing countries designed for both tea-loving world travelers and tea professionals wanting to expand their professional experience.
www.worldteatours.com

Tea Books: Nonfiction

This is a sampling of some of the diverse tea topics by tea-dedicated writers.

Antol, Marie Nadine. *Healing Teas: How to Prepare and Use Teas to Maximize Your Health.* (Garden City Park, NY: Avery Publishing Group, 1996).

Blofeld, John. *The Chinese Art of Tea.* (Boston, MA: Shambhala Publications, Inc., 1985).

Chen, Jason. *Four World-Famous Chinese Green Teas: Dragonwell Bi Luo Chun, Mao Feng, Ping Shui Ri Zhu.* (Seattle, WA: A Tea Master Book, 2012).

Cousineau, Phil and Hoyt, Scott Chamberlin. *The Soul and Spirit of Tea.* (New York, NY: Talking Leaves Press, 2013).

Donaldson, Babette. *A Tea Sipper's Tea Journal.* (Nevada City, CA: Blue Gate Books, 2014).

Fellman, Donna and Tizer, Lhasha. *Tea Here Now: Rituals, Remedies, and Meditations.* (Maui, HI: Inner Ocean Publishing, Inc. 2005).

Fisher, Aaron. *The Way of Tea: Reflections on a Life with Tea.* (Rutland, VT: Tuttle Publishing, 2010).

Fong, Roy. *The Great Teas of China.* (Oakland, CA: Tea Journey Books, 2009).

Gold, Cynthia and Stern, Lise. *Culinary Tea.* (Philadelphia, PA: Running Press, 2010).

Gustafson, Helen. *The Agony of the Leaves: The Ecstasy of My Live with Tea.* (New York, NY: Henry Hold and Company, 1996).

Gustafson, Helen. *The Green Tea User's Manual.* (New York, NY: Clarkson Potter, 2001).

Hohenegger, Beatrice. *Liquid Jade: The Story of Tea from East to West.* (New York, NY: St. Martin's Press, 2006).

Hoyt, Scott Chamberlin. *The Meaning of Tea: A Tea Inspired Journey.* (New York, NY: Talking Leaves Press, 2009).

Kakuzo, Okakura. *The Book of Tea.* (Rutland, VT: Tuttle Company, 1956).

Martin, Laura C. *Tea, The Drink That Changed the World.* (North Clarendon, VT: Tuttle Publishing, 2007).

Munichiello, Katrina Avila. *A Tea Reader: Living Life One Cup at a Time.* (Rutland, VT: Tuttle Publishing, 2011).

Murphy, Frank Hadley. *The Spirit of Tea.* (Santa Fe, NM: Sherman Asher Publishing, 2008).

Pettigrew, Jane. *The Tea Companion: A Connoisseur's Guide.* (Philadelphia, PA: Running Press, 2004).

Pettigrew, Jane and Richardson, Bruce. *The New Tea Lover's Companion: A Guide to Teas Throughout the World.* (Perryville, KY: Benjamin Press, 2008).

Pratt, James Norwood. *The Tea Dictionary.* (San Francisco, CA: Tea Society, 2005).

Pratt, James Norwood. *The Ultimate Tea Lover's Treasury: The Classic True Story of Tea.* (San Francisco, CA: Tea Society 2011).

Rose, Sarah. *For All the Tea in China: How England Stole the World's Favorite Drink and Changed History.* (New York, NY: Penguin Books, 2010).

Tea Books: Fiction

Avery, Ellis. *The Teahouse Fire.* (Riverhead Trade, 2007).
Historical fiction set in nineteenth-century Japan featuring the tea ceremony during the time when the West was becoming more acquainted with Japanese culture and the mysterious rite of tea.

Childs, Laura. *The Tea Shop Mysteries.* (New York, NY: The Berkley Publishing Group, 2001–2014).
A series of fifteen mysteries feature tea shop owner Theodosia Browning and her Charleston, South Carolina, tearoom.

Donaldson, Babette. *The Emma Lea Books.* (Nevada City, CA: Blue Gate Books, 2007–2014).
A series of books with tea themes, beginning with four story books for young children but expanding into young adult novels.

Ferguson, Sarah. *Tea for Ruby.* (New York, NY: A Paula Wiseman Book, 2008).
Duchess of York, Sarah "Fergie" Ferguson, offers a touching tea story for young children and the families who love them.

Haasse, Hella S. *The Tea Lords.* (London, GB: Portobello Books, 2013).
Historical fiction of Dutch tea plantations in the 1800s on the tropical island of Java.

Schaefer, Laura. *The Teashop Girls Series.* (New York, NY: Simon and Schuster, 2009–2012).
Tea-themed novels for young adult tea lovers with two books currently in print and possibilities of more to come.

Sheraidan, Sara. *The Secret Mandarin.* (New York, NY: Avon, 2009).
Historical fiction exploring the life of Robert Fortune and his family.

Conditions That Have Been Researched for Potential Tea Benefits

Because every kind of tea has not been tested for each of these conditions, we can only list those conditions that have been researched and the teas used in various studies. Scientific research is very much in the early stages of *proving* the health benefits of *C. sinensis*. No single piece of research will ever be considered conclusive. It will be laboratory-based studies on tissue and animals that will eventually lead to tests on human subjects. This, combined with population studies that screen subjects for specific variables—such as amount of tea consumed, age, family health history, and known health issues. Ultimately, should the findings continue to show consistent results, the entire body of evidence will be considered as the necessary validation, but we are still several years from that goal that would, for example, satisfy the USDA.

Condition	Tea Types
Age-Related Dementia	Green
Alzheimer's	Green
Antioxidant Benefits	Green and Black
Bone Health	Green
Bone Loss Prevention	Black
Breast Cancer	Green and Black
Colorectal Cancer	Green
Digestive Cancer	Green and Black
Lung Cancer	Green and Black
Oral Cancer	Green
Ovarian Cancer	Green and Black
Prostate Cancer	Green
Skin Cancer	Green and Black
Cardiovascular Health	Black
Cholesterol Management	Green, Black, and Oolong
Diabetes	Green, Black, and Oolong
Digestive Aid	Pu'erh
Cholesterol Reduction	Black and Pu'erh
Energy and Endurance	Green and Black
Gastric Ulcer Management	Black
Glaucoma	Green
Gout	Green and Pu'erh
Hypertension Management	Pu'erh
Immune Function	Black
Inflammation Reduction	Green and Black
Inflammatory-Related Diseases	Green and Black
Kidney Stones	Green
Metabolic Increase	Green and Black
Oral Health	Green, Black, and White
Parkinson's	Black
Stroke Prevention	Green and Black
Weight Management	Green, Black, Oolong, and Pu'erh

Teas and the Conditions Generally Considered to Be Supported by Them

There is a general agreement that tea provides some measurable health benefits; both on the cellular level that can be measured scientifically and in ways that you can observe in yourself and in others. As the amount of research increases, we can begin to speak more confidently about tea's benefits and look forward to a greater understanding of the beneficial properties of *Camellia sinensis*, the true tea.

Green Tea

Green tea is known for its support of the immune system, for reducing inflammation throughout the body, and for a high antioxidant value. Of great interest are studies suggesting a potential benefit to protect the body against developing cancer by scavenging free radicals. Green tea is also known to control blood pressure and aid in general heart health.

Black Tea

The higher levels of theaflavins and thearubinins in black tea, generated by the complete oxidation, are considered beneficial for additional energy, for reducing the risk of heart disease, stroke, and cancer, as well as maintaining healthy cholesterol levels.

Oolong Tea

The polyphenols in oolong tea are associated with reducing the likelihood of stroke and protecting the body against dementia, heart disease, and cancer. Some oolong teas are believed to aid in digestion. Several studies suggest that some oolong teas also help with an organized weight loss program.

Pu'erh Tea

Pu'erh teas have long been known to aid with the digestion of fatty foods and help manage healthy cholesterol levels. Studies are also showing that it offers aid in weight loss and increased metabolism. Studies on patients with gout have also shown benefits with drinking pu'erh tea.

White Tea

Studies have shown that white tea has many of the same properties to fight free radicals as green tea. It may help prevent heart disease, stroke, and cancer in regular tea drinkers. It is also proving to have benefits for people with diabetes and has high levels of fluoride and calcium to benefit oral health and maintain bone strength.

Herbal—Functional Tea

The hundreds of different botanicals from which tea is made provide a large array of benefits. Many of them have properties to help with relaxation and sleep, to aid digestion, to lessen headaches, and to support the body nutritionally. Herbal teas generally have no caffeine, which is especially important to children and to pregnant women and nursing mothers.

APPENDIX D

Scientific Studies

Recent Scientific Studies on Caffeine

Chiang W.F., Liao M.T., Cheng C.J., and Lin S.H. "Rhabdomyolysis induced by excessive coffee drinking." *Human and Experimental Toxicology* 33, no. 2 (November 2013).

Einother S.J., and Martens V.E. "Acute effects of tea consumption on attention and mood." *American Journal of Clinical Nutrition* 98, no. 4 (October 2013).

Jabbar S.B., and Hanly M.G. "Fatal Caffeine Overdose: A Case Report and Review of Literature." *American Journal of Forensic Medicine and Pathology* 34, no. 4 (December 2013): 321–4.

Kamath, Arati B., Lisheng Wang, Hiranmoy Das, Lin Li, Vernon N. Reinhold, and Jack F. Bukowski. "Antigens in tea-beverage prime human Vγ2Vδ2 T cells *in vitro* and *in vivo* for memory and nonmemory antibacterial cytokine responses." *Proceedings of the National Academy of Sciences* 100, no. 10 (13 May 2003): 6009–14.

Kim N.H., Jeong H.J., and Kim H.M. "Theanine is a candidate amino acid for pharmacological stabilization of mast cells." *Amino Acids* 42, no. 5 (May 2012): 1609–18.

Kponee K.Z., Siegel M., and Jernigan D.H. "The use of caffeinated alcoholic beverages among underage drinkers: Results of a national survey." *Addictive Behavior* 39, no. 1 (January 2014): 253–8 (ePub 8 October 2013).

Lyon M.R., Kapoor M.P., and Juneja L.R. "The effects of L-theanine on objective sleep quality in boys with attention deficit hyperactivity disorder: a randomized, double blind, placebo-controlled clinical trial." *Alternative Medicine Review* 16, no. 4 (December 2011): 348–54.

Samples of Modern Scientific Research on Green Tea

Ahmad N., and Mukhtar H. "Cutaneous photochemoprotection by green tea: a brief review." *Skin Pharmacology and Applied Skin Physiology* 14, no. 2 (March-April 2001): 69–76.

Dulloo A.G., Duret C., Rohrer D., Girardier L., Mensi N., Fathi M., Chantre P., and Vandermander J. "Efficacy of a green tea extract rich in catechin polyphenols and caffeine in increasing 24-h energy expenditure and fat oxidation in humans." *The American Journal of Clinical Nutrition* 70, no. 6 (December 1999): 1040–5.

Paulson, Henry L. "Green Tea and Its Effects on Alzheimer's." University of Michigan Health System, *Neurohealth* (blog), 25 June 2013. *http://uofmhealthblogs.org/neurohealth/memory-care/green-tea-and-its-effects-on-alzheimers/6253/*

Issa A.Y., Volate S.R., et al. "Green tea selectively targets initial stages of intestinal carcinogenesis in the AOM -Apc^Min mouse model." *Carcinogenesis* 28, no. 9 (8 September 2007): 1978–84(7).

Ji B.T., Chow W.H., Hsing A.W., McLaughlin J.K., Dai Q., Gao Y.T., Blot W.J., and Fraumeni J.F. Jr. "Green tea consumption and the risk of pancreatic and colorectal cancers." *International Journal of Cancer* 70, no. 3 (27 January 1997): 255–8.

Katiyar S.K., Bergamo B.M., Vyalil P.K., and Elmets C.A. "Green tea polyphenols: DNA photodamage and photoimmunology." *Journal of Photochemistry and Photobiology B: Biology* 65, no. 2–3 (31 December 2001): 109–14.

Katiyar S.K., Perez A., and Mukhtar H. "Green tea polyphenol treatment to human skin prevents formation of ultraviolet light B-induced pyrimidine dimers in DNA." *Clinical Cancer Research* 6, no. 10 (October 2000): 3864–9.

Kushiyama M., Shimazaki Y., Murakami M., and Yamashita Y. "Relationship between intake of green tea and periodontal disease." *Journal of Periodontology* 80, no. 3 (March 2009): 372–7.

Kuriyama S., Shimazu T., Ohmori K., Kikuchi N., Nakaya N., Nishino Y., Tsubono Y., and Tsuji I. "Green tea consumption and mortality due to cardiovascular disease, cancer, and all causes in Japan: the Ohsaki study." *JAMA* 296, no. 10 (13 September 2006): 1255–65.

Lardner, A.L. "Neurobiological effects of the green tea constituent theanine and its potential role in the treatment of psychiatric and neurodegenerative disorders." *Nutritional Neuroscience*. ePub 23 July 2013.

Mervat A. Kassem, Nourhan H. Fanaki, Mohamed A. Fawzi, and Fatma S.E. Dabbous. "Effect of Green Tea Extract on some Virulence Factors of selected Multiresistant Clinical Isolates." *Egyptian Journal of Medical Microbiology* 16, no. 3 (July 2007): 461–71.

Nagao T., Hase T., and Tokimitsu I. "A green tea extract high in catechins reduces body fat and cardiovascular risk in humans." *Obesity* 15, no. 6 (June 2007): 1473–83.

Rezai-Zadeh K., Shytle D., Sun N., Mori T., Hou H., Jeanniton D., Ehrhart J., Townsend K., Zeng J., Morgan D., Hardy J., Town T., and Tan J. "Green tea epigallocatechin-3 gallate(EGCG)modulates amyloid precursor protein cleavage and reduces cerebral amyloidosis in Alzheimer transgenic mice." *The Journal of Neuroscience* 25, no. 38 (21 September 2005): 8807–14.

Shimotoyodome A., Haramizu S., Inaba M., Murase T., and Tokimitsu I. "Exercise and green tea extract stimulate fat oxidation and prevent obesity in mice." *Medicine and Science in Sports and Exercise* 37, no. 11 (November 2005): 1884–92.

Venables M.C., Hulston C.J., Cox H.R., and Jeukendrup A.E. "Green tea extract ingestion, fat oxidation, and glucose tolerance in healthy humans." *The American Journal of Clinical Nutrition* 87, no. 3 (March 2008): 778–84.

Vinson J.A., Teufel K., and Wu N. "Green and black teas inhibit atherosclerosis by lipid, antioxidant, and fibrinolytic mechanisms." *Journal of Agricultural and Food Chemistry* 52, no. 11 (June 2004): 3661–5.

Xi Jin, Ruo-heng Zheng, and You-ming Li. "Green Tea Consumption and Liver Disease." *Liver International* 28, no. 7 (2008): 990–6.

Some Published Medical Research on Black Tea

Conney A.H., Lu Y-P., Lou Y-R., Xie J-G., and Huang M-T. "Inhibitory effect of green and black tea on tumor growth." *Proceedings of the Society for Experimental Biology and Medicine* 220, no. 4 (April 1999): 229–33.

Dora I., Arab L., Martinchik A., Sdvizhkov A., Urbanovich L., and Weisgerber U. "Black tea consumption and risk of rectal cancer in Moscow population." *Annals of Epidemiology* 13, no. 6 (July 2003): 405–11.

Duffy S.J., Keaney J.F. Jr, Holbrook M., Gokce N., Swerdloff P.L., Frei B., and Vita J.A. "Short-and long-term black tea consumption reverses endothelial dysfunction in patients with coronary artery disease." *Circulation* 104 (2001): 151–6.

Geleijnse J.M., Launer L.J., Van der Kuip D.A., Hofman A., and Witteman J.C. "Inverse association of tea and flavonoid intakes with incident myocardial infarction: the Rotterdam Study." *The American Journal of Clinical Nutrition* 75, no. 5 (May 2002): 880–6.

Hakim I.A., Alsaif M.A., Alduwaihy M., Al-Rubeaan K., Al-Nuaim A.R., and Al-Attas O.S. "Tea consumption and the prevalence of coronary heart disease in Saudi adults: results from a Saudi national study." *Preventive Medicine* 36, no. 1 (January 2003): 64–70.

Henning S.M., Aronson W., Niu Y., et al. "Tea polyphenols and theaflavins are present in prostate tissue of humans and mice after green and black tea consumption." *Journal of Nutrition* 136, no. 7 (July 2006): 1839–43.

Hirata K., Shimada K., Watanabe H., Otsuka R., Tokai .K, Yoshiyama M., Homma S., and Yoshikawa J. "Black tea increases coronary flow velocity reserve in healthy male subjects." *American Journal of Cardiology* 93, no. 11 (June 2004): 1384–8.

Hodgson J.M., Puddey I.B., Burke V., Watts G.F., and Beilin L.J. "Regular ingestion of black tea improves brachial artery vasodilator function." *Clinical Science* 102, no. 2 (February 2002): 195–201.

Hodgson J.M., Woodman R.J., Puddey I.B., Mulder T., Fuchs D., Croft K.D. "Short-term effects of polyphenol-rich black tea on blood pressure in men and women." *Food & Function* 4, no. 1 (January 2013): 111–5. Epub 5 October 2012.

Isemura M., Saeki K., Kimura T., Hayakawa S., Minami T., and Sazuka M. "Tea catechins and related polyphenols as anti-cancer agents." *BioFactors* 13, no. 1–4 (2000): 81–5.

Keli S.O., Hertog M.G.L., Feskens E.J.M., and Kromhout D. "Dietary flavonoids, antioxidant vitamins, and incidence of stroke." *Archives of Internal Medicine* 156, no. 6 (25 March 1996): 637–42.

Linke H.A., and LeGeros R.Z. "Black tea extract and dental caries formation in hamsters." *International Journal of Food Sciences and Nutrition* 54, no. 1 (January 2003): 89–95.

Lodovici M., Casalini C., De Filippo C., Copeland E., Xu X., Clifford M., and Dolara P. "Inhibition of 1,2-dimethylhydrazine-induced oxidative DNA damage in rat colon mucosa by black tea complex polyphenols." *Food and Chemical Toxicology* 38, no. 12 (December 2000): 1085–8.

Sarkar, S., Sett, P., Chowdhury, T., and Ganguly, D.K. "Effect of black tea on teeth." *Journal of Indian Society of Pedodontics and Preventive Dentistry* 18, no. 4 (December 2000): 139–140.

Van Duynhoven J., Vaughan E.E., van Dorsten F., Gomez-Roldan V., de Vos R., Vervoort J., van der Hooft J.J., Roger L., Draijer R., and Jacobs DM. "Interactions of black tea polyphenols with human gut microbiota: implications for gut and cardiovascular health." *The American Journal of Clinical Nutrition.* 30 October 2013.

Vermeer M.A., Mulder T.P., and Molhuizen H.O. "Theaflavins from black tea, especially theaflavin-3-gallate, reduce the incorporation of cholesterol into mixed micelles." *Journal of Agriculture and Food Chemistry* 56, no. 24 (24 December): 12031–6.

Vinson J.A., Teufel K., and Wu N. "Green and black teas inhibit atherosclerosis by lipid, antioxidant, and fibrinolytic mechanisms." *Journal of Agricultural and Food Chemistry* 52, no. 11 (2 June 2004): 36615.

Yang G., Wang Z-Y., Kim S., et al. "Characterization of early pulmonary hyperproliferation and tumor progression and their inhibition by black tea in a 4-(methylnitrosamino)-1-(3-pyridyl)-1-butanone-induced lung tumorigenesis model with A/J mice." *Cancer Research* 57, no. 10 (15 May1997): 1889–94.

Yoshino S., Mitoma T., Tsuruta K., Todo H., and Sugibayashi K. "Effect of emulsification on the skin permeation and UV protection of catechin." *Pharmaceutical Development and Technology* 19, no. 4 (June 2014): 395–400. Epub 2 May 2013.

Current Medical Research on Oolong Tea

Chen W., Yang Zl, Hosoda, K et al. "Clinical efficacy of oolong tea on anti-simple obesity." *Journal of Japanese Society of Clinical Nutrition* 20 (1998): 83–90.

He R.R., Chen L., Lin B.H., Matsui Y., Yao X.S., and Kurihara H. "Beneficial effects of oolong tea consumption on diet-induced overweight and obese subjects." *Chinese Journal of Integrative Medicine* 15, no. 1 (February 2009): 34–41.

Hursel R., and Westerterp-Plantenga M.S. "Catechin- and caffeine-rich teas for control of body weight in humans." *American Journal of Clinical Nutrition* 98, no. 6 (December 2013): 1682S–93S. Epub 30 October 2013.

Lin J., Zhang P., Pan Z., Xu H., Luo Y., and Wang X. "Discrimination of oolong tea (*Camellia sinensis*) varieties based on feature extraction and selection from aromatic profiles analyzed by HS-SPME/GC-MS." *Food Chemistry* 141, no. 1 (November 2013): 259–65.

Current Medical Research on White Tea

Camouse M.M., Domingo,D.S., Swain F.R., Conrad E.P., Matsui M.S., Maes D., Declercqu L., Cooper K.D., Stevens S.R., and Baron, E.D. "Topical application of green and white tea extracts provides protection from solar-simulated ultraviolet light in human skin." *Experimental Dermatology* 18, no. 6 (June 2009): 522–6.

Espinosa C., Lopez-Jimenez J.A., Cabrera L., Larque E., Almajano M.P., Arnao M.B., Zamora S., and Perez-Llamas F. "Protective effect of white tea extract against acute oxidative injury caused by adriamycin in different tissues." *Food Chemistry* 134, no. 4 (15 October 2012): 1780–5. Epub 29 March 2012.

Serio K.J., Mao J.T., Nie W.X., Tsu I.H., Jin Y.S., Rao J.Y., Lu Q.Y., Zhang Z.F., and Go V.L. "White tea extract induces apoptosis in non-small cell lung cancer cells." *Cancer Prevention Research* 3, no. 9 (September 2010): 1132–1140.

Thring S.A., Hili P., and Naughton D.P. "Anti-collagenase, anti-elastase and anti-oxidant activities of extracts from 21 plants." *BMC Complementary and Alternative Medicine* 9, no. 7 (4 August 2009).

Current Medical Research on Pu'erh Tea

Chiang C.T., Weng M.S., Lin-Shiau S.Y, Kuo K. L., Tsai Y.J., Lin J.K. "Pu-erh tea supplementation suppresses fatty acid synthase expression in the rat liver through downregulating Akt and JNK signalings as demonstrated in human hepatoma HepG2 cells." *Oncology Research* 16 (3): 119–28 (2005).

Lin, J.K., Shoei Y.L. "Mechanisms of hypolipidemic and anti-obesity effects of tea and tea polyphenols." *Molecular Nutrition and Food Research*, 50 (2): 211–217 (September 28, 2005).

Lu, Chi-Hua, Hwang, Lucy Sun. "Polyphenol contents of Pu-Erh teas and their abilities to inhibit cholesterol biosynthesis in Hep G2 cell line." *Food Chemistry* 111 (1): 67–71 (1 November 2008).

Wang B.S., Yu H.M., Chang L.W., Yen W.J., Duh P.D. "Protective effects of pu-erh tea on LDL oxidation and nitric oxide generation in macrophage cells." *LWT Food Science and Technology* 41, 1122–1132 (2008).

Zhang L, Ma Z.Z., Che, Y.Y., Li N., Tu P.F., "Protective effect of a new amide compound from pu-erh tea on human microvascular endothelial cell against cytotoxicity induced by hydrogen peroxide." *Fitoterapia* 82, 267–271 (2011).

Zhao Z.J., Pan Y.Z., Liu Q.J., Li X.H. "Exposure assessment of lovastatin in Pu-erh tea." *International Journal of Food Microbiology*. 2013 Jun 3; 164 (1): 26–31.

Cao Z.H., Gu D.H., Lin Z.Y, Xu, Z.Q., Rao, H., Liu, E.W., Jia J.J., Ge C.R. "Effect of puerh tea on body fat and lipid profiles in rats with diet-induced obesity." *Phytotherapy Research* 25 (2), 234–238.

Current Medical Research on Other Infused Beverages and Forms of Tea

Gadow A.V., Joubert E., Hansmann C.F. "Comparison of the antioxidant activity of rooibos tea with green, oolong and black tea." *Food Chemistry* 60: 73 (1997).

Mayo Clinic Women's Healthsource. "Is Kombucha tea safe to drink?" 2011 July; 15(7)8.

McKay D.L, Blumbert J.B. "A review of the bioactivity of South African herbal teas: Rooibos and Honeybush." *Phytotherapy Research* 21 (1): 1–16 (2007).

Standley L., Winterton P., Marnewick J.L., Gelderblom, W.C., Joubert E., Britz T.J. "Influence of processing stages on antimutagenic and antioxidant potentials of rooibos tea." *Journal of Agricultural and Food Chemistry*, 49(1) 112–117 (2001).

Utah State University Cooperative Extension. "Kombucha brewing under the Food and Drug Administration model Food Code: risk analysis and processing guidance." *Journal of Environmental Health*. 2013 November; 76 (4): 8–11.

Some Well-Known U.S. Tea Retailers

Adagio Teas, Chicago, IL
www.adagio.com

Afternoon to Remember, Bothell, WA
www.afternoontoremember.com

Bottom of the Cup, New Orleans, LA
www.bottomofthecup.com

Chado Tea Rooms, Los Angeles and Pasadena, CA
www.chadotea.com

Charleston Tea Plantation, Wadmalaw Island, SC
www.charlestonteaplantation.com

Davidson's Organics, Sparks, NV
www.davidsonstea.com

Dushanbe Tea House, Boulder, CO
www.boulderteahouse.com

Harney & Sons, Soho and Millerton, NY
www.harney.com

Imperial Tea Court, San Francisco and Berkeley, CA
www.imperialtea.com

Perennial Tea Room, Seattle, WA
www.perennialtearoom.com

Queen Mary's Tearoom, Seattle, WA
www.queenmarytea.com

Rose Garden Tea Room, Huntington Library and Gardens, San Marina, CA
www.huntington.org/WebAssets/ Templates/content .aspx?id=310&terms=tea room

The Tao of Tea, Portland, OR
www.taooftea.com

Savvy Tea Gourmet, Madison, CT
www.savvyteagourmet.com

Seven Cups Tea House, Tucson, AZ
www.sevencups.com

St. James Tearoom, Albuquerque, New Mexico
www.stjamestearoom.com/wp

TeaGschwendner, Chicago, IL (and worldwide)
www.teagschwendner.com

Tea's Etc., West Palm Beach, FL
www.teasetc.com

Teance, Berkeley, CA
www.teance.com

Tea Source, St. Paul and Eden Prairie, MN
www.teasource.com/teas/stores.html

Time Well Spent, Summerville, SC
www.timewellspenttearoom.com

The Cultured Cup, Dallas, TX
www.theculturedcup.com

The Steeping Room, Austin, TX
www.thesteepingroom.com

The Tea House, Naperville, IL
www.theteahouse.com

Smith Teamaker, Portland, OR
www.smithtea.com

Red Blossom, San Francisco, CA
www.redblossomtea.com

Samovar Tea Lounge, San Francisco, CA
www.samovarlife.com

Upton Tea Imports, Hopkinson, MA
www.uptontea.com

Index